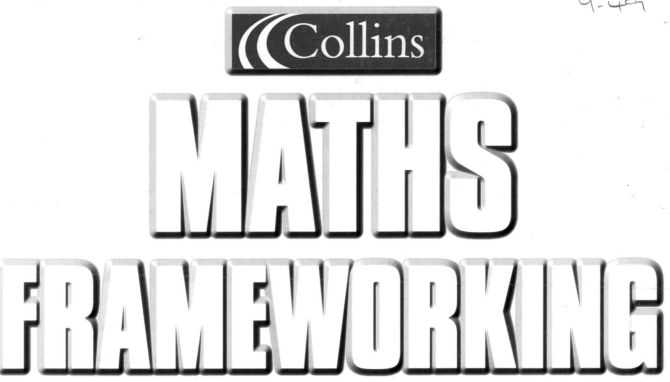

Collins

MATHS FRAMEWORKING

Complete success for Mathematics at KS3

YEAR 7

PUPIL BOOK 3

D0453093

KEVIN EVANS   KEITH GORDON   TREVOR SENIOR   BRIAN SPEED

CHAPTER 1 Algebra 1

This chapter is going to show you

- some simple number patterns that you may have seen before, and how to describe them
- how to create sequences and describe them using some basic algebraic techniques
- how to generate and describe simple whole-number sequences

What you should already know

- Odd and even numbers
- Times tables up to 10×10

Sequences and rules

You can make up many different sequences with integers (whole numbers) using simple rules.

Example 1.1

Rule | add 3 | Starting at 1 gives the sequence 1, 4, 7, 10, 13, …

Starting at 6 gives the sequence 6, 9, 12, 15, 18, …

Rule | double | Starting at 1 gives the sequence 1, 2, 4, 8, 16, …

Starting at 5 gives the sequence 5, 10, 20, 40, 80, …

So you see, with *different* **rules** and *different* **starting points**, there are very many *different* **sequences** you may make.

The numbers in a sequence are called **terms** and the starting point is called the **1st term**. The rule is often referred to as the **term-to-term rule**.

Exercise 1A

1 Use each of the following term-to-term rules with the 1st terms **i** 1 and **ii** 5.

Create each sequence with five terms in it.

   a   add 9   **b**   multiply by 5   **c**   add 7   **d**   multiply by 9

2 Use each of the following term-to-term rules with the first term 99.

Create each sequence with five terms in it.

   a   subtract 4   **b**   multiply by 11   **c**   subtract 9   **d**   add 99

3 Give the next two terms in each of these sequences. Describe the term-to-term rule you have used.

   a   2, 4, 6, …   **b**   3, 6, 9, …   **c**   1, 10, 100, …   **d**   1, 2, 4, …

   e   2, 10, 50, …   **f**   0, 7, 14, …   **g**   7, 10, 13, …   **h**   2, 6, 18 , …

4 For each pair of numbers find at least two sequences, writing the next two terms. Describe the term-to-term rule you have used.

    a 1, 4, ...   **b** 3, 7, ...   **c** 2, 6, ...

    d 3, 6, ...   **e** 4, 8, ...   **f** 5, 15, ...

5 Find at least one sequence involving each pair of numbers below, fully describing the term-to-term rule you have used.

    a 1, ..., 8   **b** 0, ..., 12   **c** 5, ..., 15

    d 4, ..., 10   **e** 10, ..., 20   **f** 16, ..., 20

6 **i** Make up some of your own sequences and describe them.

    ii Give your sequences to someone else and see if they can find out what your term-to-term rule is.

Extension Work

1 Choose a target number, say 50, and try to write a term-to-term rule which has 50 as one of its terms.

2 See how many different term-to-term rules you can find with the same 1st term that get to the target number. (Try to find at least five.)

3 Use a spreadsheet or graphics calculator for this investigation.

Here is an incomplete rule to find the next term in a sequence:

Add on ☐

Find a 1st term for the sequence and a number to go in the box so that all the terms in the sequence are:

    a odd   **b** even   **c** multiples of 5   **d** numbers ending in 7

Finding missing terms

In any sequence, you will have a 1st term, 2nd term, 3rd term, 4th term and so on.

Example 1.2

In the sequence 3, 5, 7, 9, ..., what is the 5th term, and what is the 50th term?

You first need to know what the term-to-term rule is. You can see that you add 2 from one term to the next:

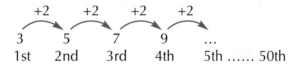

To get to the 5th term, you add 2 to the 4th term, which gives 11.

To get to the 50th term, you will have to add on 2 a total of 49 times (50 − 1) to the first term, 3. This will give $3 + 2 \times 49 = 3 + 98 = 101$

Exercise 1B

1 In each of the following sequences, find the 5th and the 50th term.

    a 4, 6, 8, 10, ...   **b** 1, 6, 11, 16, ...   **c** 3, 10, 17, 24, ...

    d 5, 8, 11, 14, ...   **e** 1, 5, 9, 13, ...   **f** 2, 10, 18, 26, ...

    g 20, 30, 40, 50, ...   **h** 10, 19, 28, 37, ...   **i** 3, 9, 15, 21, ...

2 In each of the sequences below, find the 1st term, then find the 50th term.

In each case, you have been given the 4th, 5th and 6th terms.
a ..., ..., ..., 13, 15, 17, ...
b ..., ..., ..., 18, 23, 28, ...
c ..., ..., ..., 19, 23, 27, ...
d ..., ..., ..., 32, 41, 50, ...

3 In each of the following sequences, find the missing terms and the 50th term.

Term	1st	2nd	3rd	4th	5th	6th	7th	8th	50th
Sequence A	...	...	...	...	17	19	21	23	...
Sequence B	...	9	...	19	...	29	...	39	...
Sequence C	...	...	16	23	...	37	44	...	...
Sequence D	...	...	25	...	45	...	...	75	...
Sequence E	...	5	...	11	...	...	20	...	...
Sequence F	...	...	12	...	...	18	...	22	...

4 Find the 40th term in the sequence with the term-to-term rule ADD 5 and a 1st term of 6.

5 Find the 80th term in the sequence with the term-to-term rule ADD 4 and a 1st term of 9.

6 Find the100th term in the sequence with the term-to-term rule ADD 7 and 1st term of 1.

7 Find the 30th term in the sequence with the term-to-term rule ADD 11 and 1st term of 5.

Extension Work

1 You have a simple sequence where the 50th term is 349, the 51st is 354 and the 52nd is 359. Find the 1st term and the 100th term.

2 You are laying a new path in the park using this pattern.

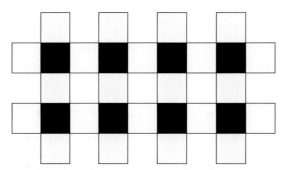

If you have 50 black slabs, how many yellow slabs do you need?

Finding the general term (*n*th term)

We can describe a sequence by finding the **nth term**. This is the **generalisation** that will allow us to find any specific term we want.

Example 1.3 Look at the sequence with the following pattern.

Pattern (term) number   1   2   3

 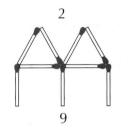 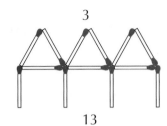

Number of matchsticks   5   9   13

a Find the generalisation (*n*th term) of the pattern.

b Find the 50th term in this sequence.

What is the term-to-term rule here? It is add 4, so the rule is based on **4*n***.

This 1st term is 5. Adding 4 gives the 2nd term, $5 + 4 = 9$, which could be written as $4 + 4 + 1 = 2 \times 4 + 1$. For the 2nd term, $n = 2$, which means that the generalisation is:

nth term = 4*n* + 1

The generalisation can be justified by the following statement.

> Each time, a triangle with a leg is added, which is four matches. Starting with one leg and repeatedly adding four matches generates the pattern and gives the generalisation $1 + 4n$.

You can use this to find the 50th term in the pattern.

When $n = 50$, $4n + 1 = 4 \times 50 + 1 = 201$

Exercise 1C

a Find the generalisation (*n*th term) for the number of matchsticks in each of the following patterns.

b Write a justification for each generalisation.

c Use this generalisation to find the 50th term in each pattern.

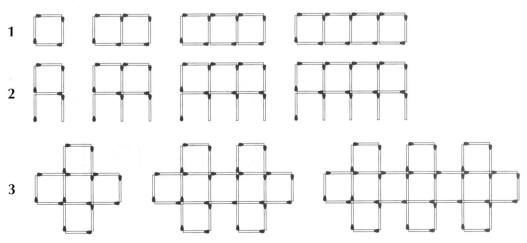

4

d Patterns 5 and 6 contain two different colours of matchsticks. Find a generalisation for
   i the number of red-tipped matchsticks   **ii** the number of blue tipped matchsticks
   iii the total number of matchsticks.

e Use your generalisations to describe the 50th term in the patterns by finding:
   i the number of red-tipped matchsticks   **ii** the number of blue tipped matchsticks
   iii the total number of matchsticks.

5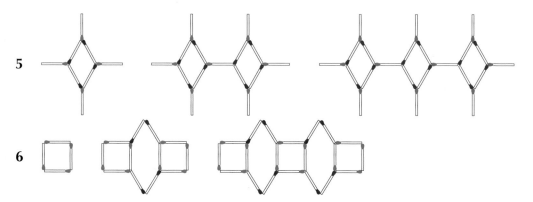

6

Extension Work

1 Make up some of your own patterns, find their generalisations, and justify them.

2 Try creating patterns which have the generalisations:
   i $5n$ **ii** $5n + 1$ **iii** $3n + 2$ **iv** $4n + 3$

3 We haven't seen many generalisations with a negative number. Try to create a pattern that has the generalisation of $4n - 1$.

Functions and mappings

Example 1.4

Complete the function machine to show the output.

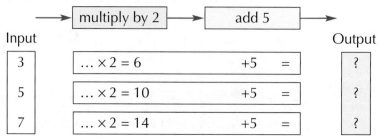

The output box can be seen to be

11
15
19

1 Complete the outputs for each of the following function machines.

a →| divide by 10 |→

input	output
100	?
80	?
60	?
50	?

b →| subtract 2 |→

input	output
4	?
5	?
8	?
11	?

c →| multiply by 5 |→

input	output
4	?
5	?
8	?
11	?

2 Express each of these functions in words.

a →| |→

input	output
2	4
3	5
4	6
5	7

b →| |→

input	output
3	9
4	12
5	15
6	18

c →| |→

input	output
1	6
2	12
3	18
4	24

d →| |→

input	output
24	12
12	6
8	4
6	3

e →| |→

input	output
2	9
3	10
4	11
5	12

f →| |→

input	output
2	16
4	32
6	48
8	64

3 Draw diagrams to illustrate each of the following functions.

Start with any numbers you like for the inputs. But remember, the larger the numbers the more difficult the problems are to work out.

a →| multiply by 2 |→| add 3 |→
  input   output

b →| multiply by 3 |→| add 1 |→
  input   output

c →| add 2 |→| multiply by 3 |→
  input   output

d →| add 5 |→| multiply by 2 |→
  input   output

4 Each of the following functions is made up from two operations, as above.

Find the **combined functions** in each case.

a

1	3
2	5
3	7
4	9

b

1	2
2	5
3	8
4	11

c

1	7
2	12
3	17
4	22

5 Work backwards from each output to find the input to each of the following functions.

a ?, ?, ?, ? → × 3 → + 4 → 7, 13, 16, 25

b ?, ?, ?, ? → + 5 → × 2 → 14, 16, 20, 26

c ?, ?, ?, ? → × 4 → − 3 → 9, 17, 33, 37

1 From the following single functions, see how many different combined functions you can make.

   × 3   + 4   − 1   × 2   + 5

2 Here is an incomplete function:

   multiply by ☐ add on ☐

   a Find numbers to go in the boxes such that:

   i 5 → 17   **ii** 8 → 60   **iii** 13 → 101

   b See how many different numbers you can find in each case.

Using letter symbols to represent functions

Here is some algebra shorthand that is useful to know:

   $2x$ means two multiplied by x
   $2g$ means two multiplied by g
   $5h$ means five multiplied by h

The idea of algebra is that we use a letter to represent a situation where we don't know a number (value) or where we know the value can vary (be lots of different numbers).

Each of the above is an **expression**. An expression is often a mixture of letters, numbers and signs. We call the letters **variables**, because the values they stand for vary.

For example, $3x$, $x + 5$, $2x + 7$ are expressions, and x is a variable in each case.

When the variable in an expression is a particular number, the expression has a particular value.

For example, in the expression $x + 6$, when $x = 4$, the expression has the value $4 + 6$, which is 10.

Exercise 1E

1 Write down what the expression $\boxed{n + 5}$ is equal to when:

   i $n = 3$ **ii** $n = 7$ **iii** $n = 10$ **iv** $n = 2$ **v** $n = 21$

2 Write down what the expression $\boxed{6x}$ is equal to when:

   i $x = 4$ **ii** $x = 5$ **iii** $x = 11$ **iv** $x = 2$ **v** $x = 7$

3 Write down what the expression $\boxed{x-1}$ is equal to when:

    i $x = 8$ **ii** $x = 19$ **iii** $x = 100$ **iv** $x = 3$ **v** $x = 87$

4 Write each of the following rules in symbolic form. For example, add 4 can be written as $x \rightarrow x + 4$.

    a add 3   **b** multiply by 5   **c** subtract 2   **d** divide by 5

    e subtract 4   **f** double   **g** multiply by 8   **h** halve

5 Express each of the following functions in symbols as in Question 4.

a
$2 \rightarrow 9$
$3 \rightarrow 10$
$4 \rightarrow 11$
$5 \rightarrow 12$

b
$2 \rightarrow 10$
$3 \rightarrow 15$
$4 \rightarrow 20$
$5 \rightarrow 25$

c
$2 \rightarrow 1$
$3 \rightarrow 2$
$4 \rightarrow 3$
$5 \rightarrow 4$

d
$2 \rightarrow 8$
$3 \rightarrow 12$
$4 \rightarrow 16$
$5 \rightarrow 20$

6 Draw mapping diagrams to illustrate each of these functions.

    a $x \rightarrow 2x + 3$ **b** $x \rightarrow 3x - 2$ **c** $x \rightarrow 5x + 1$ **d** $x \rightarrow 10x - 3$

7 Describe each of the following mappings as functions in the symbolic form, as above.

a
$1 \rightarrow 1$
$2 \rightarrow 3$
$3 \rightarrow 5$
$4 \rightarrow 7$

b
$1 \rightarrow 7$
$2 \rightarrow 11$
$3 \rightarrow 15$
$4 \rightarrow 19$

c
$1 \rightarrow 1$
$2 \rightarrow 4$
$3 \rightarrow 7$
$4 \rightarrow 10$

d
$1 \rightarrow 11$
$2 \rightarrow 21$
$3 \rightarrow 31$
$4 \rightarrow 41$

Extension Work

Think about a group of people who meet and want to shake each other's hands.

One person alone would have no one to shake hands with.

Two people would shake hands just once.

Three people would have three handshakes altogether.

Four people would have six handshakes altogether.

a Draw a simple diagram to represent these cases and so predict how many handshakes there will be with five people in the group.

b Put your results into a table and write any number sequences you see.

c Find the rule linking the number of people and the number of handshakes. Write this rule as a function.

Every two-digit whole number can be written as $10a + b$.

For example, $28 = 10 \times 2 + 8$.

Consider the function $\boxed{10x + y \rightarrow 10y - x}$ $\boxed{\begin{array}{l} 36 \rightarrow 60 - 3 = 57 \\ 19 \rightarrow 90 - 1 = 89 \\ 75 \rightarrow 50 - 7 = 43 \end{array}}$

1 Start with any two-digit number, and make a chain out of the successive results until you get a repeated number. You have found a loop.

For example:

$\boxed{17} \rightarrow 70 - 1 \rightarrow \boxed{69} \rightarrow 90 - 6 \rightarrow \boxed{84} \rightarrow 40 - 8 \rightarrow \boxed{32} \rightarrow 20 - 3 \rightarrow \boxed{17}$

We start and finish with 17. So, we have the loop of 17.

Warning: If you ever have a result which is *not* a two-digit number, then you cannot have a loop – so you stop.

2 Find at least six of these loops.

Describe what you have noticed about each loop.

3 Do you think this will happen with every two-digit number?

Explain your answer.

4 What happens if you change the function to $\boxed{10x + y \rightarrow 9y - x}$?

Describe what happens.

5 Try other changes. Describe what you notice.

What you need to know for level 5

- ○ Be able to recognise and describe simple number patterns
- ○ How to construct functions with more than one rule
- ○ Be able to express functions in symbolic form

What you need to know for level 6

- ○ Be able to describe in words the rule for the next term or the nth term of a sequence where the rule is linear
- ○ How to represent functions expressed algebraically
- ○ Be able to justify generalisations

National Curriculum SATs questions

LEVEL 5

1 *1999 Paper 2*

Jeff makes a sequence of patterns with black and grey tiles.

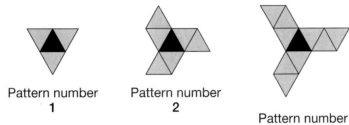

Pattern number 1   Pattern number 2

Pattern number 3

The rule for finding the number of tiles in pattern number N in Jeff's sequence is:

Number of tiles = $1 + 3N$

a   The 1 in this rule represents the black tile. What does the $3N$ represent?

b   Jeff makes pattern number 12 in his sequence.

i   How many black tiles and   **ii**   how many grey tiles does he use?

c   Jeff uses 61 tiles altogether to make a pattern in his sequence. What is the number of the pattern he makes?

d   Barbara makes a sequence of patterns with hexagonal tiles.

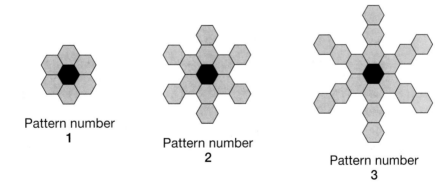

Pattern number 1

Pattern number 2

Pattern number 3

Each pattern in Barbara's sequence has 1 black tile in the middle. Each new pattern has 6 more grey tiles than the pattern before.

Write the rule for finding the number of tiles in pattern number N in Barbara's sequence.

e   Gwenno uses some tiles to make a different sequence of patterns. The rule for finding the number of tiles in pattern number N in Gwenno's sequence is

Number of tiles = $1 + 4N$

Draw what you think the first three patterns in Gwenno's sequence could be.

You can make 'huts' with matches.

 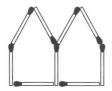 

| 1 hut needs | 2 huts need | 3 huts need |
| 5 matches | 9 matches | 13 matches |

A rule to find how many matches you need is

$$m = 4h + 1$$

m stands for the number of matches

h stands for the number of huts.

a   Use the rule to find how many matches you need to make 8 huts.
(Show your working.)

b   I use 81 matches to make some huts. How many huts do I make?
(Show your working.)

Here is a different hut pattern.

  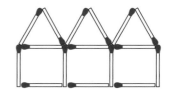

| 1 hut needs | 2 huts need | 3 huts need |
| 6 matches | 11 matches | 16 matches |

Choose the rule below that shows how many matches you need.

Remember: *m* stands for the number of matches.
$\quad\quad\quad\quad\quad$ *h* stands for the number of huts.

| $m = h + 5$ | $m = 4h + 2$ | $m = 4h + 3$ |
| $m = 5h + 1$ | $m = 5h + 2$ | $m = h + 13$ |

LEVEL 6

3 *1998 Paper 1*

This is a series of patterns with grey and white tiles.

Pattern number
1

Pattern number
2

Pattern number
3

The series of patterns continues by adding  each time

a Complete this table:

Pattern number	Number of grey tiles	Number of white tiles
5		
16		

b Complete this table by writing expressions:

Pattern number	Expression for the number of grey tiles	Expression for the number of white tiles
n		

c Write an expression to show the total number of tiles in pattern number n. Simplify your expression.

d A different series of patterns is made with tiles.

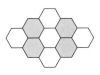 

Pattern number
1

Pattern number
2

Pattern number
3

The series of patterns continues by adding each time.

For this series of patterns, write an expression to show the total number of tiles in pattern number n.

Show your working and simplify your expression.

CHAPTER 2

Number 1

This chapter is going to show you

- how to work with decimals and whole numbers
- how to use estimation to check your answers
- how to solve problems using decimals and whole numbers, with and without a calculator

What you should already know

- How to write and read whole numbers and decimals
- How to write decimal fractions
- Times tables up to 10×10
- How to use a calculator to do simple calculations

Decimals

Look at this picture. What do the decimal numbers mean? How would you say them?

When you multiply by 100, all the digits are moved two places to the left.

Example 2.1

Work out 3.5×100.

Thousands	Hundreds	Tens	Units	Tenths	Hundredths	Thousandths	Ten thousandths
			3 •	5			
	3	5	0 •				

The digits move one place to the left when you multiply by 10, and three places to the left when you multiply by 1000.

When you divide by 1000, all the digits move three places to the right.

Example 2.2

Work out $2.3 \div 1000$.

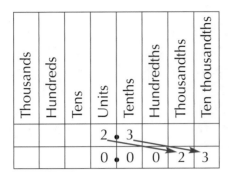

In the same way, the digits move one place to the right when you divide by 10, and two places to the right when you divide by 100.

Exercise 2A

1. Without using a calculator work out:
   a 3.4×10
   b 0.045×10
   c 0.6×10
   d 0.89×100
   e 0.053×100
   f 0.03×100
   g $0.4 \div 1000$
   h $5.8 \div 1000$
   i $3.4 \div 10$
   j $0.045 \div 10$
   k $0.6 \div 10$
   l $0.89 \div 100$

2. Fill in the missing operation in each case.
   a $0.37 \rightarrow \boxed{} \rightarrow 370$
   b $567 \rightarrow \boxed{} \rightarrow 0.0567$
   c $0.07 \rightarrow \boxed{} \rightarrow 70$
   d $650 \rightarrow \boxed{} \rightarrow 6.5$

3. Find the missing number in each case.
   a $0.03 \times 10 = \boxed{}$
   b $0.3 \times \boxed{} = 30$
   c $0.3 \div 10 = \boxed{}$
   d $3 \div \boxed{} = 0.03$
   e $0.3 \times 10 = \boxed{}$
   f $0.03 \times \boxed{} = 300$
   g $0.03 \div 100 = \boxed{}$
   h $0.3 \div \boxed{} = 0.003$
   i $\boxed{} \div 100 = 0.03$

4. 10^2 means $10 \times 10 = 100$, 10^3 means $10 \times 10 \times 10 = 1000$.

   Copy and complete each of the following
   $$10^4 = \ldots \times \ldots \times \ldots \times \ldots = \ldots\ldots$$
   $$10^5 = \qquad\qquad = \ldots\ldots$$
   $$10^6 = \qquad\qquad = \ldots\ldots$$

5. Write down the answers to each of these.
   a 3.5×10^2
   b 0.4×10^3
   c 0.07×10^2
   d 2.7×10^5
   e 0.6×10
   f 7.08×10^3
   g $3.5 \div 10^2$
   h $0.4 \div 10^3$
   i $0.07 \div 10$
   j $0.06 \div 10^3$
   k $700 \div 10^4$
   l $80 \div 10^3$

Extension Work

Design a poster to explain clearly how to multiply and/or divide a number by a power of 10 such as 10^3, 10^5.

Ordering decimals

Name	Leroy	Myrtle	Jack	Baby Jane	Alf	Doris
Age	37.4	21	$32\frac{1}{2}$	9 months	57	68 yrs 3 mths
Height	170 cm	1.54 m	189 cm	0.55 m	102 cm	1.80 m
Weight	75 kg	50.3 kg	68 kg	7.5 kg	85 kg	76 kg 300 g

Look at the people in the picture. How would you put them in order?

When you compare the size of numbers, you have to consider the **place value** of each digit.

It helps if you fill in the numbers in a table like the one shown on the right.

The decimal point separates the whole-number part of the number from the decimal-fraction part.

Thousands	Hundreds	Tens	Units	Tenths	Hundredths	Thousandths	Ten thousandths
			2	3	3	0	
			2	0	3	0	
			2	3	0	4	

Example 2.3 ▷

Put the numbers 2.33, 2.03 and 2.304 in order, from smallest to largest.

The numbers are shown in the table. Zeros have been added to make up the missing decimal places.

Working across the table from the left, you can see that all of the numbers have the same units digit. Two of them have the same tenths digit, and two have the same hundredths digit. But only one has a digit in the thousandths. The order is

   2.03, 2.304 and 2.33

Example 2.4 ▷

Put the correct sign, > or <, between each of these pairs of numbers

   a   6.05 and 6.046   **b**   0.06 and 0.065.

   a   Both numbers have the same units and tenths digits, but the hundredths digit is bigger in the first number. So the answer is 6.05 > 6.046.

   b   Both numbers have the same units, tenths and hundredths digits, but the second number has the bigger thousandths digit, as the first number has a zero in the thousandths. So the answer is 0.06 < 0.065.

1 **a** Copy the table on page 16 (but not the numbers). Write the following numbers in the table, placing each digit in the appropriate column.

4.57, 0.0045, 4.057, 4.5, 0.0457, 0.5, 4.05

b Use your answer to part **a** to write the numbers in order from smallest to largest.

2 Write each of these sets of numbers in order from smallest to largest.

a 0.0073, 0.073, 0.008, 0.7098, 0.7

b 1.2033, 1.0334, 1.405, 1.4045, 1.4

c 34, 3.4, 0.34, 0.034, 3.0034

3 Put the correct sign, > or <, between each of these pairs of numbers.

a 0.315 0.325 **b** 0.42 0.402 **c** 6.78 6.709

d 5.25 km 5.225 km **f** 0.345 kg 0.4 kg **g** £0.05 7p

4 Put these amounts of money in order.

a 56p £1.25 £0.60 130p £0.07

b £0.04 £1.04 101p 35p £0.37

5 Put these times in order: 1hour 10 minutes, 25 minutes, 1.25 hours, 0.5 hours.

6 One metre is 100 centimetres. Change all the lengths below to metres and then put them in order from smallest to largest.

6.25 m, 269 cm, 32 cm, 2.7 m, 0.34 m

7 One kilogram is 1000 grams. Change all the weights below to kilograms and then put them in order from smallest to largest.

467 g, 1.260 kg, 56 g, 0.5 kg, 0.055 kg

8 Write each of the following statements in words.

a 3.1 < 3.14 < 3.142

b £0.07 < 32p < £0.56

Extension Work

Choose a set of five consecutive integers (whole numbers), such as 3, 4, 5, 6, 7.

Use a calculator to work out the **reciprocal** of each of the five numbers. The reciprocal is the number divided into 1. That is:

1 ÷ 3, 1 ÷ 4, 1 ÷ 5, 1 ÷ 6, 1 ÷ 7

Put the answers in order from smallest to largest.

Repeat with any five two-digit whole numbers, such as 12, 15, 20, 25, 30.

What do you notice?

Directed numbers

Temperature 32 °C
Latitude 17° South
Time 09 30 h GMT

Temperature –13 °C
Latitude 84° North
Time 23 24 h GMT

Look at the two pictures. What are the differences between the temperatures, the latitudes and the times?

All numbers have a sign. Positive numbers have a + sign in front of them although we do not always write it. Negative (or minus) numbers have a – sign in front of them. We *always* write the negative sign.

The positions of positive and negative numbers can be put on a number line, as below.

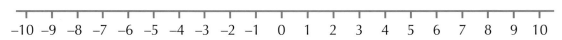

$$-10 \quad -9 \quad -8 \quad -7 \quad -6 \quad -5 \quad -4 \quad -3 \quad -2 \quad -1 \quad 0 \quad 1 \quad 2 \quad 3 \quad 4 \quad 5 \quad 6 \quad 7 \quad 8 \quad 9 \quad 10$$

This is very useful, as it helps us to compare positive and negative numbers and also to add and subtract them.

Example 2.5 ▷ Work out the answers to **a** $3 - 2 - 5$ **b** $-3 - 5 + 4 - 2$

    a Starting at zero and 'jumping' along the number line give an answer of –4.

    b $-3 - 5 + 4 - 2 = -6$

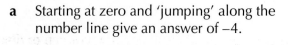

Example 2.6 ▷ Work out the answers to **a** $-2 - +4$ **b** $-6 - -3 + -2$

    a Rewrite as $-2 - 4$ and count along the number line $-2 - 4 = -6$

    b Rewrite as $-6 + 3 - 2$ and count along the number line $-6 + 3 - 2 = -5$

Example 2.7 ▷ Work out the answers to each of these.

    a $-2 \times +4$ **b** -6×-3 **c** $-15 \div -5$ **d** $+6 \times -4 \div -2$

    a $2 \times 4 = 8$, and – + are equivalent to –. So, $-2 \times +4 = -8$.

    b $6 \times 3 = 18$, and – – are equivalent to +. So, $-6 \times -3 = +18$.

    c $15 \div 5 = 3$, and – – are equivalent to +. So $-15 \div -5 = +3$.

    d $+6 \times -4 = -24$. So, $-24 \div -2 = +12$.

Exercise 2C

1 Work out the answer to each of these.

    a $6 - 9$ **b** $4 - 3$ **c** $2 - 7$ **d** $3 + 9$ **e** $1 - 3$ **f** $4 - 4$

    g $-6 + 9$ **h** $-4 - 1$ **i** $-7 - 3$ **j** $-1 + 8$ **k** $-2 - 3$ **l** $-14 + 7$

    m $-2 - 3 + 4$ **n** $-1 + 1 - 2$ **o** $-3 + 4 - 7$ **p** $-102 + 103 - 5$

2 Copy each of these calculations and then fill in the missing numbers.

a
$3 + +1 = 4$
$3 + 0 = 3$
$3 + -1 = 2$
$3 + -2 = ...$
$3 + ... = ...$
$3 + ... = ...$

b
$-2 - +1 = -3$
$-2 - 0 = -2$
$-2 - -1 = -1$
$-2 - -2 = ...$
$-2 - ... = ...$
$-2 - ... = ...$

c
$4 - +2 = 2$
$3 - +1 = 2$
$2 - 0 = 2$
$1 - -1 = ...$
$0 - ... = ...$
$... - ... = ...$

3 Work out the answer to each of these.

a $+3 - +2$ **b** $-4 - -3$ **c** $+7 - -6$ **d** $-7 + -3$ **e** $+7 - +3$
f $-9 - -5$ **g** $-6 + +6$ **h** $+6 - -7$ **i** $-6 + -6$ **j** $-1 + -8$
k $+5 - +7$ **l** $7 - -5$ **m** $-2 - -3 + -4$ **n** $- +1 + +1 - +2$

4 Find the missing number to make each of these true.

a $+2 + -6 = \boxed{}$ **b** $+4 + \boxed{} = +7$ **c** $-4 + \boxed{} = 0$

d $+5 + \boxed{} = -1$ **e** $+3 + +4 = \boxed{}$ **f** $\boxed{} - -5 = +7$

g $\boxed{} - +5 = +2$ **h** $+6 + \boxed{} = 0$ **i** $\boxed{} - -5 = -2$

j $+2 + -2 = \boxed{}$ **k** $\boxed{} - +2 = -4$ **l** $-2 + -4 = \boxed{}$

5 In a magic square, the numbers in any row, column or diagonal add up to give the same answer. Copy and complete each of these magic squares.

a

-7	0	-8
-2		-3

b

-2		-4
		-3
		-8

c

0		-13	-3
	-5		
-7	-9	-10	
-12			-15

6 Copy and complete each of these patterns.

a
$3 \times 3 = 9$
$2 \times 3 = 6$
$1 \times 3 = ...$
$0 \times 3 = ...$
$... \times 3 = ...$
$... \times 3 = ...$

b
$3 \times -2 = -6$
$2 \times -2 = -4$
$1 \times -2 = ...$
$0 \times -2 = ...$
$... \times -2 = ...$
$... \times -2 = ...$

c
$-2 \times +1 = -2$
$-1 \times +1 = ...$
$... \times +1 = ...$
$... \times +1 = ...$
$... \times +1 = ...$
$... \times +1 = ...$

7 Work out the answer to each of these.

a $+2 \times -3$ **b** $-3 \times +4$ **c** $-5 \times +2$ **d** -6×-3
e $-3 \times +8$ **f** $-4 \times +5$ **g** -3×-4 **h** -6×-1
i $+7 \times -2$ **j** $+2 \times +8$ **k** $+6 \times -10$ **l** $+8 \times +4$
m -15×-2 **n** $-6 \times -3 \times -1$ **o** $-2 \times +4 \times -2$

8 Work out the answer to each of these.

a $+12 \div -3$	**b** $-24 \div +4$	**c** $-6 \div +2$	**d** $-6 \div -3$
e $-32 \div +8$	**f** $-40 \div +5$	**g** $-32 \div -4$	**h** $-6 \div -1$
i $+7 \div -2$	**j** $+12 \div +6$	**k** $+60 \div -10$	**l** $+8 \div +4$
m $-15 \div -2$	**n** $-6 \times -3 \div -2$	**o** $-2 \times +6 \div -3$	

Extension Work

A maths test consists of 20 questions. Three points are given for a correct answer and two points are deducted if an answer is wrong or not attempted.

Show that it is possible to get a score of zero.

Show clearly that all the possible scores are multiples of 5.

What happens when there are four points for a correct answer and minus two for a wrong answer? Investigate what happens when the points awarded and deducted are changed.

A computer spreadsheet is useful for this activity.

Estimates

UNITED v CITY

CROWD	41 923
SCORE	2 – 1
TIME OF FIRST GOAL	42 min 13 sec
PRICE OF A PIE	95p
CHILDREN	33% off normal ticket prices

Which of the numbers above can be approximated? Which need to be given exactly?

You should have an idea if the answer to a calculation is about the right size or not. There are some ways of checking answers. First, when it is a multiplication, you can check that the final digit is correct. Second, you can round numbers off and do a mental calculation to see if an answer is about the right size. Third, you can check by doing the inverse operation.

Example 2.8 Explain why these calculations must be wrong.

a $23 \times 45 = 1053$ **b** $19 \times 59 = 121$

a The last digit should be 5, because the product of the last digits is 15. That is, $23 \times 45 = \ldots 5$.

b The answer is roughly $20 \times 60 = 1200$.

Example 2.9

Estimate the answers to these calculations.

   a $\dfrac{21.3 + 48.7}{6.4}$ **b** 31.2×48.5 **c** $359 \div 42$ **d** 57×0.42

   a   Round off the numbers on the top to $20 + 50 = 70$. Round off 6.4 to 7.
Then $70 \div 7 = 10$.

   b   Round off to 30×50, which is $3 \times 5 \times 100 = 1500$.

   c   Round off to $360 \div 40$, which is $36 \div 4 = 9$.

   d   Round off to 60×0.4, which is $6 \times 4 = 24$.

Example 2.10

By using the inverse operation, check if each calculation is correct.

   a $450 \div 6 = 75$ **b** $310 - 59 = 249$

   a   By the inverse operation, $450 = 6 \times 75$. This is true and can be checked
mentally: $6 \times 70 = 420$, $6 \times 5 = 30$, $420 + 30 = 450$.

   b   By the inverse operation, $310 = 249 + 59$. This must end in 8 as $9 + 9 = 18$, so it
cannot be correct.

Exercise 2D

1 Explain why these calculations must be wrong.

   a $24 \times 42 = 1080$ **b** $51 \times 73 = 723$ **c** $\dfrac{34.5 + 63.2}{9.7} = 20.07$

   d $360 \div 8 = 35$ **e** $354 - 37 = 323$

2 Estimate the answer to each of these problems.

   a $2768 - 392$ **b** 231×18 **c** $792 \div 38$ **d** $\dfrac{36.7 + 23.2}{14.1}$

   e 423×423 **f** $157.2 \div 38.2$ **g** $\dfrac{135.7 - 68.2}{15.8 - 8.9}$ **h** $\dfrac{38.9 \times 61.2}{39.6 - 18.4}$

3 Delroy had £10. In his shopping basket he had a magazine costing £2.65, some
batteries costing £1.92, and a tape costing £4.99. Without adding up the numbers,
how could Delroy be sure he had enough to buy the goods in the basket? Explain a
quick way for Delroy to find out if he could afford a 45p bar of chocolate as well.

4 Amy bought 6 bottles of pop at 46p per bottle. The shopkeeper asked her for £3.16.
Without working out the correct answer, explain why this is wrong.

5 A first class stamp is 27p. I need eight. Will £2 be enough to pay for them? Explain
your answer clearly.

6 Round off each of the following to one decimal place.

   a   0.56   **b**   0.67   **c**   0.89   **d**   1.23   **e**   3.45

   f   1.38   **g**   4.72   **h**   9.99   **i**   0.12   **j**   0.07

   k   1.46   **l**   5.216   **m**   8.765   **n**   5.032   **o**   5.067

7 Work out each of these.

a	60×0.7	**b**	50×0.2	**c**	90×0.7	**d**	30×0.4
e	80×0.4	**f**	40×0.8	**g**	40×0.2	**h**	20×0.9
i	40×0.9	**j**	30×0.8	**k**	30×0.5	**l**	120×0.2

8 Estimate the answer to each of the following.

a	72×0.56	**b**	61×0.67	**c**	39×0.81	**d**	42×0.17
e	57×0.33	**f**	68×0.68	**g**	38×0.19	**h**	23×0.91
i	43×0.86	**j**	28×0.75	**k**	34×0.52	**l**	116×0.18

9 $62 \div 0.39$ can be approximated as $60 \div 0.4 = 600 \div 4 = 150$. Estimate the answer to each of the following divisions.

a	$62 \div 0.56$	**b**	$139 \div 0.67$	**c**	$39 \div 0.81$	**d**	$42 \div 0.17$
e	$57 \div 0.33$	**f**	$68 \div 0.68$	**g**	$38 \div 0.19$	**h**	$178 \div 0.91$
i	$269 \div 0.86$	**j**	$38 \div 0.75$	**k**	$34 \div 0.52$	**l**	$116 \div 0.18$

Extension Work

The first 15 **square numbers** are 1, 4, 9, 16, 25, 36, 49, 64, 81, 100, 121, 144, 169, 196 and 225. The inverse operation of squaring a number is to find its **square root**. So $\sqrt{121} = 11$. Only the square numbers have integer square roots. Other square roots have to be estimated or found from a calculator.

For example, to find the square root of 30 use a diagram like that on the right, to estimate that $\sqrt{30} \approx 5.48$.
(A check shows that $5.48^2 = 30.03$.)

Here is another example. Find $\sqrt{45}$.
The diagram shows that $\sqrt{45} \approx 6.7$.
(Check: $6.7^2 = 44.89$)

Use the above method to find $\sqrt{20}$, $\sqrt{55}$, $\sqrt{75}$, $\sqrt{110}$, $\sqrt{140}$, $\sqrt{200}$. Check your answers with a calculator.

Column method for addition, subtraction and multiplication

1.2 + 5 + 0.06
= 0.23

Look at the picture. What is wrong?

You may have several ways of adding and subtracting numbers, such as estimation or using a number line. Here you will be shown how to set out additions and subtractions using the column method. You may already have learnt about 'lining up the units digit'. This is not strictly correct. What you do is 'line up the decimal points'.

1.2
5
0.06
0.23

Example 2.11 Work out, without using a calculator: **a** 3.27 + 14.8   **b** 12.8 – 3.45

  a Write the numbers in columns, lining up the decimal points. You should fill the gap with a zero.

$$\begin{array}{r} 3.27 \\ + \, 14.80 \\ \hline 18.07 \\ {\scriptstyle 1} \end{array}$$

Note the carry digit in the units column, because 2 + 8 = 10.

  b Write the numbers in columns and fill the gap with a zero.

$$\begin{array}{r} {\scriptstyle 0\ 1\ 7\ 1} \\ 12.80 \\ - \, 3.45 \\ \hline 9.35 \end{array}$$

Note that, because you cannot take 5 from 0, you have to borrow from the next column. This means that 8 becomes 7 and zero becomes 10.

Example 2.12 Work out 3.14 + 14.5 – 8.72.

This type of problem needs to be done in two stages. First, do the addition and then do the subtraction.

$$\begin{array}{r} 3.14 \\ + \, 14.50 \\ \hline 17.64 \end{array} \qquad \begin{array}{r} {\scriptstyle 0\ 16\ 1} \\ 17.64 \\ - \, 8.72 \\ \hline 8.92 \end{array}$$

Example 2.13   Work out **a** 3.7×9 **b** 6.24×8

Do these as 'short' multiplications and keep the decimal points lined up.

a
$$
\begin{array}{r}
3.7 \\
\times\ \ 9 \\
\hline
33.3 \\
\end{array}
$$
$_6$

b
$$
\begin{array}{r}
6.24 \\
\times\ \ \ \ 8 \\
\hline
49.92 \\
\end{array}
$$
$_{1\ \ 3}$

Exercise 2E

1 By means of a drawing, show how you would use a number line to work out the answers to these.

   a $2.4 + 3.7$ **b** $8.4 - 5.6$

2 Repeat the calculations in Question 1 using the column method. Show all your working.

3 Use the column method to work out the following additions.

   a $37.1 + 14.2$ **b** $32.6 + 15.73$ **c** $6.78 + 4.59$ **d** $9.62 + 0.7$
   e $4.79 + 1.2$ **f** $6.08 + 2.16$ **g** $1.2 + 3.41 + 4.56$
   h $76.57 + 312.5 + 6.08$

4 Use the column method to work out the following subtractions.

   a $37.1 - 14.2$ **b** $32.6 - 15.73$ **c** $6.78 - 4.59$ **d** $9.62 - 0.7$
   e $4.79 - 1.2$ **f** $6.08 - 2.16$ **g** $1.2 + 3.41 - 4.56$
   h $76.57 + 312.5 - 6.08$

5 Work out the cost of a pair of socks at £4.99, a pair of laces at 79p, a tin of shoe polish at £1.23 and two shoe brushes at £1.34 each.

6 Write the change you would get from £10 if you bought goods worth

   a £4.56   **b** £3.99   **c** £7.01   **d** 34p

7 Use the column method to work out each of the following.

   a 2.6×7 **b** 3.1×9 **c** 4.8×8 **d** 4.3×7
   e 3.14×3 **f** 7.06×8 **g** 6.84×7 **h** 3.79×5
   i 9.26×4 **j** 8.23×9 **k** 1.47×9 **l** 3.89×6
   m 6.25×8 **n** 2.49×5 **o** 3.65×8 **p** 9.83×6

8 Work out the cost of six cassettes that are £2.95 each.

9 A bar of soap costs £1.37. Work out the cost of seven bars.

10 A bottle of grape juice costs £2.62. Work out the cost of nine bottles.

$$6 \times 8 = 48 \qquad 6 \times 0.8 = 4.8 \qquad 0.6 \times 0.8 = 0.48$$

When these calculations are set out in columns, they look like this:

$$
\begin{array}{r}
8 \\
\times\ 6 \\
\hline
48
\end{array}
\qquad
\begin{array}{r}
0.8 \\
\times\ 6.0 \\
\hline
4.8
\end{array}
\qquad
\begin{array}{r}
0.8 \\
\times\ 0.6 \\
\hline
0.48
\end{array}
$$

The column method does not work when we multiply decimals.

Use a calculator to find out the rules for where the decimal point goes in multiplication problems such as

$$3 \times 0.2 \qquad 5 \times 0.7 \qquad 0.3 \times 0.9 \qquad 0.2 \times 0.6 \qquad 0.03 \times 0.5$$

Solving problems

A bus starts at Barnsley and makes four stops before reaching Penistone. At Barnsley 23 people get on. At Dodworth 12 people get off and 14 people get on. At Silkstone 15 people get off and 4 people get on. At Hoylandswaine 5 people get off and 6 people get on. At Cubley 9 people get off and 8 get on. At Penistone the rest of the passengers get off. How many people are on the bus?

When you solve problems, you need to develop a strategy: that is, a way to go about the problem. You also have to decide which mathematical operation you need to solve it. For example, is it addition, subtraction, multiplication or division or a combination of these? Something else you must do is to read the question fully before starting. The answer to the problem above is one! The driver.

Read the questions below carefully.

Exercise 2F

1. It cost six people £15 to go to the cinema. How much would it cost eight people?

2. Ten pencils cost £4.50. How much would seven pencils cost?

3. A water tank holds 500 litres. How much has been used if there is 143.7 litres left in the tank?

4. Strips of paper are 40 cm long. They are stuck together with a 10 cm overlap.

   a   How long would two strips glued together be?
   b   How long would four strips glued together be?

5. A can of coke and a Kit-Kat together cost 80p. Two cans of coke and a Kit-Kat together cost £1.30. How much would three cans of coke and four Kit-Kats cost?

6 To make a number chain, start with any number.

When the number is even, divide it by 2.

When the number is odd, multiply it by 3 and add 1.

If you start with 13, the chain becomes 13, 40, 20, 10, 5, 16, 8, 4, 2, 1, 4, 2, 1, …

The chain repeats 4, 2, 1, 4, 2, 1. So, stop the chain when it gets to 1.

Start with other numbers below 20. What is the longest chain you can make before you get to 1?

7 If $135 \times 44 = 5940$, write down, without calculating, the value of:

    a 13.5×4.4 **b** 1.35×44 **c** 1.35×4.4 **d** 1350×440

8 Find four consecutive odd numbers that add up to 80.

9 30 can be worked out as $33 - 3$. Can you find two other ways of working out 30 using three equal digits?

10 Arrange the numbers 1, 2, 3 and 4 in each of these to make the problem correct.

    a $\square + \square = \square + \square$ **b** $\square \times \square = \square\square$ **c** $\square\square \div \square = \square$

Extension Work

Using the numbers 1, 2, 3 and 4 and any mathematical signs, make all of the numbers from 1 to 10.

For example: $2 \times 3 - 4 - 1 = 1$, $12 - 3 - 4 = 5$

Once you have found all the numbers up to 10, can you find totals above 10?

What you need to know for level 5

- How to estimate answers and check if an answer is about right
- How to multiply and divide decimals by 10, 100 and 1000
- How to add and subtract using negative and positive numbers
- How to solve problems using a variety of mathematical methods

What you need to know for level 6

- How to order and approximate decimals
- How to approximate to one decimal place
- How to multiply and divide by powers of 10
- How to solve more complex problems using a variety of mathematical methods

National Curriculum SATs questions

LEVEL 5

1 *1997 Paper 2*

Look at these number cards.

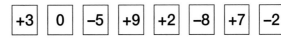

$$\boxed{+3}\ \boxed{0}\ \boxed{-5}\ \boxed{+9}\ \boxed{+2}\ \boxed{-8}\ \boxed{+7}\ \boxed{-2}$$

a Choose a card to give the answer

$$\boxed{+2} + \boxed{-5} + \boxed{} = 4$$

b Choose a card to give the lowest possible answer.
Work out the answer.

$$\boxed{-2} + \boxed{} = \dots$$

c Choose a card to give the lowest possible answer.
Work out the answer.

$$\boxed{-2} - \boxed{} = \dots$$

d Now choose a card to give the highest possible answer.
Work out the answer.

$$\boxed{-2} - \boxed{} = \dots$$

2 *1999 Paper 1*

Here is a list of numbers: -7 -5 -3 -1 0 2 4 6

a What is the total of all eight of the numbers on the list?

b Choose the three numbers from the list which have the lowest possible total.

Write the numbers and their total. You must not use the same number more than once.

$$\dots + \dots + \dots = \dots$$

LEVEL 6

3 *1996 Paper 1*

A calculator can be used in this question.

Bill, Ravi and Eric are three divers in a competition. Each dive has a dive rating. Each dive is marked by five judges who give a mark out of 10.

The highest and lowest of the five marks are removed. The other three are added together. This total is then multiplied by the dive rating to get the final score.

a Bill does a dive with a dive rating of 3.34. The judges give 7.0, 7.5, 8.0, 8.0, 8.5.

What is Bill's score ?

b Ravi scored 82.68 on a dive with a dive rating of 3.18.

What was the total of the middle three marks given by the judges ?

c Eric needs to score at least 102.69 to win the competition. He decides to do a dive with a dive rating of 3.26. Explain why Eric has made a poor decision.

4 *1998 Paper 1*

Each of these calculations has an answer of 60. Copy and fill in the gaps.

a $2.4 \times 25 = 60$, $\quad 0.24 \times \ldots\ldots = 60$

b $60 \div 1 = 60$, $\quad 6 \div \ldots\ldots = 60$

5 *1999 Paper 2* (adapted)

a Use £1 = 11.35 kroner to work out how much 45p is in kroner.

b Use 180 yen = £1 to work out how much 468 yen is in pounds.

6 *2000 Paper 1*

a Write the best estimate of the answer to $72.34 \div 8.91$: $\quad$ 6 $\quad$ 7 $\quad$ 8 $\quad$ 9 $\quad$ 10 $\quad$ 11

b Write the best estimate of the answer to 32.7×0.48: $\quad$ 1.2 $\quad$ 1.6 $\quad$ 12 $\quad$ 16 $\quad$ 120 $\quad$ 160

7 *2001 Paper 2*

A drink from a machine costs 55p. The table shows the coins that were put in the machine one day.

Coins	Number of coins
50p	31
20p	22
10p	41
5p	59

How many cans of drink were sold that day?

Shape, Space and Measures 1

This chapter is going to show you

- how to estimate and calculate perimeters and areas of 2-D shapes
- how to calculate the area of a rectangle, of a triangle, of a parallelogram and of a trapezium
- how to draw 3-D shapes on an isometric grid
- how to calculate the surface area and the volume of a cuboid

What you should already know

- How to measure and draw lines
- How to find the perimeter of a shape
- Area is measured in square centimetres
- How to draw the net of a cube
- The names of 3-D shapes such as the cube and cuboid

Length, perimeter and area

The metric units of length in common use are:
the millimetre (mm)
the centimetre (cm)
the metre (m)
the kilometre (km)

The metric units of area in common use are:
the square millimetre (mm^2)
the square centimetre (cm^2)
the square metre (m^2)
the square kilometre (km^2)

Example 3.1

The length of this line is 72 mm or 7.2 cm.

Example 3.2

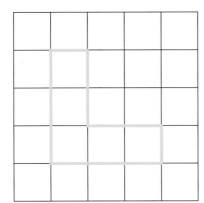

The side of each square on the grid represents 1 cm.

The perimeter of the L-shape = 1 + 2 + 2 + 1 + 3 + 3
= 12 cm

By counting the squares, the area of the L-shape = 5 cm^2

Example 3.3

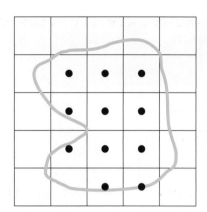

Estimate the area of the shape.

Each square on the grid has an area of 1 cm².

Mark each square which is at least half a square with a dot.

There are 11 dotted squares. So, an estimate for the area of the shape is 11 cm².

Length (*l*)

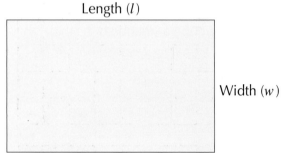

Width (*w*)

The perimeter of a rectangle is the total distance around the shape.

Perimeter = 2 Lengths + 2 Widths

$P = 2l + 2w$ Unit is mm, cm or m.

The area of the rectangle is the amount of space inside the shape.

Area = Length × Width

$A = l \times w$ or $A = lw$ Unit is mm², cm² or m².

Example 3.4

Find the perimeter and area of each of the following.

a

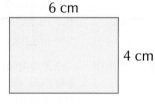

6 cm

4 cm

$P = 2 \times 6 + 2 \times 4$
$ = 12 + 8$
$ = 20 \text{ cm}$

$A = 6 \times 4$
$ = 24 \text{ cm}^2$

b

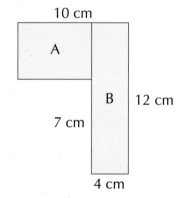

10 cm

A

B   12 cm

7 cm

4 cm

$P = 10 + 12 + 4 + 7 + 6 + 5$
$ = 44 \text{ cm}$

Total area = Area of A + Area of B
$ = 6 \times 5 + 12 \times 4$
$ = 30 + 48$
$ = 78 \text{ cm}^2$

Exercise 3A

1 Measure the length of each of the following lines. Give your answer in centimetres.

a ————————

b ————————

c ————————————

d ————————————

e ————————————————

2 The following lines are drawn using a scale of 1 cm represents 10 m. Write down the length that each line represents.

a _____

b _____

c _____

d _____

e _____

3 Each square on the grid represents one square centimetre. Find the perimeter and area of each shape.

a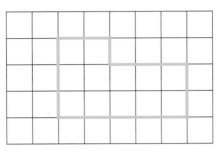

b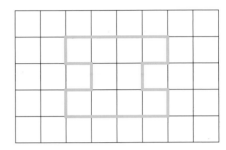

c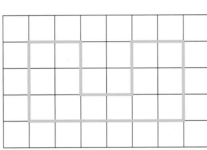

d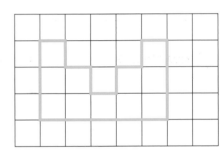

4 Estimate the area of each of these shapes. Each square on the grid represents one square centimetre.

a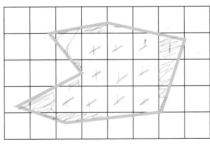

b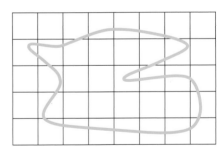

c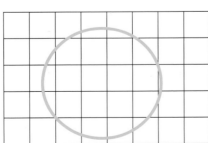

d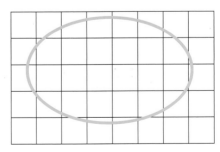

5 Find **i** the perimeter and **ii** the area of each rectangle.

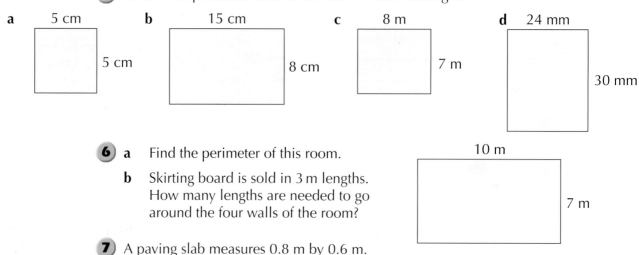

a   5 cm — 5 cm

b   15 cm — 8 cm

c   8 m — 7 m

d   24 mm — 30 mm

6 a Find the perimeter of this room.

   b Skirting board is sold in 3 m lengths. How many lengths are needed to go around the four walls of the room?

10 m — 7 m

7 A paving slab measures 0.8 m by 0.6 m. Find the perimeter of the slab.

8 A football pitch measures 100 m by 75 m. Calculate the area of the pitch.

9 A room measures 6 m by 4 m.

   a What is the area of the floor?

   b The floor is to be covered using square carpet tiles measuring 50 cm by 50 cm. How many tiles are needed to cover the floor?

10 Calculate the perimeter of this square.   25 cm²

11 Copy and complete the table for rectangles **a** to **f**.

	Length	Width	Perimeter	Area
a	8 cm	6 cm		
b	20 cm	15 cm		
c	10 cm		30 cm	
d		5 m	22 m	
e	7 m			42 m²
f		10 mm		250 mm²

12 Find **i** the perimeter and **ii** the area of each of the following compound shapes.

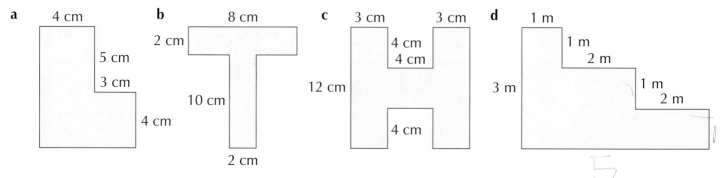

a   4 cm, 5 cm, 3 cm, 4 cm

b   8 cm, 2 cm, 10 cm, 2 cm

c   3 cm, 3 cm, 4 cm, 4 cm, 12 cm, 4 cm

d   1 m, 1 m, 2 m, 3 m, 1 m, 2 m

13 Phil finds the area of this compound shape.

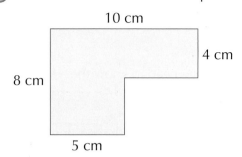

10 cm

4 cm

8 cm

5 cm

This is his working:

Area = 10 x 4 + 8 x 5
= 40 + 40
= 80 cm²

a Explain why he is wrong.

b Calculate the correct answer.

14 Sandra makes a picture frame from a rectangular piece of card for a photograph of her favourite group.

a Find the area of the photograph.

b Find the area of the card she uses.

c Find the area of the border.

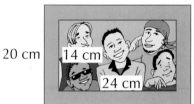

20 cm

14 cm

24 cm

30 cm

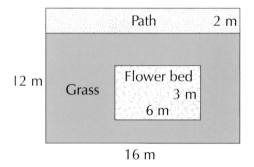

Path   2 m

12 m

Grass

Flower bed

3 m

6 m

16 m

15 A garden is in the shape of a rectangle measuring 16 m by 12 m.

a On centimetre squared paper, make a scale drawing of the garden. Use a scale of 1 cm to represent 1 m.

b Calculate the area of the grass.

16 How many rectangles can you draw with a fixed perimeter of 20 cm but each one having a different area?

Extension Work

1 Equable rectangles

Investigate whether a rectangle can have the same numerical value for its perimeter and its area.

2 Sheep pens

A farmer has 60 m of fence to make a rectangular sheep pen against a wall. Find the length and width of the pen in order to make its area as large as possible.

3 Squares on a chessboard

How many squares on a chessboard?

Areas of some 2-D shapes

Area of a triangle

To find the area of a triangle, you need to know the length of its base and its perpendicular height.

The diagram below shows that the area of the triangle is half of the area of a rectangle with the same base and height:

Area 1 = Area 2
Area 3 = Area 4

So, the area of a triangle is

$\frac{1}{2}$ × Base × Height.

The formula for the triangle is

$A = \frac{1}{2} \times b \times h = \frac{1}{2}bh$

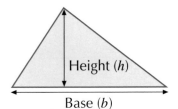

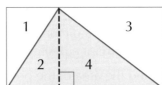

Example 3.5

Calculate the area of this triangle.

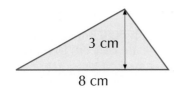

$A = \frac{1}{2} \times 8 \times 3 = 4 \times 3 = 12$ cm^2

Area of a parallelogram

To find the area of a parallelogram, you need to know the length of its base and its perpendicular height.

The diagrams on the right show that the parallelogram has the same area as a rectangle with the same base and height.

So, the area of a parallelogram is

Base × Height.

The formula for the area of a parallelogram is

$A = b \times h = bh$

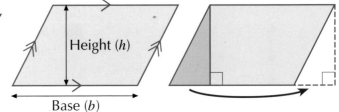

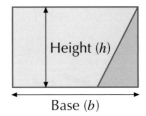

Example 3.6

Calculate the area of this parallelogram.

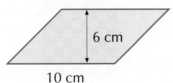

$A = 6 \times 10 = 60$ cm^2

Area of a trapezium

To find the area of a trapezium, you need to know the length of its two parallel sides, a and b, and the perpendicular height, h, between the parallel sides.

The diagram below shows how two of the same trapezia fit together to form a parallelogram.

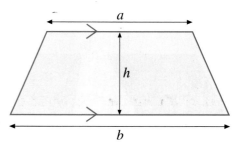

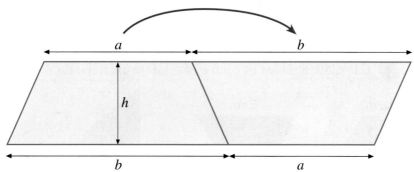

So, the area of a trapezium is

$\frac{1}{2} \times$ Sum of the lengths of the parallel sides $\times$ Height

The formula for the area of a trapezium is

$A = \frac{1}{2} \times (a + b) \times h = \frac{1}{2}(a + b)h$

Example 3.7

Calculate the area of this trapezium.

5 cm
4 cm
9 cm

$A = \frac{1}{2} \times (9 + 5) \times 4$
$= \frac{14 \times 4}{2}$
$= 28 \text{ cm}^2$

Exercise 3B

1 Calculate the area of each of the following triangles.

a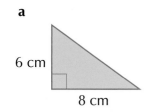
6 cm
8 cm

b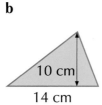
10 cm
14 cm

c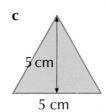
5 cm
5 cm

d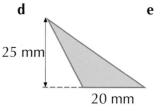
25 mm
20 mm

e
4 m
5 m

2 Copy and complete the table for triangles **a** to **e**.

	Base	Height	Area
a	5 cm	4 cm	
b	7 cm	2 cm	
c	9 m	5 m	
d	12 mm		60 mm²
e		8 m	28 m²

3 Calculate the area of each of the following parallelograms.

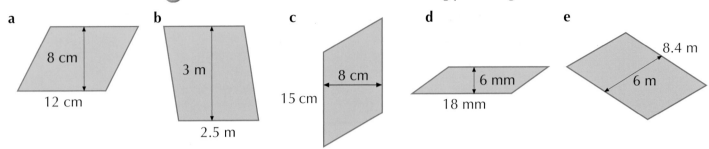

a
8 cm
12 cm

b
3 m
2.5 m

c
8 cm
15 cm

d
6 mm
18 mm

e
8.4 m
6 m

4 Calculate the area of each of the following trapezia.

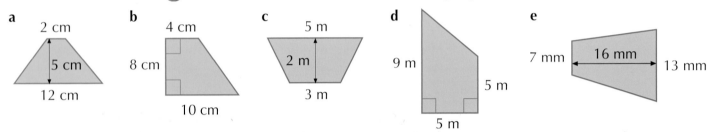

a
2 cm
5 cm
12 cm

b
4 cm
8 cm
10 cm

c
5 m
2 m
3 m

d
9 m
5 m
5 m

e
7 mm
16 mm
13 mm

5 The diagram shows the end wall of a garden shed.

   a Find the area of the door.

   b Find the area of the brick wall.

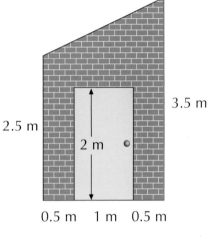

3.5 m

2.5 m

2 m

0.5 m   1 m   0.5 m

6 Find the area of this mathematical stencil with the shapes cut out.

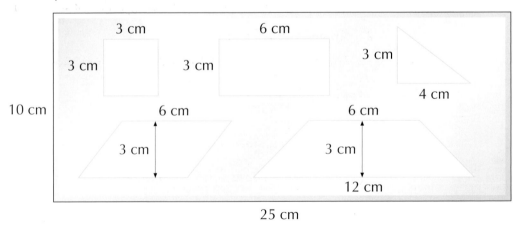

3 cm
6 cm
3 cm
3 cm
3 cm
3 cm
4 cm
10 cm
6 cm
3 cm
6 cm
3 cm
12 cm
25 cm

7 The area of this trapezium is 8 cm².
Find different values of a, b and h, with $b > a$.

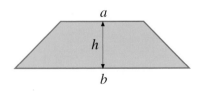

a
h
b

1 **Pick's formula**

The shapes below are drawn in a 1 cm grid of dots.

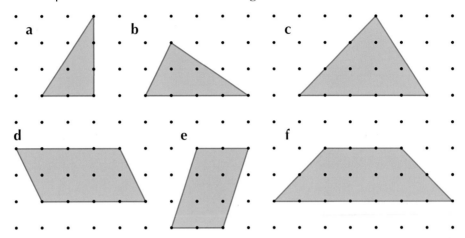

	Number of dots on perimeter of shape	Number of dots inside shape	Area of shape (cm²)
a			
b			
c			
d			
e			
f			

i   Copy and complete the table for each shape.

ii Find a formula that connects the number of dots on the perimeter (P), the number of dots inside (I) and the area (A) of each shape.

iii Check your formula by drawing different shapes on a 1 cm grid of dots.

2 **Changing units of area**

Draw diagrams to show that $1 \text{ cm}^2 = 100 \text{ mm}^2$ and that $1 \text{ m}^2 = 10\,000 \text{ cm}^2$.

3-D shapes

You should be able to recognise and name the following 3-D shapes or solids.

Cube   Cuboid   Pyramid   Tetrahedron   Triangular prism   Cone   Cylinder   Sphere   Hemisphere

Some of these solids can be drawn in several ways, as Example 3.8 shows.

Example 3.8   For a cube

On a square grid	As a net	On an isometric grid
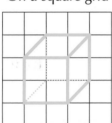	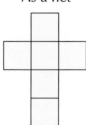	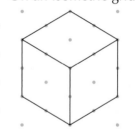

Not easy to draw to scale. Hidden edges can be dotted.   Used to make the shape when tabs are added.   Used to draw accurately. Each column of dots must be vertical.

Exercise 3C

1 On a square grid, draw as many different nets to make a cube as you can.

2 On squared paper, draw accurate nets for each of the following cuboids.

a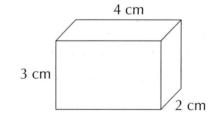

b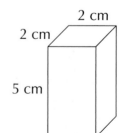

3 A cuboid has six faces, eight vertices and 12 edges.

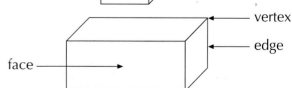

How many faces, vertices and edges do each of the following 3-D shapes have?

a

Square-based pyramid

b

Triangular prism

c

Tetrahedron

4 Draw each of the following cuboids accurately on an isometric grid.

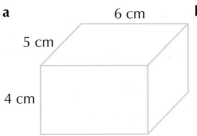

a 6 cm 5 cm 4 cm

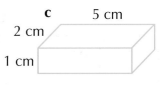

b 2 cm 2 cm 5 cm

c 5 cm 2 cm 1 cm

5 Draw this T-shape accurately on an isometric grid.

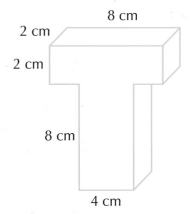

2 cm 2 cm 8 cm 8 cm 4 cm

6 How many cubes are required to make this solid?

Draw other similar solids of your own on an isometric grid.

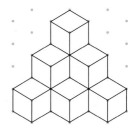

7 How many cubes are required to make this cuboid?

Can you find a quick way of working out the number of cubes inside any cuboid?

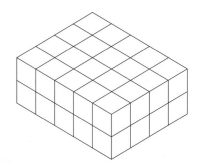

1 Euler's theorem

Copy and complete the following table for seven different polyhedrons.
Ask your teacher to show you these 3-D shapes.

Solid	Number of faces	Number of vertices	Number of edges
Cuboid			
Square-based pyramid			
Triangular prism			
Tetrahedron			
Hexagonal prism			
Octahedron			
Dodecahedron			

Find a formula that connects the number of faces, vertices and edges.

This formula is named after Léonard Euler, a famous eighteenth-century Swiss mathematician.

2 Pentominoes

A pentomino is a 2-D shape made from five squares that touch side to side. Here are two examples.

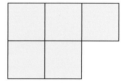

a Draw on squared paper as many different pentominoes as you can.

b How many of these pentominoes are nets that make an open cube?

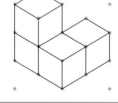

3 Four cubes

On an isometric grid, draw all the possible different solids that can be made from four cubes. Here is an example.

Surface area and volume of cuboids

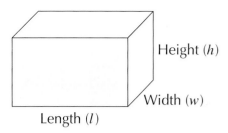

Length (*l*)   Width (*w*)   Height (*h*)

The surface area of a cuboid is found by calculating the total area of its six faces.

Area of top and bottom faces = 2 × length × width = $2lw$

Area of front and back faces = 2 × length × height = $2lh$

Area of the two sides = 2 × width × height = $2wh$

Surface area of cuboid = $S = 2lw + 2lh + 2wh$

Volume is the amount of space inside a 3-D shape.

The volume of a cuboid is found by multiplying its length by its width by its height.

Volume of a cuboid = Length × Width × Height

$$V = l \times w \times h = lwh$$

The metric units of volume in common use are:

cubic millimetre (mm³)

cubic centimetre (cm³)

cubic metre (m³)

Example 3.9

Find the surface area and volume of this cuboid.

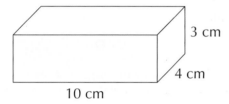

3 cm   4 cm   10 cm

$S = (2 \times 10 \times 4) + (2 \times 10 \times 3) + (2 \times 4 \times 3)$

$= 80 + 60 + 24$

$= 164 \text{ cm}^2$

$V = 10 \times 4 \times 3$

$= 120 \text{ cm}^3$

Exercise 3D

1 Find **i** the surface area and **ii** the volume for each of the following cuboids.

a

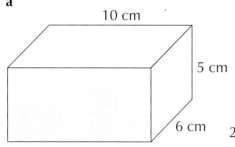

10 cm   5 cm   6 cm

b

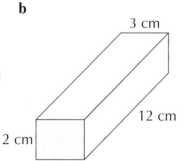

3 cm   12 cm   2 cm

c

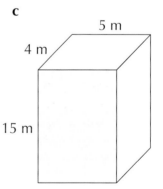

5 m   4 m   15 m

d

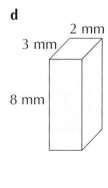

2 mm   3 mm   8 mm

2 Find the surface area of this unit cube.

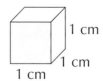

1 cm   1 cm   1 cm

3 Find **i** the surface area and **ii** the volume of each of the cubes with the following edge lengths.

   a   2 cm   **b**   5 cm   **c**   10 cm   **d**   8 m

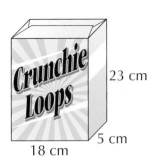

Crunchie Loops

23 cm

18 cm   5 cm

4 Find the surface area of the cereal packet on the left.

5 Find the surface area of the outside of this open water tank.
(A cuboid without a top.)

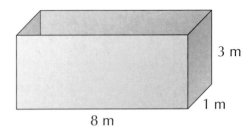

3 m

1 m

8 m

6 For the 3-D shape right, find:
  a its total surface area
  b its volume.

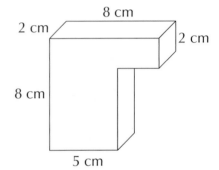

2 cm

8 cm

2 cm

8 cm

2 cm

5 cm

7 Draw some 3-D shapes on isometric paper using five unit cubes. Find the surface area of each of your shapes.

8 Find the volume of a hall which is 30 m long, 20 m wide and 10 m high.

9 How many packets of sweets, each measuring 8 cm by 5 cm by 2 cm, can be packed into a cardboard box measuring 32 cm by 20 cm by 12 cm?

10 Find the volume of this block of wood, giving your answer in cubic centimetres.

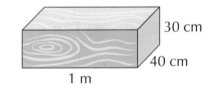

30 cm

40 cm

1 m

Extension Work

1 Estimating

Estimate the surface area and the volume of various everyday objects in the shape of cuboids.

Check your estimates by measuring.

20 cm

16 cm

2 Open box problem

An open box is made from a piece of card, measuring 20 cm by 16 cm, by cutting off a square from each corner.

Investigate the surface area of the open box formed for different sizes of square cut off.

You may wish to put your data on a computer spreadsheet.

3 Cubes to cuboids.

Twenty unit cubes are arranged to form a cuboid.

How many different cuboids can you make?

Which one has the greatest surface area?

What you need to know for level 5

- How to calculate the area of a rectangle by using the formula $A = lw$
- How to draw nets for 3-D shapes
- How to draw 3-D shapes on an isometric grid
- How to calculate the surface area of a cuboid

What you need to know for level 6

- How to calculate the area of a triangle, of a parallelogram and of a trapezium by using the appropriate formula
- How to calculate the volume of a cuboid

National Curriculum SATs questions

LEVEL 5

1 *1999 Paper 1*

The diagram shows a rectangle 18 cm long and 14 cm wide.

It has been split into four smaller rectangles.

What is the area of each small rectangle on the diagram?

One has been done for you.

What is the area of the whole rectangle?

What is 18×14?

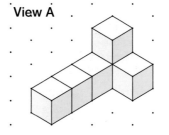

2 *2000 Paper 2*

I make a model with 6 cubes.

The drawings show my model from two different views.

View A   View B

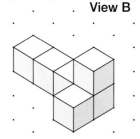

a I join one more cube to my model.

The drawing from view A shows where I join the cube.

Copy and complete the drawing from view B.

View A   View B

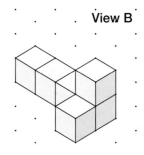

b Then I move the cube to a different position.

Copy and complete the drawing from view B.

View A   View B

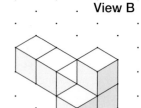

3 *1999 Paper 2*

This cuboid is made from 4 small cubes

a Draw a cuboid which is twice as high, twice as long and twice as wide.

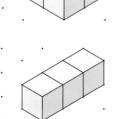

b Graham made this cuboid from 3 small cubes.

Mohinder wants to make a cuboid which is twice as high, twice as long and twice as wide as Graham's cuboid.

How many small cubes will Mohinder need altogether?

LEVEL 6

4 *1993 Paper 1*

Darren has a large empty match box.

He decorates it to make a gift box.

He wraps a rectangle of felt around the box. The edges of the felt do not overlap.

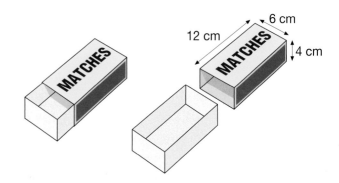

a What are the length and width of the felt?

Darren sticks ribbon around the two ends of the match box, like this. The ends of the ribbon do not overlap.

b What is the total length of ribbon Darren uses?

5   *1998 Paper 2*

A box for coffee is in the shape of a hexagonal prism.

One end of the box is shown below. Each of the six triangles in the hexagon has the same dimensions.

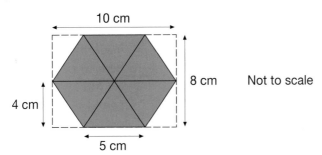

10 cm

8 cm   Not to scale

4 cm

5 cm

Calculate the total area of the hexagon.

6   *1998 Paper 1*

Each shape in this question has an area of 10 cm².

No diagram is drawn to scale.

a   Calculate the height of this parallelogram.

Area = 10 cm²   Height = ... cm

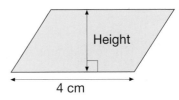

Height

4 cm

b   Calculate the length of the base of this triangle.

Area = 10 cm²   Base = ... cm

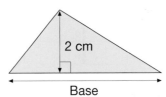

2 cm

Base

c   What might be the values of *h*, *a* and *b* in this trapezium? (*a* is greater than *b*)

Area = 10 cm²   *h* = ... cm

a = ... cm   *b* = ... cm

b

h

a

What else might the values of *h*, *a* and *b* be?

Area = 10 cm²   *h* = ... cm   *a* = ... cm   *b* = ... cm

Fractions

These diagrams show you five ways to split a 4 by 4 grid into quarters.

How many more different ways can you find to do this?

What about splitting the 4 by 4 grid into halves?

Example 4.1 ▷ Fill in the missing number in each of these equivalent fractions.

a $\dfrac{1}{3} = \dfrac{\square}{15}$ **b** $\dfrac{5}{8} = \dfrac{\square}{32}$ **c** $\dfrac{15}{27} = \dfrac{5}{\square}$

a Multiply by 5   **b** Multiply by 4   **c** Divide by 3

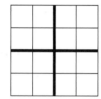 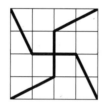 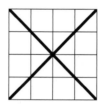 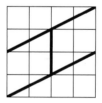

Example 4.2 ▷ Write each of the following as mixed numbers.

a $\dfrac{48}{15}$ **b** The fraction of a kilometre given by 3150 metres

a $48 \div 15 = 3$ remainder 3. So, $48 = 3\frac{3}{15}$ which cancels to $3\frac{1}{5}$

(Note: it is usually easier to cancel after the fraction has been written as a mixed number than before.)

b 1 kilometre is 1000 metres. So, the fraction is $\dfrac{3150}{1000} = 3\frac{150}{1000} = 3\frac{3}{20}$

1 Find the missing number in each of these equivalent fractions.

a $\frac{2}{3} = \frac{\square}{9}$ b $\frac{3}{8} = \frac{\square}{16}$ c $\frac{5}{9} = \frac{\square}{27}$ d $\frac{2}{5} = \frac{\square}{15}$

e $\frac{3}{7} = \frac{\square}{28}$ f $\frac{4}{9} = \frac{\square}{36}$ g $\frac{1}{5} = \frac{\square}{25}$ h $\frac{2}{11} = \frac{14}{\square}$

i $\frac{4}{9} = \frac{20}{\square}$ j $\frac{8}{5} = \frac{\square}{15}$ k $\frac{7}{2} = \frac{\square}{6}$ l $\frac{13}{3} = \frac{52}{\square}$

2 Cancel each of these fractions to its simplest form.

a $\frac{4}{12}$ b $\frac{6}{9}$ c $\frac{14}{21}$ d $\frac{15}{20}$ e $\frac{18}{20}$ f $\frac{20}{50}$

g $\frac{8}{24}$ h $\frac{6}{12}$ i $\frac{4}{24}$ j $\frac{12}{20}$ k $\frac{16}{24}$ l $\frac{25}{35}$

m $\frac{6}{14}$ n $\frac{12}{9}$ o $\frac{18}{27}$ p $\frac{45}{20}$ q $\frac{28}{10}$ r $\frac{120}{40}$

3 Clocks have 12 divisions around the face. What fraction of a full turn does

a   the minute hand turn through from 7:15 to 7:35?
b   the minute hand turn through from 8:25 to 9:25?
c   the hour hand turn through from 1:00 to 4:00?
d   the hour hand turn through from 4:00 to 5:30?

4 This compass rose has eight divisions around its face. What fraction of a turn takes you from

a   NW to SW clockwise?   b   E to S anticlockwise?
c   NE to S clockwise?   d   S to NE anticlockwise?
e   W to SE clockwise?   f   N to NW clockwise?

5 Give each answer in its lowest terms.

a   1 metre is 100 cm. What fraction of a metre is 35 cm?
b   1 kilogram is 1000 grams. What fraction of a kilogram is 550 grams?
c   1 hour is 60 minutes. What fraction of 1 hour is 33 minutes?
d   1 kilometres is 1000 metres. What fraction of a kilometre is 75 metres?

6 Write each of these fractions as a mixed number. Cancel down if appropriate.

a   seven thirds   b   sixteen sevenths   c   twelve fifths   d   nine halves

e $\frac{20}{7}$ f $\frac{24}{5}$ g $\frac{13}{3}$ h $\frac{19}{8}$

i $\frac{146}{12}$ j $\frac{78}{10}$ k $\frac{52}{12}$ l $\frac{102}{9}$

7 Use the information in Questions **3** and **5** to write each of these fractions as a mixed number.

a   The fraction of a turn the minute hand of a clock goes through from
     i   7:15 to 9:45   ii   8:25 to 10:10   iii   6:12 to 7:24
b   The fraction of a metre given by
     i   715 cm   ii   2300 mm   iii   405 cm
c   The fraction of a kilogram given by
     i   2300 g   ii   4050 g   iii   7500 g

There are 360° in one full turn. 90° is $\frac{90°}{360°} = \frac{1}{4}$ of a full turn.

1 What fraction of a full turn is each of these?

    a 60°   **b** 20°   **c** 180°   **d** 30°

    e 45°   **f** 36°   **g** 5°   **h** 450°

2 How many degrees is   **a** $\frac{1}{8}$ of a full turn?   **b** $\frac{1}{5}$ of a full turn?

3 360 was the number of days in a year according to the Ancient Egyptians. They also thought that numbers with lots of factors had magical properties. Find all the factors of 360.

4 Explain how the factors can be used to work out what fraction of a full turn is 40°.

Fractions and decimals

All of the grids below contain 100 squares. Some of the squares have been shaded in. In each case, write down the amount that has been shaded as a fraction, a percentage and a decimal. What connections can you see between the equivalent values?

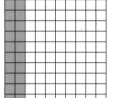 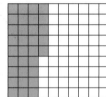 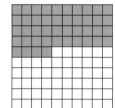 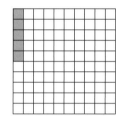 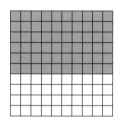 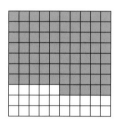

Example 4.3   Convert each of the following decimals to a fraction: **a** 0.65   **b** 0.44

  a $0.65 = \frac{65}{100} = \frac{13}{20}$ (cancel by 5)   **b** $0.44 = \frac{44}{100} = \frac{11}{25}$ (cancel by 4)

Example 4.4   Convert each of the following fractions to a decimal: **a** $\frac{7}{8}$ **b** $\frac{40}{25}$

  a Multiply top and bottom by 12.5:

$$\frac{7}{8} \frac{(\times 12.5)}{(\times 12.5)} = \frac{87.5}{100} = 0.875$$

  b First change to a mixed number: $\frac{40}{25} = 1\frac{15}{25}$.

    Then multiply the top and the bottom of the fraction by 4:

$$\frac{15}{25} \frac{(\times 4)}{(\times 4)} = \frac{60}{100} = 0.6$$

    So, the mixed number is 1.6.

Example 4.5 Put the correct sign, < or >, between each pair of fractions **a** $\frac{5}{8} \ldots \frac{3}{5}$ **b** $\frac{42}{25} \ldots \frac{17}{10}$

a Convert to fractions out of 100 (or decimals):

$$\frac{5}{8} = \frac{62.5}{100} = 0.625, \ \frac{3}{5} = \frac{60}{100} = 0.6. \ \text{So}, \frac{5}{8} > \frac{3}{5}.$$

b Convert first to mixed numbers then to fractions out of 100 (or decimals):

$$\frac{42}{25} = 1\frac{17}{25} = 1\frac{68}{100} = 1.68, \frac{17}{10} = 1\frac{70}{100} = 1.7. \ \text{So}, \frac{42}{25} < \frac{17}{10}.$$

Exercise 4B

1 Convert each of the following decimals to a fraction.

a 0.2	**b** 0.28	**c** 0.35	**d** 0.85	**e** 0.9	**f** 0.16
g 0.24	**h** 0.48	**i** 0.95	**j** 0.05	**k** 0.99	**l** 0.27

2 Convert each of the following fractions to a decimal.

a $\frac{3}{10}$	**b** $\frac{4}{25}$	**c** $\frac{3}{20}$	**d** $\frac{3}{8}$	**e** $\frac{23}{100}$	**f** $\frac{6}{25}$
g $\frac{7}{50}$	**h** $\frac{14}{25}$	**i** $\frac{13}{20}$	**j** $\frac{11}{10}$	**k** $\frac{115}{50}$	**l** $\frac{26}{25}$

3 Convert each of these top-heavy fractions to a decimal.

a $\frac{3}{2}$	**b** $\frac{7}{5}$	**c** $\frac{9}{8}$	**d** $\frac{17}{8}$	**e** $\frac{15}{2}$	**f** $\frac{22}{5}$
g $\frac{33}{20}$	**h** $\frac{17}{5}$	**i** $\frac{12}{5}$	**j** $\frac{33}{25}$	**k** $\frac{9}{4}$	**l** $\frac{41}{10}$

4 Convert each of these decimals to a mixed number.

a 1.25	**b** 2.5	**c** 3.125	**d** 4.4	**e** 5.375	**f** 2.6

5 Put the correct sign, <, > or =, between each pair of fractions.

a $\frac{7}{50} \ldots \frac{2}{20}$ **b** $\frac{27}{50} \ldots \frac{13}{25}$ **c** $\frac{10}{8} \ldots \frac{25}{20}$

6 Put each set of fractions in order of size, smallest first.

a $\frac{7}{25}, \frac{3}{10}, \frac{1}{4}$ **b** $\frac{3}{4}, \frac{37}{50}, \frac{7}{10}$ **c** $1\frac{6}{25}, 1\frac{1}{4}, 1\frac{11}{50}$

7 Which of these fractions is nearer to 1: $\frac{5}{8}$ or $\frac{8}{5}$? Show all your working.

Extension Work

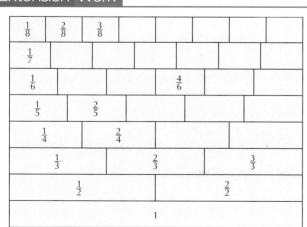

On squared paper outline an 8 × 8 grid.

Mark it off as shown. Then fill in the rest of the values in the boxes.

Use the diagram to put the correct sign (<, > or =) between each pair of fractions.

a $\frac{2}{7} \ldots \frac{1}{5}$ **b** $\frac{3}{8} \ldots \frac{1}{3}$ **c** $\frac{3}{4} \ldots \frac{6}{8}$

d $\frac{1}{2} \ldots \frac{4}{7}$ **e** $\frac{2}{8} \ldots \frac{1}{4}$ **f** $\frac{3}{7} \ldots \frac{1}{3}$

g $\frac{3}{5} \ldots \frac{2}{3}$ **h** $\frac{1}{2} \ldots \frac{5}{8}$ **i** $\frac{8}{5} \ldots \frac{5}{3}$

j $\frac{3}{6} \ldots \frac{1}{2}$ **k** $\frac{7}{4} \ldots \frac{4}{3}$ **l** $\frac{3}{2} \ldots \frac{6}{4}$

Adding and subtracting fractions

Look at the fraction chart and the number line.
Explain how you could use them to show that

$1\frac{1}{2} + \frac{7}{8} = 2\frac{3}{8}$ and $1\frac{1}{2} - \frac{7}{8} = \frac{5}{8}$.

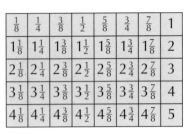

Example 4.6

Work out each of these: **a** $2\frac{1}{4} + 1\frac{3}{8}$ **b** $1\frac{1}{4} - \frac{5}{8}$

a   Start at $2\frac{1}{4}$ on the fraction chart. Add 1 to take you to $3\frac{1}{4}$.
Then count on $\frac{3}{8}$ to $3\frac{5}{8}$.

b   Start at $1\frac{1}{4}$ on the number line and count back $\frac{5}{8}$ to take you to $\frac{5}{8}$.

Example 4.7

Work out each of the following: **a** $\frac{3}{7} + \frac{5}{7}$ **b** $\frac{2}{9} + \frac{5}{9} - \frac{1}{9}$

Unless you can use a fraction chart or a number line, fractions must have the same denominator before they can be added or subtracted. The numerator of the answer is just the sum (or difference) of the original numerators. The denominator does not change. Sometimes it is possible to cancel the answer to its lowest terms.

a $\frac{3}{7} + \frac{5}{7} = \frac{8}{7} = 1\frac{1}{7}$

b $\frac{2}{9} + \frac{5}{9} - \frac{1}{9} = \frac{6}{9} = \frac{2}{3}$

Example 4.8

Work out each of these: **a** $\frac{2}{3} + \frac{1}{4}$ **b** $\frac{8}{9} - \frac{5}{6}$

When denominators are not the same, they must be made the same before the numerators can be added or subtracted. To do this, you need to find the **least common multiple** (**LCM**) of the denominators.

a   The LCM of 3 and 4 is 12. So, the two fractions need to be written as twelfths:
$$\frac{2}{3} + \frac{1}{4} = \frac{8}{12} + \frac{3}{12} = \frac{11}{12}$$

b   The LCM of 9 and 6 is 18. So, the two fractions need to be written as eighteenths:
$$\frac{8}{9} - \frac{5}{6} = \frac{16}{18} - \frac{15}{18} = \frac{1}{18}$$

Example 4.9

Work out each of the following: **a** $\frac{2}{3}$ of 45p   **b** $\frac{3}{7}$ of 140 cm

a   First find $\frac{1}{3}$ of 45: $45 \div 3 = 15$. So, $\frac{2}{3}$ of 45p $= 2 \times 15 = 30$p.

b   First find $\frac{1}{7}$ of 140: $140 \div 7 = 20$. So, $\frac{3}{7}$ of 140 cm $= 3 \times 20 = 60$ cm.

1 Work out each of the following. The fraction chart and the number line on page 50 may help.

a $\frac{5}{8} + \frac{1}{2}$ b $1\frac{1}{8} + \frac{3}{8}$ c $2\frac{2}{8} + 1\frac{5}{8}$ d $1\frac{1}{2} + \frac{7}{8}$

e $1\frac{5}{8} + 1\frac{3}{4}$ f $2\frac{7}{8} + 1\frac{1}{4}$ g $1\frac{3}{8} + 2\frac{3}{8}$ h $\frac{3}{8} + 1\frac{1}{2} + 1\frac{3}{4}$

i $\frac{5}{8} - \frac{1}{2}$ j $2\frac{1}{8} - \frac{5}{8}$ k $2\frac{3}{8} - 1\frac{5}{8}$ l $1\frac{1}{2} - \frac{7}{8}$

m $2\frac{3}{4} - 1\frac{3}{8}$ n $2\frac{7}{8} - 1\frac{1}{4}$ o $3\frac{3}{8} - 1\frac{3}{4}$ p $1\frac{3}{4} + 1\frac{1}{2} - 1\frac{7}{8}$

2 Work out each of the following. Convert to mixed numbers or cancel down to lowest terms.

a $\frac{1}{3} + \frac{1}{3}$ b $\frac{5}{6} + \frac{5}{6}$ c $\frac{3}{10} + \frac{3}{10}$ d $\frac{1}{9} + \frac{2}{9}$

e $\frac{4}{15} + \frac{13}{15}$ f $\frac{7}{9} + \frac{5}{9}$ g $\frac{5}{12} + 1\frac{1}{12}$ h $\frac{3}{7} + \frac{5}{7} + \frac{2}{7}$

i $\frac{5}{7} - \frac{2}{7}$ j $\frac{5}{6} - \frac{1}{6}$ k $\frac{9}{10} - \frac{3}{10}$ l $\frac{8}{9} - \frac{2}{9}$

m $\frac{14}{15} - \frac{2}{15}$ n $\frac{7}{9} - \frac{4}{9}$ o $\frac{11}{12} - \frac{5}{12}$ p $\frac{3}{10} + \frac{9}{10} - \frac{5}{10}$

3 Convert each pair of fractions to their equivalent fractions with a common denominator. Then work out the answer, cancelling down or writing as a mixed number if appropriate.

a $\frac{1}{3} + \frac{1}{4}$ b $\frac{1}{6} + \frac{1}{3}$ c $\frac{3}{10} + \frac{1}{4}$ d $\frac{1}{9} + \frac{5}{6}$

e $\frac{4}{15} + \frac{3}{10}$ f $\frac{7}{8} + \frac{5}{6}$ g $\frac{7}{12} + \frac{1}{4}$ h $\frac{3}{4} + \frac{1}{3} + \frac{1}{2}$

i $\frac{1}{3} - \frac{1}{4}$ j $\frac{5}{6} - \frac{1}{3}$ k $\frac{3}{10} - \frac{1}{4}$ l $\frac{8}{9} - \frac{1}{6}$

m $\frac{4}{15} - \frac{1}{10}$ n $\frac{7}{8} - \frac{5}{6}$ o $\frac{7}{12} - \frac{1}{4}$ p $\frac{3}{4} + \frac{1}{3} - \frac{1}{2}$

4 Work out each of the following.

a Half of twenty-four   b A third of thirty-six   c A quarter of forty-four

d A sixth of eighteen   e A fifth of thirty-five   f An eighth of forty

5 Work out each of the following.

a $\frac{2}{3}$ of 36 m   b $\frac{3}{4}$ of 44p   c $\frac{5}{6}$ of £18   d $\frac{4}{5}$ of 35 kg

e $\frac{3}{8}$ of 40 cm   f $\frac{3}{7}$ of 42 km   g $\frac{4}{9}$ of 36 mm   h $\frac{5}{6}$ of £24

i $\frac{3}{10}$ of £1   j $\frac{7}{8}$ of 84 m   k $\frac{7}{12}$ of 48 cm   l $\frac{9}{10}$ of 55 km

6 Work out each of these. Convert to mixed numbers or cancel down to lowest terms.

a $5 \times \frac{2}{3}$ b $3 \times \frac{3}{4}$ c $4 \times \frac{3}{8}$ d $6 \times \frac{2}{9}$

e $8 \times \frac{5}{6}$ f $4 \times \frac{7}{12}$ g $5 \times \frac{3}{7}$ h $4 \times \frac{3}{10}$

i $\frac{2}{3} \div 5$ j $\frac{3}{4} \div 3$ k $\frac{3}{8} \div 4$ l $\frac{2}{9} \div 6$

m $\frac{5}{6} \div 8$ n $\frac{7}{12} \div 4$ o $\frac{3}{7} \div 5$ p $\frac{3}{10} \div 4$

The Ancient Egyptians thought that 360 was a magical number because it had lots of factors.

They also used only fractions with 1 or 2 as the numerator, together with the commonly occurring fractions such as two-thirds, three-quarters, four-fifths and five-sixths.

Write down all the factors of 360 (or use your results from the extension work in Exercise 4A).

Write down the following fractions as equivalent fractions with a denominator of 360.

$$\frac{1}{2}, \frac{1}{3}, \frac{1}{4}, \frac{1}{5}, \frac{1}{6}, \frac{1}{8}, \frac{1}{9}, \frac{1}{10}, \frac{1}{12}$$

Use these results to work out:

a $\frac{1}{2} + \frac{1}{3}$ **b** $\frac{1}{2} + \frac{1}{6}$ **c** $\frac{1}{2} + \frac{1}{5}$ **d** $\frac{1}{3} + \frac{1}{4}$ **e** $\frac{1}{6} + \frac{1}{8}$

f $\frac{1}{3} - \frac{1}{5}$ **g** $\frac{1}{4} - \frac{1}{6}$ **h** $\frac{1}{8} - \frac{1}{10}$ **i** $\frac{1}{3} + \frac{1}{4} + \frac{1}{5}$ **j** $\frac{1}{6} + \frac{1}{12} - \frac{1}{4}$

Cancel down your answers to their simplest form.

Equivalences

Explain why BAG = 70%, HIDE = 2.2 and FED = $1\frac{1}{5}$.

Find the percentage value of CABBAGE. Find the decimal value of BADGE. Find the fraction value of CHIDE. Find the percentage, decimal and fraction values of other words you can make with these letters.

Example 4.10 ▷ Work out the equivalent fraction, decimal and/or percentage for each of the following.

a 0.14 **b** 0.55 **c** 66% **d** 45% **e** $\frac{9}{25}$ **f** $\frac{3}{8}$

a $0.14 = 14\% = \frac{14}{100} = \frac{7}{50}$ **b** $0.55 = 55\% = \frac{55}{100} = \frac{11}{20}$

c $66\% = 0.66 = \frac{66}{100} = \frac{33}{50}$ **d** $45\% = 0.45 = \frac{45}{100} = \frac{9}{20}$

d $\frac{9}{25} = \frac{36}{100} = 36\% = 0.36$ **f** $\frac{3}{8} = \frac{37.5}{100} = 37\frac{1}{2}\% = 0.375$

Example 4.11 ▷ Work out: **a** 35% of 620 **b** 40% of 56

a 10% of 620 = 62, 5% of 620 = 31. So 35% of 620 = 62 + 62 + 62 + 31 = 217.

b 10% of 56 = 5.6. So, 40% of 56 = 4 × 5.6 = 22.4.

Example 4.12 **a** A clothes shop has a sale and reduces its prices by 20%. How much is the sale price of these two items?

  i Jacket costing £45   **ii** Dress costing £125

  i 20% of 45 is 2 × 10% of 45 = 2 × 4.5 = 9. So, the jacket costs £45 – £9 = £36.

  ii 20% of 125 is 2 × 10% of 125 = 2 × 12.50 = 25. So, the dress costs £125 – £25 = £100.

b A company gives all its workers a 5% pay rise. How much is the new wage of each of these workers?

  i Joan who now gets £240 per week   **ii** Jack who gets £6.60 per hour

  i 5% of 240 is $\frac{1}{2}$ × 10% of 240 = $\frac{1}{2}$ × 24 = 12. So, Joan gets £240 + £12 = £252 per week.

  ii 5% of 6.60 is $\frac{1}{2}$ × 10% of 6.60 = $\frac{1}{2}$ × 66p = 33p. So, Jack gets £6.60 + 33p = £6.99 per hour.

Exercise 4D

1 Work out the equivalent percentage and fraction to each of these decimals.

  a 0.3   **b** 0.44   **c** 0.65   **d** 0.8   **e** 0.78
  f 0.27   **g** 0.05   **h** 0.16   **i** 0.96   **j** 0.25

2 Work out the equivalent decimal and fraction to each of these percentages.

  a 35%   **b** 70%   **c** 48%   **d** 40%   **e** 64%
  f 31%   **g** 4%   **h** 75%   **i** 18%   **j** 110%

3 Work out the equivalent percentage and decimal to each of these fractions.

  a $\frac{2}{25}$ **b** $\frac{7}{50}$ **c** $\frac{9}{10}$ **d** $\frac{17}{20}$ **e** $\frac{1}{8}$
  f $\frac{3}{5}$ **g** $\frac{17}{25}$ **h** $1\frac{3}{4}$ **i** $\frac{1}{10}$ **j** $\frac{19}{20}$

4 Write down the equivalent decimal and percentage to each of these.

  a $\frac{1}{3}$ **b** $\frac{2}{3}$

5 Calculate:

  a 10% of 240   **b** 35% of 460   **c** 60% of 150   **d** 40% of 32
  e 15% of 540   **f** 20% of 95   **g** 45% of 320   **h** 5% of 70
  i 75% of 280   **j** 10% of 45   **k** 30% of 45

6 Work out the final amount when:

  a £45 is increased by 10%   **b** £48 is decreased by 10%
  c £120 is increased by 20%   **d** £90 is decreased by 20%
  e £65 is increased by 15%   **f** £110 is decreased by 15%
  g £250 is increased by 25%   **h** £300 is decreased by 25%
  i £6.80 is increased by 35%   **j** £5.40 is decreased by 15%

7 a In a sale all prices are reduced by 15%. What is the new price of an item which costs:

    i £17.40   **ii** £26   **iii** £52.80   **iv** £74

  b An electrical company increases its prices by 5%. What is the new price of an item which costs:

    i £230   **ii** £130   **iii** £385   **iv** £99

Extension Work

As a decimal, a fraction and a percentage are all different ways of writing the same thing, we can sometimes make a calculation easier by using an equivalent form instead of the decimal, fraction or percentage given.

Example 1: 20% of 35. As 20% is $\frac{1}{5}$, this is the same as $\frac{1}{5} \times 35 = 7$.

Example 2: 0.3×340. As 0.3 is 30%, this the same as 30% of 340. 10% of 340 is 34. So, 30% of 340 is $3 \times 34 = 102$.

Example 3: $\frac{3}{25}$ of 40. As $\frac{3}{25}$ is 0.12, this is the same as $0.12 \times 40 = 4.8$.

Rewrite the following using an alternative to the percentage, decimal or fraction given. Then work out the answer.

  a 20% of 75   **b** $\frac{2}{25}$ of 60   **c** 25% of 19   **d** 60% of 550

  e $\frac{3}{20}$ of 90   **f** 0.125×64 **g** $\frac{3}{5}$ of 7   **h** 0.4×270

  i 75% of 44   **j** 0.3333×180

Solving problems

Mrs Bountiful decided to give £10 000 to her grandchildren, nieces and nephews. She gave $\frac{1}{5}$ to her only grandson, $\frac{1}{8}$ to each of her two granddaughters, $\frac{1}{10}$ to each of her three nieces and $\frac{1}{20}$ to each of her four nephews. What was left she gave to charity. How much did they each receive? What *fraction* of the £10 000 did she give to charity?

The best way to do this problem is to work with amounts of money rather than fractions.

The grandson gets $\frac{1}{5} \times £10\,000 = £2000$. Each granddaughter gets $\frac{1}{8} \times £10\,000 = £1250$. Each niece gets $\frac{1}{10} \times £10\,000 = £1000$. Each nephew gets $\frac{1}{20} \times £10\,000 = £500$.

Altogether she gives away $2000 + 2 \times (1250) + 3 \times (1000) + 4 \times (500) = £9500$. This leaves £500. As a fraction of £10 000, this is $\frac{500}{10\,000} = \frac{1}{20}$.

Solve the problems in Exercise 4E. Show all your working and explain what you are doing.

Exercise 4E

1 What number is halfway between the two numbers shown on each scale?

  a

  b

  c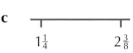

2 Which of these is greater?

  a $\frac{3}{5}$ of 45 or $\frac{2}{3}$ of 39?   **b** $\frac{3}{4}$ of 64 or $\frac{7}{9}$ of 63?   **c** $\frac{3}{10}$ of 35 or $\frac{1}{4}$ of 39?

3 There are 360 passengers on a Jumbo Jet. $\frac{1}{4}$ of them are British, $\frac{2}{5}$ of them are French, $\frac{1}{6}$ of them are German, $\frac{1}{12}$ of them are Italian and the rest are Dutch. How many of each nationality are there? What fraction of the passengers are Dutch?

4 Which of these dealers is giving the better value?

Jack's Fita Duo!
$\frac{1}{6}$ off the normal price of £45 000

Jill's Fita Duo!
$\frac{1}{5}$ off the normal price of £48,000

5 $\frac{4}{15}$ and $\frac{24}{9}$ are examples of three-digit fractions.

    a There is only one three-digit fraction equal to $1\frac{1}{2}$. What is it?

    b There are three three-digit fractions equal to $2\frac{1}{2}$, $3\frac{1}{2}$ and $4\frac{1}{2}$. Find them and explain why there cannot be more than three equivalent three-digit fractions for these numbers.

    c In the series of fractions $2\frac{1}{2}$, $3\frac{1}{2}$, $4\frac{1}{2}$, $5\frac{1}{2}$, ..., the last one that has three equivalent three-digit fractions is $16\frac{1}{2}$. Explain why.

6 There are 54 fractions in the sequence: $\frac{1}{54}$, $\frac{2}{54}$, $\frac{3}{54}$, $\frac{4}{54}$, ..., $\frac{54}{54}$. How many of them will not cancel down to a simpler form?

7 A shop is taking 10% off all its prices. How much will these items cost after a 10% reduction?

    a Saucepan £16.00   **b** Spoon 60p   **c** Coffee pot £5.80

    d Bread maker £54.00   **e** Cutlery set £27.40   **f** Tea set £20.80

8 A company is offering its workers a 5% pay rise. How much will the salary of each of the following people be after the pay rise?

    a Fred the storeman £12 000   **b** Alice the office manager £25 000

    c Doris the director £40 000   **d** John the driver £15 500

9 Another company is offering its workers a 4% or £700 per annum pay rise, whichever is the greater.

    What will the pay of the following people be after the pay rise?

    a Alf the storeman £12 000

    b Mark the office manager £25 000

    c Joe the driver £15 500

    d At what salary will a 4% pay rise be the same as a £700 pay rise?

National Curriculum SATs questions

LEVEL 5

1 *1998 Paper 1*

This is how Caryl works out 15% of 120 in her head.

10% of 120 is 12
5% of 120 is 6
so 15% of 120 is 18

a Show how Caryl can work out $17\frac{1}{2}$ % of 240 in her head.

b Work out 35% of 520. Show your working.

2 *2001 Paper 1*

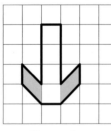 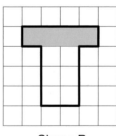 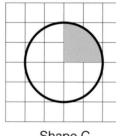 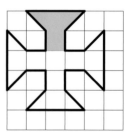

| Shape A | Shape B | Shape C | Shape D |

a What fraction of shape A is shaded?

b What percentage of shape B is shaded?

c Which of shape C or shape D has the greater percentage shaded or are they both the same?

Explain how you know.

LEVEL 6

3 *1997 Paper 2*

The table shows some information about pupils in a school.

	Left-handed	Right-handed
Girls	32	180
Boys	28	168

There are 408 pupils in the school. What percentage of the pupils are boys?

4 *1998 Paper 2*

The table shows the land area of each of the world's continents

Continent	Land area (in 1000 km²)
Africa	30 264
Antarctica	13 209
Asia	44 250
Europe	9 907
North America	24 398
Oceania	8 534
South America	17 793
World	148 355

a Which continent is approximately 12% of the world's land area?

b What percentage of the world's land area is Antarctica?

5 *1999 Paper 1*

a In a magazine there are three adverts on the same page. In total, what fraction of the page do the three adverts use ?

b An advert costs £10 for each $\frac{1}{32}$ of a page. An advert uses $\frac{3}{16}$ of a page. How much does the advert cost?

> Advert 1 uses $\frac{1}{4}$ of the page
>
> Advert 2 uses $\frac{1}{8}$ of the page
>
> Advert 3 uses $\frac{1}{16}$ of the page

6 *2001 Paper 1*

On a farm 80 sheep gave birth to lambs. 30% of the sheep gave birth to two lambs. The rest gave birth to just one lamb.

In total, how many lambs were born?

This chapter is going to show you

- how to calculate the mode, the median, the mean and the range for a set of data
- how to interpret statistical diagrams and charts
- how to calculate probabilities using equally likely outcomes
- how to collect data from experiments and calculate probabilities

What you should already know

- How to interpret data from tables, graphs and charts
- How to draw line graphs, frequency tables and bar charts

Mode, median and range

Statistics is concerned with the collection and organisation of data, the representation of data on diagrams and the interpretation of data.

When interpreting data we often need to find an **average**. For example: the average rainfall in Britain, the average score of a batsman, the average weekly wage, the average mark in an examination.

An average is a useful statistic because it represents a whole set of values by just a single or typical value. This section explains how to find two types of average: the **mode** and the **median**. It also explains how to find the **range** of a set of values.

The **mode** is the value that occurs most often in a set of data. It is the only average that can be used for non-numerical data. Sometimes there may be no mode because either all the values are different, or no single value occurs more often than other values. For grouped data, a mode cannot be found, so, instead, we find the **modal class**.

The **median** is the middle value for a set of values when they are put in numerical order. It is often used when one value in the set of data is much larger or much smaller than the rest. This value is called a **rogue value**.

The **range** of a set of values is the largest value minus the smallest value. A small range means that the values in the set of data are similar in size, whereas a large range means that the values differ considerably and therefore are more spread out.

Example 5.1 ▷ Here are the ages of 11 players in a football squad. Find the mode, median and range.

23, 19, 24, 26, 28, 27, 24, 23, 20, 23, 26

First, put the ages in order: 19, 20, 23, 23, 23, 24, 24, 26, 26, 27, 28

The mode is the number which occurs most often. So, the mode is 23.

The median is the number in the middle of the set. So, the median is 24.

The range is the largest number minus the smallest number: 28 − 19 = 9. The range is 9.

Example 5.2

Below are the marks of ten pupils in a mental arithmetic test. Find the mode, median and range.

19, 18, 16, 15, 13, 14, 20, 19, 18, 15

First, put the marks in order: 13, 14, 15, 15, 16, 18, 18, 19, 19, 20

There is no mode because no number occurs more often than the others.

There are two numbers in the middle of the set: 16 and 18. The median is the number in the middle of these two numbers. So, the median is 17.

The range is the largest number minus the smallest number: 20 − 13 = 7. The range is 7.

Exercise 5A

1 Find the mode of each of the following sets of data.

   a   red, white, blue, red, white, blue, red, blue, white, red

   b   rain, sun, cloud, fog, rain, sun, snow, cloud, snow, sun, rain, sun

   c   E, A, I, U, E, O, I, E, A, E, A, O, I, U, E, I, E

   d   ♠, ♣, ♥, ♦, ♣, ♠, ♥, ♣, ♦, ♥, ♣, ♥, ♦, ♥

2 Find the median of each of the following sets of data.

   a   7, 6, 2, 3, 1, 9, 5, 4, 8

   b   36, 34, 45, 28, 37, 40, 24, 27, 33, 31, 41

   c   14, 12, 18, 6, 10, 20, 16, 8

   d   99, 101, 107, 103, 109, 102, 105, 110, 100, 98

3 Find the range of each of the following sets of data.

   a   23, 37, 18, 23, 28, 19, 21, 25, 36

   b   3, 1, 2, 3, 1, 0, 4, 2, 4, 2, 6, 5, 4, 5

   c   2.1, 3.4, 2.7, 1.8, 2.3, 2.6, 2.9, 1.7, 2.2

   d   2, 1, 3, 0, −2, 3, −1, 1, 0, −2, 1

4 Find the mode, median and range of each set of data.

   a   £2.50   £1.80   £3.65   £3.80   £4.20   £3.25   £1.80

   b   23 kg, 18 kg, 22 kg, 31 kg, 29 kg, 32 kg

   c   132 cm, 145 cm, 151cm, 132 cm, 140 cm, 142 cm

   d   32°, 36°, 32°, 30°, 31°, 31°, 34°, 33°, 32°, 35°

5 A group of nine Year 7 students had their lunch in the school cafeteria. Given below is the amount that each of them spent.

     £2.30   £2.20   £2.00   £2.50   £2.20
     £2.90   £3.60   £2.20   £2.80

   a   Find the mode for the data.

   b   Find the median for the data.

   c   Which is the better average to use? Explain your answer.

6 Mr Kent draws a grouped frequency table to show the marks obtained by 32 students in his science test.

Mark	Tally	Frequency
21–40	⅃⅂⅂⅂	
41–60	⅃⅂⅂⅂ IIII	
61–80	⅃⅂⅂⅂ ⅃⅂⅂⅂ I	
81–100	⅃⅂⅂⅂ II	

    a Copy and complete the frequency column in the table.

    b Write down the modal class for Mr Kent's data.

    c What is the greatest range of marks possible for the data in the table?

    d Explain why it is not possible to find the exact median for the data in the table.

7 **a** Write down a list of seven numbers which has a median of 10 and a mode of 12.

    b Write down a list of eight numbers which has a median of 10 and a mode of 12.

    c Write down a list of seven numbers which has a median of 10, a mode of 12 and a range of 8.

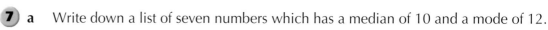
Extension Work

Surveys

Carry out a survey for any of the following. For each one, collect your data on a survey sheet, find the modal category and draw diagrams to illustrate your data.

1 The most popular colour of cars in the staff car park.

2 The most common letter in a page of text.

3 The favourite TV soap opera of students in your class.

The mean

The **mean** is the most commonly used average. It is also called the **mean average** or simply the **average**. The mean can be used only with numerical data.

The mean of a set of values is the sum of all the values divided by the number of values in the set. That is:

$$\text{Mean} = \frac{\text{Sum of all values}}{\text{Number of values}}$$

The mean is a useful statistic because it takes all values into account, but it can be distorted by rogue values.

Example 5.3   Find the mean of 2, 7, 9, 10.

$$\text{Mean} = \frac{2 + 7 + 9 + 10}{4} = \frac{28}{4} = 7$$

For more complex data, we can use a calculator. When the answer is not exact, the mean is usually given to one decimal place (1 dp).

Example 5.4 ▷ The ages of seven people are 40, 37, 34, 42, 45, 39, 35. Calculate their mean age.

$$\text{Mean age} = \frac{40 + 37 + 34 + 42 + 45 + 39 + 35}{7} = \frac{272}{7} = 38.9 \,(1\,\text{dp})$$

If you don't have a calculator, the mean can sometimes be worked out more quickly by using an **assumed mean**, as the following example shows.

Example 5.5 ▷ Find the mean of 46, 47, 37, 41, 39.

First, choose a value as an initial estimate for the mean. This is the assumed mean and will usually be a central value. It does not have to be a value in the list.

Take the assumed mean for the list to be 40. Then find the difference between each value in the list and the assumed mean. These are 6, 7, −3, 1, −1.

The mean of the differences is

$$\frac{6 + 7 + -3 + 1 + -1}{5} = \frac{10}{5} = 2 \quad \text{(This answer can be negative for some examples.)}$$

The actual mean is

Assumed mean + Mean of the differences

So, the actual mean for the list of numbers is 40 + 2 = 42.

The mean can also be calculated from a frequency table, as the following example shows.

Example 5.6 ▷ The frequency table shows the scores obtained when a dice is thrown 20 times. Find the mean score.

Score	1	2	3	4	5	6
Frequency	4	3	4	3	2	4

The table is redrawn in the way shown on the right in order to calculate the sum of the 20 scores.

Score	Frequency	Score × Frequency
1	4	4
2	3	6
3	4	12
4	3	12
5	2	10
6	4	24
Total	**20**	**68**

$$\text{Mean score} = \frac{68}{20} = 3.4$$

Exercise 5B

1. Find the mean of each of the following sets of data.

   a 8, 7, 6, 10, 4

   b 23, 32, 40, 37, 29, 25

   c 11, 12, 9, 26, 14, 17, 16

   d 2.4, 1.6, 3.2, 1.8, 4.2, 2.5, 4.5, 2.2

2 Find the mean of each of the following sets of data, giving your answer to 1 dp.

    a   6, 7, 6, 4, 2, 3   **b**   12, 15, 17, 11, 18, 16, 14

    c   78, 72, 82, 95, 47, 67, 77, 80   **d**   9.1, 7.8, 10.3, 8.5, 11.6, 8.9

3 Use an assumed mean to find the mean of each of the following sets of data.

    a   27, 32, 39, 34, 26, 28

    b   97, 106, 89, 107, 98, 104, 95, 104

    c   237, 256, 242, 251, 238, 259, 245, 261, 255, 236

    d   30.6, 29.8, 31.2, 28.7, 32.8, 29.3, 31.8

4 The heights, in centimetres, of ten children are

       132, 147, 143, 136, 135, 146, 153, 132, 137, 149

    a   Find the mean height of the children.

    b   Find the median height of the children.

    c   Find the modal height of the children.

    d   Which average do you think is the best one to use? Explain your answer.

5 The weekly wages of 12 office staff in a small company are

       £120, £140, £110, £400, £105, £360, £150, £200, £120, £130, £125, £140

    a   Find the mean weekly wage of the staff.

    b   How many staff earn more than the mean wage?

    c   Explain why so few staff earn more than the mean wage.

6 The frequency table shows the shoe sizes of 30 students in form 7HW.

Shoe size	3	4	5	6	7	8
Frequency	3	3	8	9	6	1

Calculate the mean shoe size of the form.

7 The bar chart shows the midday temperatures for every day in February for Playa de las Américas in Tenerife.

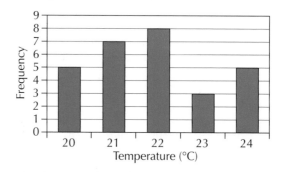

By drawing a suitable frequency table, calculate the mean daily temperature.

8 **a** | 6 | 4 | 3 | 7 | Find the mean of the four cards.

b | 3 | 7 | 6 | 8 | ? | Find the value of the fifth card, if the mean of the five cards is to be the same as in part **a**.

9 The mean age of three friends, Phil, Martin and Mike, is 42. Steve joins the three and the mean age of the four friends is now 40. How old is Steve?

1 **Vital statistics**

Working in groups, calculate the mean for the group's age, height and weight.

2 **Average score**

Throw a dice ten times. Record your results on a survey sheet. What is the mean score?

Repeat the experiment but throw the dice 20 times. What is the mean score now?

Repeat the experiment but throw the dice 50 times. What is the mean score now?

Write down anything you notice as you throw the dice more times.

Statistical diagrams

Once data has been collected from a survey, it can de displayed in various ways to make it easier to understand and interpret.

The most common ways to display data are bar charts, pie charts and line graphs.

Bar charts have several different forms. The questions in Exercise 5C will show you the different types of bar chart that can be used. Notice that data which has single categories gives a bar chart with gaps between the bars. Grouped data gives a bar chart with no gaps between the bars.

Pie charts are used to show data when you do not need to know the number of items in each category of the sample. Pie charts are used to show proportions.

Line graphs are usually used to show trends and patterns in the data.

Exercise 5C

1 The bar chart shows how the students in class 7PB travel to school.

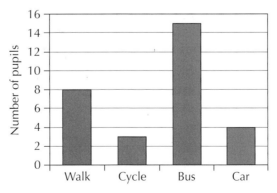

a How many students cycle to school?

b What is the mode for the way the students travel to school?

c How many students are there in class 7PB?

2 The dual bar chart shows the daily average number of hours of sunshine in London and Edinburgh over a year.

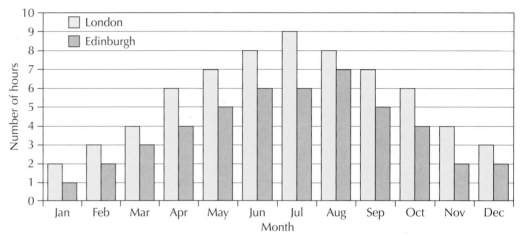

a Which city has the most sunshine?

b Which month is the sunniest for London and for Edinburgh?

c What is the range for the number of hours of sunshine over the year for London and for Edinburgh?

3 The percentage compound bar chart shows the favourite colours for a sample of Year 7 students.

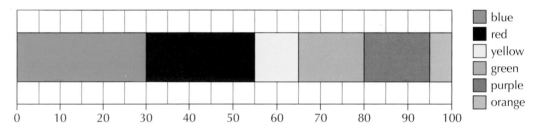

blue
red
yellow
green
purple
orange

a Which is the colour preferred by most students?

b What percentage of the students preferred yellow?

c Which two colours were equally preferred by the students?

d If there were 40 students in the sample, how many of them preferred red?

e Explain why the compound bar chart is a useful way to illustrate the data.

4 The bar chart shows the marks obtained in a mathematics test by the students in class 7KG.

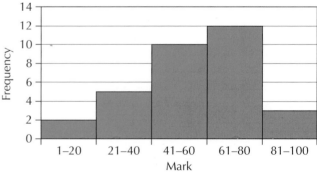

a How many students are there in class 7KG?

b What is the modal class for the data?

c How many students got a mark over 60?

d Write down the smallest and greatest range of marks possible for the data.

5 The pie chart shows the TV channel that 60 people in a survey most often watched.

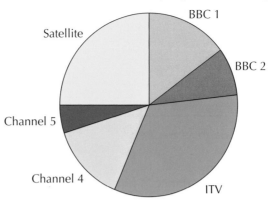

a Which is the most popular channel?

b Which is the least popular channel?

c Which channel is most often watched by 25% of the people in the survey?

d About how many people in the survey most often watched ITV?

6 The line graph shows the temperature, in °C, in Leeds over a 12-hour period.

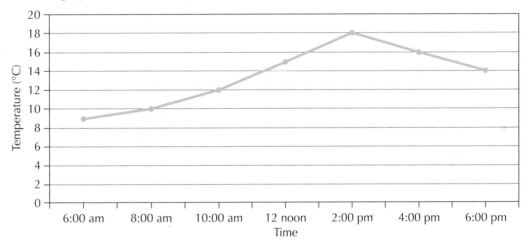

a What is the temperature at midday? **b** What is the temperature at 3pm?

c Write down the range for the temperature over the 12-hour period.

d Explain why the line graph is a useful way of showing the data.

Extension Work

Statistics in the press

Look through newspapers and magazines to find as many statistical diagrams as you can. Make a display to show the variety of diagrams used in the press.

What types of diagram are most common? How effective are the diagrams in showing the information?

Are any of the diagrams misleading? If they are, explain why.

Statistics in other areas

Do other subject areas in school make use of statistical diagrams?

Find examples in textbooks from other subjects to show where statistical diagrams are used most effectively.

Probability

Probability is the way of describing and measuring the chance or likelihood that an **event** will happen.

The chance of an event happening can be shown on a **probability scale**:

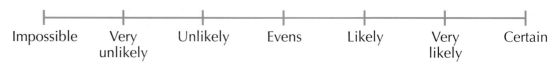

| Impossible | Very unlikely | Unlikely | Evens | Likely | Very likely | Certain |

An evens chance is often referred as 'a 50–50 chance'. Other everyday words used to describe probability are: uncertain, possible, probable, good chance, poor chance.

To measure probability, we use a scale from 0 to 1. So probabilities are written as fractions or decimals, and sometimes as percentages, as in the weather forecasts.

The probability scale is now drawn as:

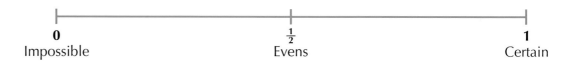

0
Impossible
$\frac{1}{2}$
Evens
1
Certain

We define the probability of an event happening as:

$$P(\text{event}) = \frac{\text{Number of outcomes in the event}}{\text{Total number of all possible outcomes}}$$

Example 5.7

When tossing a fair coin, there are two possible outcomes:
Head (H) or Tail (T).

Each outcome is **equally likely** to happen because it is a fair coin. So,

$$P(H) = \tfrac{1}{2} \text{ and } P(T) = \tfrac{1}{2}$$

This is the **probability fraction** for the event.

(Sometimes, people may say a 1 in 2 chance or a 50–50 chance.)

Example 5.8

When throwing a fair dice, there are six equally likely outcomes: 1, 2, 3, 4, 5, 6.

So, for example:

$$P(6) = \tfrac{1}{6} \text{ and } P(1 \text{ or } 2) = \tfrac{2}{6} = \tfrac{1}{3}$$

Probability fractions are *always* cancelled down.

Example 5.9

When drawing a card from a normal pack of 52 playing cards, the probability of picking a Spade is

$$P(\text{a Spade}) = \tfrac{13}{52} = \tfrac{1}{4}$$

So, the probability of *not* picking a Spade is

$$P(\text{not a Spade}) = \tfrac{39}{52} = \tfrac{3}{4}$$

The answer in Example 5.9 is the same as $1 - \frac{1}{4}$.

So, when the probability of an event occurring is p, the probability of the event not occurring is $1 - p$.

A **sample space diagram** is often used to show the equally likely outcomes for two combined events.

Example 5.10

The sample space diagram on the right shows all the possible outcomes for the total score when two fair dice are thrown.

The sample space diagram shows that there are 36 equally likely outcomes. So, for example:

a P(double 6) = P(score of 12) = $\frac{1}{36}$

b P(score of 8) = $\frac{5}{36}$

c P(score greater than 10) =
       P(score of 11 or 12) = $\frac{3}{36} = \frac{1}{12}$

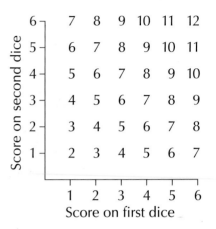

Exercise 5D

1 Cards numbered 1 to 10 are placed in a box. A card is drawn at random from the box. Find the probability that the card drawn is:

    a 5   **b** an even number   **c** a number in the 3 times table

    d 4 or 8   **e** a number less than 12   **f** not 7

2 Adam picks a card at random from a normal pack of 52 playing cards. Find each of the following probabilities.

    a P(a Jack)   **b** P(a Heart)   **c** P(a picture card)

    d P(Ace of Spades)   **e** P(a 9 or a 10)   **f** P(not an ace)

3 A bag contains five red discs, three blue discs and two green discs. Linda takes out a disc at random. Find the probability that she takes out:

    a a red disc   **b** a blue disc   **c** a green disc

    d a yellow disc   **e** a red or blue disc   **f** a disc that is not blue

4 Mitchell has a box of coloured squares with shapes drawn on them.

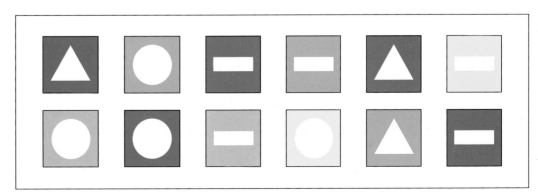

He takes out a square at random. Find the probability that he takes out :

a   a red square

b   a square with a circle in it

c   a green square with a triangle in it

d   a blue square with a rectangle or a circle in it

e   a square with no rectangle in it.

5   Marion says that the result of a football match can be win, lose or draw. She then says that, since there are three outcomes, …

Is she correct? Explain your answer.

... the probability that a team wins a match is $\frac{1}{3}$

6   The sample space diagram shows the outcomes when two fair coins are tossed.

a   Copy and complete the diagram.

b   Using the sample space diagram, find each of the following probabilities.

   i   P(2 Heads)   **ii**   P(2 Tails)

   iii   P(1 Head and 1 Tail)

   iv   P(not getting 2 Heads)

Second coin

Head –

Tail –   (T, T)

       Tail   Head
       First coin

7   The two different, fair, five-sided spinners shown here are spun together and the product of their scores is recorded.

a   Draw a sample space diagram to show all the possible outcomes.

b   How many equally likely outcomes are there?

c   Find each of the following probabilities:

   i   P(score of 18)   **ii**   P(score of 4)

   iii   P(score that is a multiple of 3)   **iv**   P(odd score)

Spinner 1: 1, 3, 5, 1, 3

Spinner 2: 2, 4, 4, 2, 6

Extension Work

You will need a set of cards numbered 1 to 10 for this experiment.

Line up the cards, face down and in random order.

1   Turn over the first card.

2   Work out the probability that the second card will be higher than the first card.

3   Work out the probability that the second card will be lower than the first card.

4   Turn over the second card.

5   Work out the probability that the third card will be higher than the second card.

6   Work out the probability that the third card will be lower than the second card.

7   Carry on the process. Write down all your results clearly and explain any patterns that you notice.

Repeat the experiment. Are your results the same?

Experimental probability

The probabilities in the previous section were calculated using equally likely outcomes. A probability worked out this way is known as a **theoretical probability**.

Sometimes, a probability can be found only by carrying out a series of experiments and recording the results in a frequency table. The probability of the event can then be estimated from these results. A probability found in this way is known as an **experimental probability**.

To find an experimental probability, the experiment has to be repeated a number of times. Each separate experiment carried out is known as a **trial**.

$$\text{Experimental probability of an event} = \frac{\text{Number of times the event occurs}}{\text{Total number of trials}}$$

It is important to remember that when an experiment is repeated, the experimental probability will be slightly different each time. The experimental probability of an event is an estimate for the theoretical probability. As the number of trials increases, the value of the experimental probability gets closer to the theoretical probability.

Example 5.11

A dice is thrown 50 times. The results of the 50 trials are shown in a frequency table.

Score	1	2	3	4	5	6
Frequency	8	9	8	10	7	8

The experimental probability of getting a 3 $= \dfrac{8}{50} = \dfrac{4}{25}$

Exercise 5E

1. Working in pairs, toss a coin 50 times and record your results in a frequency table.
   a. Use your results to find the experimental probability of getting a Head.
   b. What is the theoretical probability of getting a Head?
   c. How many Heads would you expect to get after tossing the coin 50 times?

2. Working in pairs, throw a dice 100 times and record your results in a frequency table.
   a. Find the experimental probability of getting 6, writing your answer as
      i. a fraction
      ii. a decimal
   b. The theoretical probability of getting a 6 is $\frac{1}{6}$ or 0.17. How close is your experimental probability to the theoretical probability?
   c. Explain how you could improve the accuracy of your experimental probability.

3. Working in pairs, drop a drawing pin 50 times. Record your results in the following frequency table.

	Tally	Frequency
Point up		
Point down		

   a. What is the experimental probability that the drawing pin will land point-up?
   b. Is your answer greater or less than an evens chance?
   c. Explain what would happen if you repeated the experiment.

4 Brian says: ' When I drop a piece of toast, it always lands butter-side down'.

Simulate Brian's statement by dropping a playing card 50 times and recording the number of times the card lands face down.

    a   What is the experimental probability that the card lands face down?

    b   Do you think this is a good way to test Brian's statement? Explain your answer.

5 Working in pairs, toss three coins 50 times. Record, in a frequency table, the number of Heads you get for each trial.

    a   What is the experimental probability of getting each of the following?

        i   three Heads   **ii**   two Heads   **iii**   one Head   **iv**   no Heads

    b   List all the equally likely outcomes for throwing three coins. (Hint: there are eight.) What is the theoretical probability of getting each of the following?

        i   three Heads   **ii**   two Heads   **iii**   one Head   **iv**   no Heads

Extension Work

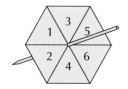

Biased spinners

Make a six-sided spinner from card and a cocktail stick.

Weight it by sticking a small piece of Plasticine below one of the numbers on the card. This will make the spinner unfair or biased.

Roll the spinner 60 times and record the scores in a frequency table.

Find the experimental probability for each score.

Compare your results with what you would expect from a fair, six-sided spinner.

Repeat the experiment by making a spinner with a different number of sides.

What you need to know for level 5

- How to find the mean and the median for a set of data
- How to find the mean from a frequency table
- How to interpret statistical diagrams
- How to calculate probability using equally likely outcomes
- How to calculate probability from experimental data

What you need to know for level 6

- How to calculate the mean for a set of data using an assumed mean
- When the probability of an event occurring is p, the probability of the event not occurring is $1 - p$
- How to calculate probabilities using a sample space diagram for two combined events

National Curriculum SATs questions

LEVEL 5

1 *2000 Paper 2*

A newspaper predicts what the ages of secondary school teachers will be in six years' time.

They print this chart.

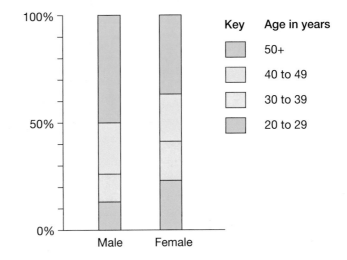

a The chart shows 24% of male teachers will be aged 40 to 49.

About what percentage of female teachers will be aged 40 to 49?

b About what percentage of female teachers will be aged 50+?

c The newspaper predicts there will be about 20 000 male teachers aged 40 to 49.

Estimate the number of male teachers that will be aged 50+.

d Assume the total number of male teachers will be about the same as the total number of female teachers.

Use the chart to decide which statement given below is correct.

Generally, male teachers will tend to be younger than female teachers.

Generally, female teachers will tend to be younger than male teachers.

Explain how you used the chart to decide.

2 *2000 Paper 2*

In each box of cereal there is a free gift of a card.

You cannot tell which card will be in a box. Each card is equally likely.

There are four different cards: A, B, C or D

a Zoe needs card A.

Her brother Paul needs cards C and D.

They buy one box of cereal.

What is the probability that the card is one that Zoe needs?

What is the probability that the card is one that Paul needs?

b Then their mother opens the box. She tells them the card is not card A.

Now what is the probability the card is one that Zoe needs?

What is the probability that the card is one that Paul needs?

LEVEL 6

3 *2000 Paper 2*

    a Paula played four games in a competition. In three games, Paula scored 8 points each time. In the other game she scored no points.

       What was Paula's mean score over the four games?

    b Jessie only played two games. Her mean score was 3 points. Her range was 4 points.

       What points did Jessie score in her two games?

    c Ali played three games. His mean score was also 3 points. His range was also 4 points.

       What points might Ali have scored in his three games? Show your working.

4 *1996 Paper 2*

A school has five year groups.

80 pupils from the school took part in a sponsored swim. Lara drew this graph.

    a Look at the graph.

       Did Year 10 have fewer pupils taking part in the swim than Year 7?

       Explain your answer.

    b Use the graph to work out the mean number of lengths swum by each of the 80 pupils. Show your working.

Number of lengths swum by each year group

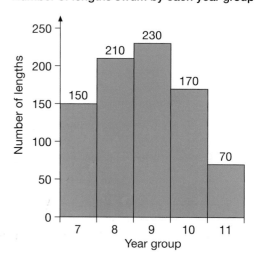

5 *1998 Paper 2*

I have two fair dice. Each of the dice is numbered 1 to 6.

    a The probability that I will throw double 6 (both dice showing number 6) is

$$\frac{1}{36}$$

       What is the probability that I will not throw double 6?

    b I throw both dice and get double 6. Then I throw the dice again.

       Which statement describes the probability that I will throw double 6 this time?

       Less than $\frac{1}{36}$

               $\frac{1}{36}$

       More than $\frac{1}{36}$

       Explain your answer.

I start again and throw both dice.

    c What is the probability that I will throw double 3 (both dice showing number 3)?

    d What is the probability that I will throw a double? (It could be double 1 or double 2 or any other double.)

This chapter is going to show you

- how to use letters in place of numbers
- how to use the rules (conventions) of algebra
- how to solve puzzles called equations
- how to solve problems using algebra.

What you should already know

- Understand and be able to apply the rules of arithmetic
- The meaning of the words term and expression

Algebraic terms and expressions

In algebra, you will keep meeting three words: **variable**, **term** and **expression**.

Variable This is the letter in a term or an expression whose value can vary. Some of the letters most used for variables are x, y, n and t.

Term This is an algebraic quantity which contains only a letter (or combination of letters) and may contain a number. For example:

$3n$ means 3 multiplied by the variable n

$\dfrac{n}{2}$ means n divided by 2

n^2 means n multiplied by itself (normally said as 'n squared')

Expression This is a combination of letters (variables) and signs, often with numbers. For example:

$8 - n$ means subtract n from 8
$n - 3$ means subtract 3 from n
$2n + 7$ means n multiplied by 2 with 7 added on

When you give a particular value to the variable in an expression, the expression takes on a particular value.

For example, if the variable n takes the value of 4, then the terms and expressions which include this variable will have particular values, as shown below:

$3n = 12$ $\dfrac{n}{2} = 2$ $n^2 = 16$ $8 - n = 4$ $n - 3 = 1$ $2n + 7 = 15$

Exercise 6A

1 Write terms, or expressions, to illustrate the following sentences.

a Add four to m.	**b** Multiply t by eight.	**c** Nine minus y.
d Multiply m by itself.	**e** Divide n by five.	**f** Subtract t from seven.
g Multiply n by three, then add five.		**h** Multiply six by t.
i Multiply m by five, then subtract three.		**j** Multiply x by x.

2 Write down the values of each term for the three values of n.

a $4n$ where **i** $n = 2$ **ii** $n = 5$ **iii** $n = 11$

b $\dfrac{n}{2}$ where **i** $n = 6$ **ii** $n = 14$ **iii** $n = 8$

c n^2 where **i** $n = 3$ **ii** $n = 6$ **iii** $n = 7$

d $3n$ where **i** $n = 7$ **ii** $n = 5$ **iii** $n = 9$

e $\dfrac{n}{5}$ where **i** $n = 10$ **ii** $n = 5$ **iii** $n = 20$

3 Write down the values of each expression for the three values of n.

a $n - 5$ where **i** $n = 8$ **ii** $n = 14$ **iii** $n = 11$

b $10 - n$ where **i** $n = 4$ **ii** $n = 7$ **iii** $n = 1$

c $2n + 3$ where **i** $n = 2$ **ii** $n = 5$ **iii** $n = 7$

d $5n - 1$ where **i** $n = 3$ **ii** $n = 4$ **iii** $n = 8$

e $20 - 2n$ where **i** $n = 1$ **ii** $n = 5$ **iii** $n = 9$

4 Write down the values of each expression for the three values of n.

a $n^2 - 1$ where **i** $n = 2$ **ii** $n = 3$ **iii** $n = 4$

b $5 + n^2$ where **i** $n = 8$ **ii** $n = 9$ **iii** $n = 10$

c $n^2 + 9$ where **i** $n = 5$ **ii** $n = 4$ **iii** $n = 3$

d $25 + n^2$ where **i** $n = 4$ **ii** $n = 5$ **iii** $n = 6$

Extension Work

1 Using the variable n and the operations {add, subtract, multiply, divide, square], write down as many different expressions, you can that use as:

a two operations

b three operations

2 Choose any value for n, say 5, and see how many of these expressions have the same value.

Rules of algebra

The rules (conventions) of algebra are the same rules that are used in arithmetic. For example:

$3 + 4 = 4 + 3$ $\qquad a + b = b + a$

$3 \times 4 = 4 \times 3$ $\qquad a \times b = b \times a$ or $ab = ba$

But remember, for example, that:

$7 - 5 \neq 5 - 7$ $\qquad a - b \neq b - a$

$6 \div 3 \neq 3 \div 6$ $\qquad \dfrac{a}{b} \neq \dfrac{b}{a}$

From one fact, other facts can be stated. For example:

$3 + 4 = 7$ $\qquad\qquad\qquad\qquad\qquad a + b = 10$

gives $7 - 4 = 3$ and $7 - 3 = 4$ $\qquad$ gives $10 - a = b$ and $10 - b = a$

$3 \times 4 = 12$ $\qquad\qquad\qquad\qquad\qquad ab = 10$

gives $\dfrac{12}{3} = 4$ and $\dfrac{12}{4} = 3$ $\qquad$ gives $\dfrac{10}{a} = b$ and $\dfrac{10}{b} = a$

1 In each of the following clouds only two expressions are equal to each other. Write down the equal pair.

a

$$a + b \quad a - b$$
$$a \times b \quad b + a$$
$$b \div a \quad b - a$$

b

$$m + p \quad m - p$$
$$m \times p \quad p \div m \quad m \div p$$
$$p \times m$$

2 In each of the following lists, write down all the expressions that equal each other.

a $ab, a + b, b - a, ba, \dfrac{a}{b}, a - b, \dfrac{b}{a}, b + a, a \div b$

b $k \times t, k + t, \dfrac{k}{t}, kt, k \div t, tk, t + k, t \times k, k - t$

3 Write down two more facts that are implied by each of the following statements.

a $a + b = 7$ **b** $ab = 24$ **c** $3 + k = 9$ **d** $\dfrac{8}{a} = 7$

4 Show by the substitution of suitable numbers that:

a $m + n = n + m$ **b** $ab = ba$ **c** $p - t \neq t - p$ **d** $\dfrac{m}{n} \neq \dfrac{n}{m}$

5 Show by the substitution of suitable numbers that:

a $a + b + c = c + b + a$ **b** $acb = abc = cba$

6 If you know that $a + b + c + d = 180$, write down as many other expressions that equal 180 as you can.

7 It is known that $abcd = 100$. Write down at least ten other expressions that must also equal 100.

8 Show, by substitution, that $3t^2 \neq (3t)^2$.

9 Write down the value of each expression when $t = 5$.
a $3t^2$ **b** $(3t)^2$ **c** $4t^2 + 1$ **d** $(4t + 1)^2$

Extension Work

1 Write down some values of a and b which make the following statement true.

$$a + b = ab$$

You will find only one pair of integers. There are lots of decimal numbers to find, but each time try to keep one of the variables an integer.

2 Write down some values of a and b which make the following statements true.

$$a - b = \dfrac{a}{b}$$

You will find only one pair of integers. There are lots of decimal numbers to find, but each time try to keep one of the variables an integer.

3 Is $(a + b) \times (a - b) = a^2 - b^2$ for all values of a and b?

4 A Fibonacci sequence is one in which each term, after the second term, is the sum of the two previous terms. For example:

1, 1, 2, 3, 5, 8, 13, 21, 34, …

How many different Fibonacci sequences can you find which have 50 as the seventh term?

Simplifying expressions

If you add 2 cups to 3 cups, you get 5 cups. In algebra, this can be represented as

$$2c + 3c = 5c$$

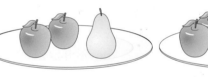

The terms here are called **like terms**, because they are all multiples of c.

Only like terms can be added or subtracted to simplify an expression. Unlike terms cannot be combined.

Check out these two boxes.

Examples of combining like terms

$$3p + 4p = 7p \qquad 5t + 3t = 8t$$

$$9w - 4w = 5w \qquad 12q - 5q = 7q$$

$$a + 3a + 7a = 11a$$

$$15m - 2m - m = 12m$$

Examples of unlike terms

$$x + y \qquad\qquad 2m + 3p$$

$$7 - 3y \qquad\qquad 5g + 2k$$

$$m - 3p$$

Like terms can be combined even when they are mixed together with unlike terms. For example:

2 apples and 1 pear added to 4 apples and 2 kiwis make 6 apples, 1 pear and 2 kiwis, or in algebra

$$2a + p + 4a + 2k = 6a + 2k + p$$

Examples of different sorts of like terms mixed together

$$4t + 5m + 2m + 3t + m = 7t + 8m$$

$$5k + 4g - 2k + g = 3k + 3g$$

NOTE $\quad g = 1g \quad m = 1m$

You **never** write the one in front of a variable

Expanding and simplifying

There are many situations in algebra where there is a need to use brackets in expressions. They keep things tidy! You can **expand** brackets, as shown in Example 6.1. This operation is also called **multiplying out**.

Example 6.1

Expand and simplify $2(3p + 4) + 3(4p + 1)$.

This means that each term in each pair of brackets is multiplied by the number outside the brackets. This gives

$$2 \times 3p + 2 \times 4 + 3 \times 4p + 3 \times 1$$
$$= 6p + 8 + 12p + 3$$
$$= 18p + 11$$

1 Simplify each of the following expressions.

   a $4c + 2c$ **b** $6d + 4d$ **c** $7p - 5p$ **d** $2x + 6x + 3x$

   e $4t + 2t - t$ **f** $7m - 3m$ **g** $q + 5q - 2q$ **h** $a + 6a - 3a$

   i $4p + p - 2p$ **j** $2w + 3w - w$ **k** $4t + 3t - 5t$ **l** $5g - g - 2g$

   m $5x + x + 2x$ **n** $8y - 2y - 3y$ **p** $6f + 3f - 7f$ **q** $8c - 4c - 3c$

2 Simplify each of the following expressions.

   a $2x + 2y + 3x + 6y$ **b** $4w + 6t - 2w - 2t$ **c** $4m + 7n + 3m - n$

   d $4x + 8y - 2y - 3x$ **e** $8 + 4x - 3 + 2x$ **f** $8p + 9 - 3p - 4$

   g $2y + 4x - 3 + x - y$ **h** $5d + 8c - 4c + 7$ **i** $4f + 2 + 3d - 1 - 3f$

3 Expand each of the following expressions.

   a $4(x + 5)$ **b** $2(3t + 4)$ **c** $5(3m + 1)$ **d** $4(3w - 2)$

   e $6(3m - 4)$ **f** $7(4q - 3)$ **g** $2(3x - 4)$ **h** $3(2t + 7)$

   i $7(3k + p - 2)$ **j** $4(3 - k + 2t)$ **k** $5(m - 3 + 6p)$ **l** $4(2 - 5k - 2m)$

4 Expand and simplify each of the following expressions.

   a $4(x + 5) + 3(x + 3)$ **b** $5(p + 7) + 3(p + 3)$

   c $3(w + 3) + 4(w - 2)$ **d** $6(d + 3) + 3(d - 5)$

   e $3(8p + 2) + 3(5p + 1)$ **f** $4(6m + 5) + 2(5m - 4)$

   g $5(3w + 7) + 2(2w - 1)$ **h** $7(3c + 2) + 2(5c - 4)$

   i $4(t + 6) + 3(4t - 1)$ **j** $5(3x + 2) + 4(3x - 2)$

1 When an expression contains brackets within brackets, first simplify the expression within the innermost brackets.

   Expand and simplify each of these.

   a $2[3x + 5(x + 2)]$ **b** $3[4y + 3(2y - 1)]$

   c $4\{m + 2[m + (m - 1)]\}$ **d** $5\{2(t + 1) + 3[4t + 3(2t - 1)]\}$

2 Find at least ten different pairs of brackets which would expand and simplify to give each of the following.

   a $12x + 11y$ **b** $12x - 11y$

Formulae

Where you have a **rule** to calculate some quantity, you can write the rule as a **formula**.

Example 6.2 A rule to calculate the cost of hiring a hall for a wedding is £200 plus £6 per person. This rule, written as a formula, is

$$c = 200 + 6n$$

where c = cost in £
       n = number of people

Example 6.3 ▸   Use the formula $c = 200 + 6n$ to calculate the cost of a wedding with 70 people.

Cost $= 200 + 6 \times 70 = 200 + 420 = £620$

Exercise 6D

1 Write each of these rules as a formula. Use the first letter of each variable in the formula. (Each letter is printed in blue.)

   a   The cost of hiring a boat is £2 per hour.

   b   The distance run each time is 300 metres round the track.

   c   Dad's age is always Joy's age plus 40.

   d   The cost of a party is £50 plus £8 per person.

   e   The number of bottles of wine needed is 5 plus the number of people divided by 3.

2 A mechanic uses the formula

$$c = 8 + 5t$$

   where c = cost in £

              t = time, in hours, to complete the work

Calculate what the mechanic charges to complete the work in:

   a   1 hour   **b**   3 hours   **c**   7 hours

3 A singer uses the formula

$$c = 25 + 15s$$

   where c = cost in £

              s = number of songs sung

Calculate what the singer charges to sing the following:

   a   2 songs   **b**   4 songs   **c**   8 songs

4 The formula for a child's dose of medicine is

$$D = \frac{10C - 10}{C}$$

   where D = dose, in millilitres, for a child

              C = child's age in years

Use the formula to calculate the dose for each of the following ages:

   a   8 years   **b**   5 years

   c $2\frac{1}{2}$ years   **d**   10 years

5 The formula for the cost of a newspaper advert is

$$C = 5W + 10A$$

   where C = charge in £

              W = number of words used

              A = area of the advert in cm^2

Use the formula to calculate the charge for the following adverts:

   a   10 words with an area of $20\,cm^2$ **b**   8 words with an area of $6\,cm^2$

   c   12 words with an area of $15\,cm^2$ **d**   17 words with an area of $15\,cm^2$

6 The cost of a badge is given by the formula

$$C = 60R^2$$

   where C = cost in pence

              R = radius of badge

Use the formula to calculate the cost of each of these badges:

   a   radius 1 cm   **b**   radius 2 cm   **c**   radius 2.5 cm

A three-tier set of number bricks looks like this:

	21	
9		12
5	4	8

The numbers on two adjacent bricks are added to create the number on the brick above them.

a Find the top brick number when the bottom bricks, in order; are:

   i 6, 7 and 10   **ii** a, b and a **iii** $a + 1$, $a + 2$ and $a + 3$

b If the bottom three bricks are a, b and c, write a formula for the total in the top brick.

c The top number is 10. Each bottom brick is a different positive number. How many different combinations of bottom brick numbers are there?

Equations

An equation states that two things are equal. These can be two expressions or an expression and a quantity.

An equation can be represented by a pair of scales. When the scales balance, both sides are equal.

The left-hand pan has 3 bags and 2 marbles.

The right-hand pan has 17 marbles.

Each bag contains the same number of marbles. How many marbles are in a bag?

Let the number of marbles in a bag be x, which gives: $\qquad 3x + 2 = 17$

Take 2 marbles away from each side: $\qquad 3x + 2 - 2 = 17 - 2$

This gives: $\qquad 3x = 15$

Now, $3x$ means $3 \times x$. This is equal to 15. So: $\qquad x = 5$

There are 5 marbles in each bag.

You will usually solve these types of equation by subtracting or adding to both sides in order to have a single term on each side of the equals sign.

Example 6.4 Solve $4x + 3 = 31$.

Subtract 3 from both sides: $4x + 3 - 3 = 31 - 3$

$$4x = 28$$
$$(4 \times ? = 28)$$
$$x = 7$$

Example 6.5 Solve $3x - 5 = 13$.

Add 5 to both sides: $3x - 5 + 5 = 13 + 5$

$$3x = 18$$
$$(3 \times ? = 18)$$
$$x = 6$$

1 Solve each of the following equations.

a	$2x + 3 = 11$	**b**	$2x + 5 = 13$	**c**	$3x + 4 = 19$	**d**	$3x + 7 = 19$
e	$4m + 1 = 21$	**f**	$5k + 6 = 21$	**g**	$4n + 9 = 17$	**h**	$2x + 7 = 27$
i	$6h + 5 = 23$	**j**	$3t + 5 = 26$	**k**	$8x + 3 = 35$	**l**	$5y + 3 = 28$
m	$7x + 3 = 10$	**n**	$4t + 7 = 39$	**p**	$3x + 8 = 20$	**q**	$8m + 5 = 21$

2 Solve each of the following equations.

a	$3x - 2 = 13$	**b**	$2m - 5 = 1$	**c**	$4x - 1 = 11$	**d**	$5t - 3 = 17$
e	$2x - 3 = 13$	**f**	$4m - 5 = 19$	**g**	$3m - 2 = 10$	**h**	$7x - 3 = 25$
i	$5m - 2 = 18$	**j**	$3k - 4 = 5$	**k**	$8x - 5 = 11$	**l**	$2t - 3 = 7$
m	$4x - 3 = 5$	**n**	$8y - 3 = 29$	**p**	$5x - 4 = 11$	**q**	$3m - 1 = 17$

3 Solve each of the following equations.

a	$2x + 3 = 11$	**b**	$3x + 4 = 10$	**c**	$5x - 1 = 29$	**d**	$4x - 3 = 25$
e	$3m - 2 = 13$	**f**	$5m + 4 = 49$	**g**	$7m + 3 = 24$	**h**	$4m - 5 = 23$
l	$6k + 1 = 25$	**j**	$5k - 3 = 2$	**k**	$3k - 1 = 23$	**l**	$2k + 5 = 15$
m	$7x - 3 = 18$	**n**	$4x + 3 = 43$	**p**	$5x + 6 = 31$	**q**	$9x - 4 = 68$

4 The solution of each of the following equations may involve a decimal or a fraction.

a	$2x + 7 = 8$	**b**	$5x + 3 = 4$	**c**	$2x + 3 = 8$	**d**	$4x + 7 = 20$
e	$5x - 3 = 9$	**f**	$2x - 7 = 10$	**g**	$4x - 5 = 6$	**h**	$10x - 3 = 8$

What you need to know for level 5

- How to construct, express in symbolic form and use simple formulae, involving one or two operations
- How to simplify expressions and expand brackets
- How to solve equations

What you need to know for level 6

- How to use formulae with more than one variable
- How to solve equations with non-integer solutions

National Curriculum SATs questions

LEVEL 5

1 *2000 Paper 1*

The area of the shaded square is 4.
The area of the semicircle is *t*

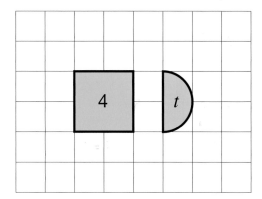

The grid below shows a shape.
The area of this shape in terms of *t* is 4 + 2*t*

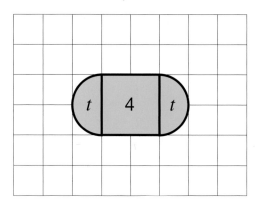

a Write down the area of the shapes below in terms of *t*.

i

ii

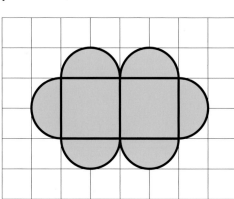

b Draw diagrams to show shapes with area   **i**   8 + 4*t*   **ii**   4 − 2*t*

2 *2000 Paper 1*

Jenny and Alan each have a rectangle made out of paper.

One side is 10 cm. The other side is *n* cm.

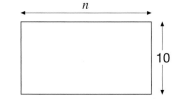

a They write expressions for the perimeter of the rectangle.

Jenny writes 2*n* + 20

Alan writes 2(*n* + 10)

Which of the following is a true statement?

Jenny is correct and Alan is wrong.   Jenny is wrong and Alan is correct.

Both Jenny and Alan are correct.   Both Jenny and Alan are wrong.

b   Alan cuts his rectangle, then puts the two halves side by side.

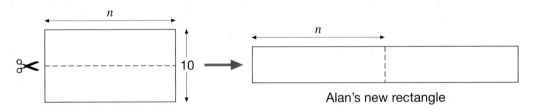

Alan's new rectangle

What is the perimeter of Alan's new rectangle? Write your expression as simply as possible.

c   Jenny cuts her rectangle a different way, and puts one half below the other half.

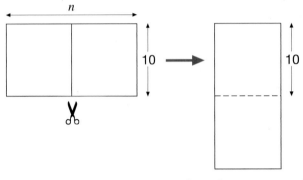

Jenny's new rectangle

What is the perimeter of Jenny's new rectangle?

Write your expression as simply as possible.

d   What value of *n* would make the perimeter of Jenny's new rectangle the same value as the perimeter of Alan's new rectangle.

LEVEL 6

3   *Paper 2 1999*

Write an expression for each missing length in these rectangles. Write each expression as simply as possible.

a

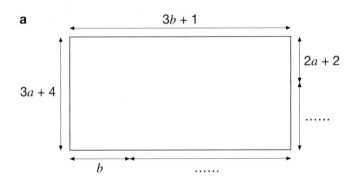

b

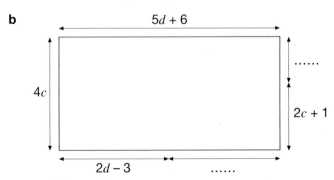

CHAPTER 7

Shape, Space and Measures **2**

This chapter is going to show you

- the vocabulary and notation for lines and angles
- how to identify alternate and corresponding angles
- how to use angles at a point, angles on a straight line, angles in a triangle and in a quadrilateral, and vertically opposite angles
- how to use coordinates in all four quadrants

What you should already know

- The geometric properties of triangles and quadrilaterals
- How to plot coordinates in the first quadrant

Lines and angles

Lines A straight line can be considered to have infinite length.

A **line segment** has finite length.

A ——————————————— B

The line segment AB has two end points, one at A and the other at B.

Two lines lie in a **plane**, which is a flat surface.

Two lines either are parallel or intersect.

   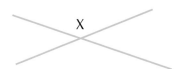   

Parallel lines never meet.　　These two lines intersect at a point X.　　These two lines intersect at right angles. The lines are said to be **perpendicular**.

Angles When two lines meet at a point, they form an **angle**. An angle is a measure of rotation and is measured in degrees (°).

Types of angle

Right angle　　Half turn　　Full turn　　Acute angle　　Obtuse angle　　Reflex angle
90°　　180°　　360°　　less than 90°　　between 90° and 180°　　between 180° and 360°

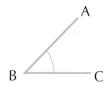

A

B ———— C

Describing angles

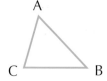

A

The angle at B can be written as:

∠ B or ∠ ABC or AB̂C

Describing triangles

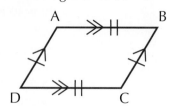

The triangle can be represented by △ABC.
It has three vertices A, B and C;
three angles, ∠A, ∠B and ∠C;
three sides, AB, AC and BC.

Example 7.1 ▷ Describe the geometric properties of these two shapes.

a Isosceles triangle ABC

AB = AC
∠ABC = ∠ACB

b Parallelogram ABCD

AB = CD and AD = BC
AB is parallel to CD or AḂ // CD
AD is parallel to BC or AD // BC

Corresponding and alternate angles

A line which intersects a set of parallel lines is called a **transversal**.

Notice in the diagram that eight distinct angles are formed by a transversal which intersects a pair of parallel lines.

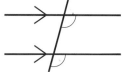

The two angles marked on the diagram above are equal and are called **corresponding angles**.

Look for the letter F to identify corresponding angles.

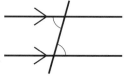

The two angles marked on the diagram above are equal and are called **alternate angles**.

Look for the letter Z to identify alternate angles.

Exercise 7A

1 Write down which of the angles below are acute, which are obtuse and which are reflex. Estimate the size of each one.

a   **b**    **c**   **d**    **e**   **f**

2 For the shape ABCDE:

a Write down two lines that are equal in length.

b Write down two lines that are parallel.

c Write down two lines that are perpendicular to each other.

d Copy the diagram and draw on the two diagonals BD and CE. What do you notice about the two diagonals?

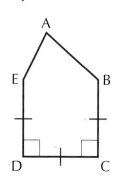

3 Write down the geometric properties of these three shapes.

a Equilateral triangle ABC **b** Square ABCD **c** Rhombus ABCD

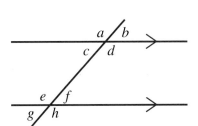
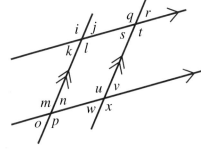

4

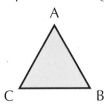
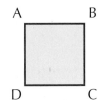

Copy and complete each of the following sentences:

a *a* and … are corresponding angles   **b** *b* and … are corresponding angles

c *c* and … are corresponding angles   **d** *d* and … are corresponding angles

e *e* and … are alternate angles   **f** *f* and … are alternate angles

g *k* and … are corresponding angles   **h** *u* and … are corresponding angles

i *l* and … are corresponding angles   **j** *r* and … are corresponding angles

k *n* and … are alternate angles   **l** *s* and … are alternate angles

Extension Work

1 For the regular hexagon ABCDEF:

   a Write down all the pairs of sides that are parallel.

   b Write down all the diagonals that are perpendicular.

2 Cut the rectangle ABCD into two parts with one straight cut. How many different shapes can you make? Draw a diagram to show each different cut you use.

Calculating angles

You can calculate the **unknown angles** in a diagram from the information given. Unknown angles are usually denoted by letters, such as *a*, *b*, *c*, … .

Remember: usually the diagrams are not to scale.

Angles around a point

Angles around a point add up to 360°.

Example 7.2   Calculate the size of the angle *a*.

$$a = 360° - 150° - 130°$$
$$a = 80°$$

Angles on a straight line

Angles on a straight line add up to 180°.

Example 7.3 Calculate the size of the angle *b*.

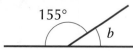

$b = 180° - 155°$

$b = 25°$

Angles in a triangle The angles in a triangle add up to 180°.

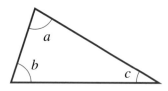

$a + b + c = 180°$

Example 7.4 Calculate the size of the angle *c*.

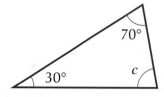

$c = 180° - 70° - 30°$

$c = 80°$

Angles in a quadrilateral

The angles in a quadrilateral add up to 360°.

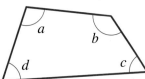

$a + b + c + d = 360°$

Example 7.5 Calculate the size of angle *d*.

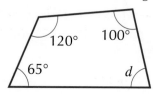

$d = 360° - 120° - 100° - 65°$

$d = 75°$

Vertically opposite angles

When two lines intersect, the opposite angles are equal.

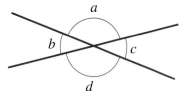

$a = d$ and $b = c$

Example 7.6 Calculate the sizes of angles *e* and *f*.

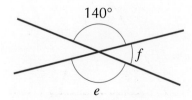

$e = 140°$ (opposite angles)

$f = 40°$ (angles on a straight line)

1 Calculate the size of each unknown angle.

a

110° 120°
a

b

110°
b

c
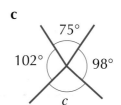
75°
102° 98°
c

d
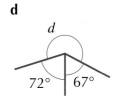
d
72° 67°

2 Calculate the size of each unknown angle.

a
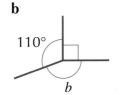
130°
a

b
52°
b

c
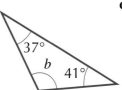
76° 25°
c

d
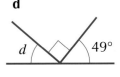
d 49°

3 Calculate the size of each unknown angle.

a
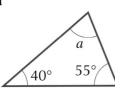
a
40° 55°

b

37°
b 41°

c
c 35°

d

d
63°

4 Calculate the size of each unknown angle.

a
100°
70°
110° *a*

b

54°
b
77°

c
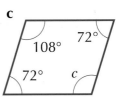
108° 72°
72° *c*

d
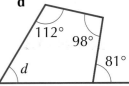
112° 98°
d 81°

5 Calculate the size of each unknown angle.

a
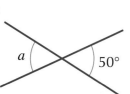
a 50°

b
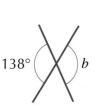
138° *b*

c
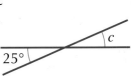
c
25°

d
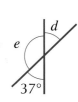
d
e
37°

6 Calculate the size of each unknown angle.

a
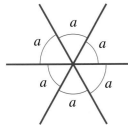
a
a *a*
a *a*
a

b
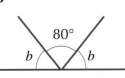
80°
b *b*

c
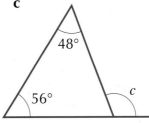
48°
56° *c*

d
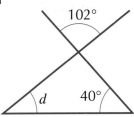
102°
d 40°

7 Geometrical proofs

a Copy the following two proofs and then write them out without looking at the answers.

i The sum of the angles of a triangle is 180°.

To prove $a + b + c = 180°$.

Draw a line parallel to one side of the triangle.
$x = b$ (alternate angles)
$y = c$ (alternate angles)
$a + x + y = 180°$ (angles on a straight line)

So, $a + b + c = 180°$.

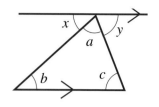

ii An exterior angle of a triangle is equal to the sum of the two interior opposite angles.

x is an exterior angle of the triangle.
To prove $a + b = x$.

$a + b + c = 180°$ (angles in a triangle)
$x + c = 180°$ (angles on a straight line)

So, $a + b = x$.

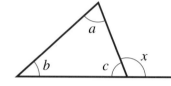

b Write out a proof that the sum of the angles of a quadrilateral is 360°.
(Hint: Divide the quadrilateral into two triangles.)

1 Calculate the size of each unknown angle.

a

b
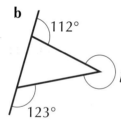

c
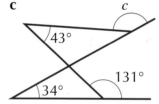

d
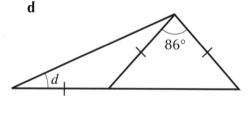

e
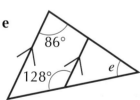

f
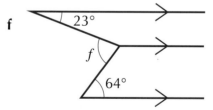

2 One angle in an isosceles triangle is 42°. Calculate the possible sizes of the other two angles.

3 Calculate the sizes of the angles marked with letters.

a
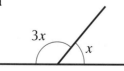

b
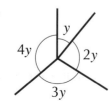

c
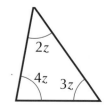

Coordinates

We use **coordinates** to locate a point on a grid.

The grid consists of two axes, called the **x-axis** and the **y-axis**. They are perpendicular to each other.

The two axes meet at a point called the **origin**, which is labelled O.

The point A on the grid is 4 units across and 3 units up.

We say that the coordinates of A are (4, 3), which is usually written as A(4, 3).

The first number, 4, is the x-coordinate of A and the second number, 3, is the y-coordinate of A. The x-coordinate is *always* written first.

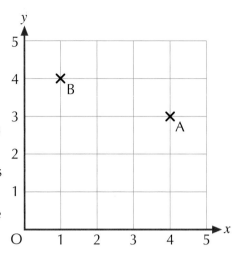

When plotting a point on a grid, a ✖ or a ● is usually used.

The coordinates of the origin are (0, 0) and the coordinates of the point B are (1, 4).

The grid system can be extended to negative numbers and points can be plotted in all **four quadrants**.

Example 7.7 ▷ The coordinates of the points on the grid are:
A(4, 2), B(–2, 3), C(–3, –1), D(1, –4)

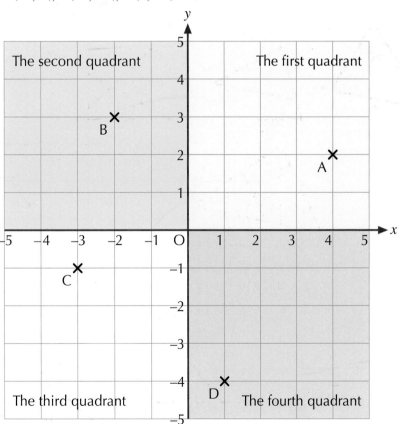

1. Write down the coordinates of the points P, Q, R, S and T.

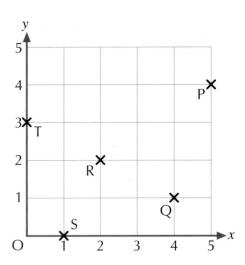

2. a Make a copy of the grid in Question 1. Then plot the points A(1, 1), B(1, 5) and C(4, 5).

    b The three points are the vertices of a rectangle. Plot point D to complete the rectangle.

    c Write down the coordinates of D.

3. Write down the coordinates of the points A, B, C, D, E, F, G and H.

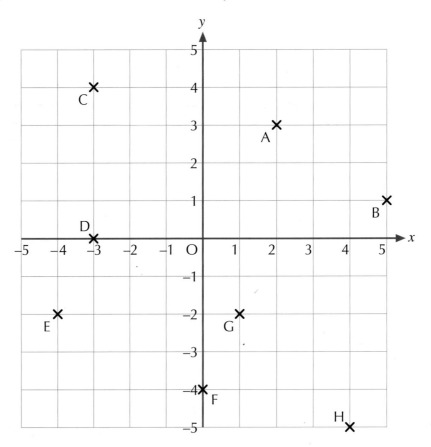

4. a Make a copy of the grid in Question 3. Then plot the points A(−4, 3), B(−2, −2), C(0, 1), D(2, −2) and E(4, 3).

    b Join the points in the order given. What letter have you drawn?

5 **a** Make a copy of the grid in Question 3. Then plot the points W(3, 4), X(3, –2) and Y(–3, –2).

b The points form three vertices of a square WXYZ. Plot the point Z and draw the square.

c What are the coordinates of the point Z?

d Draw in the diagonals of the square. What are the coordinates of the point of intersection of the diagonals?

Extension Work

Coordinates and lines

- Draw on a grid *x*-and *y*-axes from –8 to 8.
- Plot the points (0, 2) and (6, 8) and join them to make a straight line.
- Write down the coordinates of other points that lie on the line.
- Can you spot a rule that connects the *x*-coordinate and the *y*-coordinate?
- Extend the line into the third quadrant. Does your rule still work?
- The rule you have found is given by the formula $y = x + 2$.
- Now draw the following lines on different grids using these formulae:

    a $y = x + 3$ **b** $y = x$ **c** $y = x - 2$

What you need to know for level 5

- The language associated with angle
- The sum of the angles in a triangle and of angles around a point
- Use and interpret coordinates in all four quadrants

What you need to know for level 6

- How to use the geometrical properties of quadrilaterals
- How to solve problems using the angle properties of intersecting and parallel straight lines

National Curriculum SATs questions

LEVEL 5

1 *2000 Paper 1*

Look at these angles.

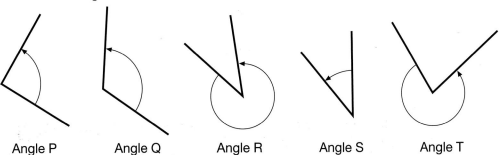

Angle P   Angle Q   Angle R   Angle S   Angle T

One of the angles measures 120°. Write its letter.

2   *1999 Paper 2*

   a   The time on this clock is 3 o'clock.

       What is the size of the angle between the hands?

   b   Use a whole number to complete this sentence:

       At … o'clock the size of the angle between the hands is 180°.

   c   What is the size of the angle between the hands at 1 o'clock?

   d   What is the size of the angle between the hands at 5 o'clock?

   e   How long does it take for the minute hand to move 360°?

LEVEL 6

3   *1999 Paper 1*

The shape on the right has three identical
white tiles and three identical grey tiles.

The sides of each tile are all the same length.
Opposite sides of each tile are parallel. One of
the angles is 70°.

   a   Calculate the size of angle k.

   b   Calculate the size of angle m.

Show your working.

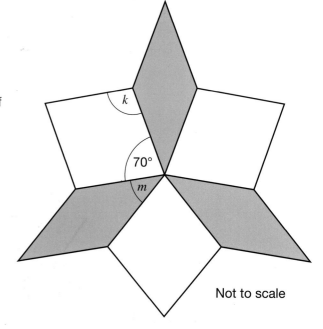

Not to scale

4   *2001 Paper 1*

The diagram shows two isosceles triangles inside
a parallelogram.

   a   On a copy of the diagram, mark another
angle that is 75°. Label it 75°.

   b   Calculate the size of the angle marked k.
Show your working.

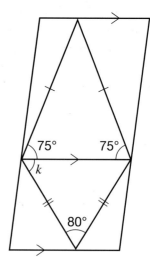

<table>
<tr><td>**This chapter is going to show you**</td><td>**What you should already know**</td></tr>
<tr><td>

- how to collect and organise discrete and continuous data
- how to create data collection forms
- how to create questionnaires
- how to use frequency tables to collate discrete and continuous data
- how to conduct surveys and experiments
- how to draw simple conclusions from data

</td><td>

- How to create a tally chart
- How to draw bar charts and pictograms

</td></tr>
</table>

Using a tally chart

Discrete data

What method of transport do students use to travel to school – and why?

When students are asked this question, they will give different methods of travelling, such as bus, car, bike, walking, train and even some others we don't yet know about!

A good way to collect this data is to fill in a tally chart as each student is asked how he or she travels to school. For example:

Type of transport	Tally	Frequency
Bus	Лፐፐ IIII	9
Car	Лፐፐ	5
Bike	II	2
Walking	Лፐፐ Лፐፐ IIII	14
Other		
	Total	30

This sort of data is called **discrete data** because there is only a fixed number of possible answers.

Continuous data

How far do you travel to school?

Because students could give any answer within a reasonable range, such as 2 miles, 1.3 miles, 1.25 miles, we say that the data is **continuous**. As all the data may be different, a good way to collect this data is to group it into distance intervals.

For example, we use 2 < Distance ≤ 4 to mean the distance is more than 2 miles and less than or equal to 4 miles. So, we include 4 miles but not 2 miles in this category.

Distance to travel to school (miles)	Tally	Frequency
0 < Distance ≤ 2	⊥⊥⊤⊤ | |	7
2 < Distance ≤ 4	| | | |	4
4 < Distance ≤ 6	| | |	3
6 < Distance ≤ 8	⊥⊥⊤⊤ ⊥⊥⊤⊤ | | |	13
	Total	27

Exercise 8A

1 Use your own class tally sheet (or the one on page 93) to draw a chart illustrating the methods of transport used by students to get to school.

2 Use your own class tally sheet (or the one above) to draw a chart illustrating the distance that students travel to school.

Extension Work

Put into a spreadsheet the data from one of the tally charts in this lesson.
Then create the statistical charts available. Pay close attention to the labelling.

Using the correct data

Do certain newspapers use more long words than the other newspapers?

There are many different newspapers about. Can you list six different national newspapers?

Now consider Ted's question. The strict way to answer this would be to count, in each newspaper, all the words and all their letters. But this would take too long, so we take what is called a **sample**. We count, say, 100 words from each newspaper to find the length of each word.

Exercise 8B

This whole exercise is a class activity.

1 a You will be given either a whole newspaper or a page from one.
  b Create a data capture form (a tally chart) like the one below.

Number of letters	Tally	Frequency
1		
2		
3		
4		
5		

c Choose a typical page from the newspaper. Then select at least two different articles. Next, count the number of letters in each word from each article (or paragraph), and fill in the tally chart. Don't miss out any words. Before you start to count, see part **f** below.

d Decide what to do with such things as:
  Numbers – 6 would count as 1, six would count as 3.
  Hyphenated words – Ignore the hyphen.
  Abbreviations – Just count what are there.

e Once you have completed this task, fill in the frequency column. Now create a bar chart of the results.

f Each of you will have taken a different newspaper. So what about comparing your results with others'? To do this, you must all use the same number of words.

Look at the following misleading conclusions that arise from not using like data.

Travelling to school Two different classes did a survey of how students travelled to school.

They both made pie charts to show their results.

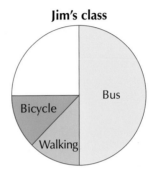
Jim's class

Sara's class

Look at both charts and ask yourself:

Which class had the most students using the bus?

Obvious – it's Jim's class!

BUT if you are told:

In Jim's class there were only 24 students, and in Sara's class there were 36 students.

Then you will see that:

  In Jim's class, half of the 24 used the bus, which is 12.
  In Sara's class, more than one third used the bus, which is about 14.

Clearly, you have to be very careful about interpreting data in its final form.

Here, you can say that a bigger proportion of Jim's class used the bus, but *not* more students used the bus than in Sara's class.

So, it is most important to try to use like numbers of items when you are going to make a comparison of data from different sources.

Extension Work

Now go back to the newspaper articles and use continuous data. For example, you could ask students in your class, and in other classes, to read the sample of 100 words and time them to see if the papers with longer words take any longer to read. Write a short report of your findings.

Grouped frequencies

How long does it take you to get to school in the morning?

A class was asked this question and the replies, in minutes, were:

6 min, 3 min, 5 min, 20 min, 15 min, 11 min, 13 min, 28 min, 30 min, 5 min, 2 min, 6 min, 8 min, 18 min, 23 min, 22 min, 17 min, 13 min, 4 min, 2 min, 30 min, 17 min, 19 min, 25 min, 8 min, 3 min, 9 min, 12 min, 15 min, 8 min.

There are too many different values here to make a sensible bar chart. So we group them to produce a **grouped frequency table**, as shown below. The different groups the data has been put into are called **classes**. Where possible, classes are kept the same size as each other.

Time (minutes)	0–5	–10	–15	–20	–25	–30
Frequency	7	6	6	5	3	3

Notice how we use –10, –15, … to mean 'over 5 minutes up to 10 minutes', and so on.

A bar chart has been drawn from this data, and information put on each bar about the method of transport.

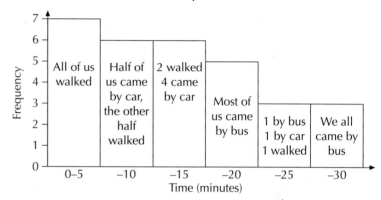

We could also use a continuous scale for this data.

Time to travel to school (minutes)	Frequency
0 < Time ≤ 5	7
5 < Time ≤ 10	6
10 < Time ≤ 15	6
15 < Time ≤ 20	5
20 < Time ≤ 25	3
25 < Time ≤ 30	3

The graph would now look like this.

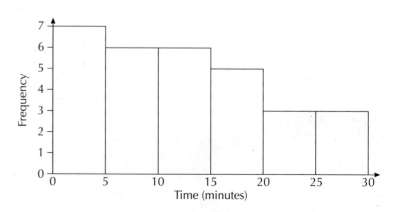

1 A class did a survey on how many pencils each student had with them in school. The results of this survey are:

4, 7, 2, 18, 1, 16, 19, 15, 13, 0, 9, 17, 4, 6, 10, 12, 15, 8, 3, 14, 20, 14, 15, 18, 5, 16, 3, 6, 5, 18, 12

a Put this data into a grouped frequency table with a class size of 5: that is, 0–4, 5–9, 10–14 …

b Draw a bar chart of the data.

2 A teacher asked her class: 'How many hours a week do you spend on a computer?'

She asked them to give an average, rounded figure in hours. This was their response:

3, 6, 9, 2, 23, 18, 6, 8, 29, 27, 2, 1, 0, 5, 19, 23, 30, 21, 7, 4, 23, 8, 7, 1, 0, 25, 24, 8, 13, 18, 15, 16

These are some of the reasons students gave for the length of time they spent on a computer:

'I haven't got one.' 'I play games on mine.' 'I always try to do my homework on the computer.' 'I can't use it when I want to, because my brother's always on it.'

a Put the above data into a grouped frequency table with a class size of 5.

b Draw a bar chart with the information. Try to include in the chart the reasons given.

3 Use the data you have from your survey on the number of letters in words to create a grouped frequency table:

a with a class size of 3   **b** with a class size of 5

c Which class size seems most sensible to use in this case?

4 The table shows the times of goals scored in football matches played on one weekend in November.

Time of goals (minutes)	Frequency
$0 <$ Time ≤ 15	3
$15 <$ Time ≤ 30	6
$30 <$ Time ≤ 45	8
$45 <$ Time ≤ 60	4
$60 <$ Time ≤ 75	2
$75 <$ Time ≤ 90	5

a One goal was scored after exactly 75 minutes. In which class was it recorded?

b Five teams scored in the last five minutes of their games. Write down what other information this tells you.

c Draw a frequency diagram to represent the data in the table.

Extension Work

Collect data about the heights of the students in your class. Design a frequency table to record the information. Draw a frequency diagram from your table of results. Comment on your results.

Data collection

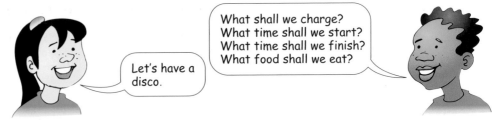

Let's ask a sample of the students in our school these questions. In other words, not everyone, but a few from each group.

You ask each question, then immediately complete your data collection form.

An example of a suitable data collection form is shown below.

Year group	Boy or girl	How much to charge?	Time to start?	Time to finish?	What would you like to eat?
Y7	B	£1	7 pm	11 pm	Crisps, beefburgers, chips
Y7	G	50p	7 pm	9 pm	Chips, crisps, lollies
Y8	G	£2	7.30 pm	10 pm	Crisps, hot dogs
Y11	B	£3	8.30 pm	11.30 pm	Chocolate, pizza

Keep track of the age	Try to ask equal numbers	Once the data is collected, it can be sorted into frequency tables.

There are five stages in running this type of survey:
- Deciding what questions to ask and who to ask.
- Creating a simple, suitable data collection form for all the questions.
- Asking the questions and completing the data collection form.
- After collecting all the data, collating it in frequency tables.
- Analysing the data to draw conclusions from the survey.

The size of your sample will depend on many things. It may be simply the first 50 people you come across. Or you may want 10% of the available people.

In the above example, a good sample would probably be about four from each class, two boys and two girls.

Exercise 8D

A class did the above survey on a sample of 10 students from each of the Key Stage 3 years. Their data collection chart is shown on the next page.

1 a Create the frequency tables for the suggested charges from each year group Y7, Y8 and Y9.

b Comment on the differences between the year groups.

2 a Create the frequency tables for the suggested starting times from each year group Y7, Y8 and Y9.

b Comment on the differences between the year groups.

3 **a** Create the frequency tables for the suggested lengths of time the disco should last from each year group Y7, Y8 and Y9.

   b Comment on the differences between the year groups.

4 Complete the survey on what food each year group suggests.

Year group	Boy or girl	How much to charge	Time to start	Time to finish	What would you like to eat?
Y7	B	£1	7 pm	11 pm	Crisps, beefburgers, chips
Y7	G	50p	7 pm	9 pm	Chips, crisps, lollies
Y8	G	£2	7.30 pm	10 pm	Crisps, hot dogs
Y9	B	£3	8.30 pm	11.30 pm	Chocolate, pizza
Y9	G	£2	8 pm	10 pm	Pizza
Y9	B	£2.50	7.30 pm	9.30 pm	Hot dogs, Chocolate
Y8	G	£1	8 pm	10.30 pm	Crisps
Y7	B	75p	7 pm	9 pm	Crisps, beefburgers
Y7	B	£1	7.30 pm	10.30 pm	Crisps, lollies
Y8	B	£1.50	7 pm	9 pm	Crisps, chips, hot dogs
Y9	G	£2	8 pm	11 pm	Pizza, chocolate
Y9	G	£1.50	8 pm	10.30 pm	Chips, pizza
Y9	G	£2	8 pm	11 pm	Crisps, pizza
Y7	G	£1.50	7 pm	9 pm	Crisps, lollies, chocolate
Y8	B	£2	7.30 pm	9.30 pm	Crisps, lollies, chocolate
Y8	B	£1	8 pm	10 pm	Chips, hot dogs
Y9	B	£1.50	8 pm	11 pm	Pizza
Y7	B	50p	7 pm	9.30 pm	Crisps, hot dogs
Y8	G	75p	8 pm	10.30 pm	Crisps, chips
Y9	B	£2	7.30 pm	10.30 pm	Pizza
Y8	G	£1.50	7.30 pm	10 pm	Chips, hot dogs, chocolate
Y8	B	£1.25	7 pm	9.30 pm	Chips, hot dogs, lollies
Y9	G	£3	7 pm	9.30 pm	Crisps, pizza
Y9	B	£2.50	8 pm	10.30 pm	Crisps, hot dogs
Y7	G	25p	7.30 pm	10 pm	Crisps, beefburgers, lollies
Y7	G	50p	7 pm	9 pm	Crisps, pizza
Y7	G	£1	7 pm	9.30 pm	Crisps, pizza
Y8	B	£2	8 pm	10 pm	Crisps, chips, chocolate
Y8	G	£1.50	7.30 pm	9.30 pm	Chips, beefburgers
Y7	B	£1	7.30 pm	10 pm	Crisps, lollies

What you need to know for level 5

- How to compare two simple distributions
- How to interpret graphs and diagrams, and draw conclusions
- Recognise the need for care when setting class boundaries

What you need to know for level 6

- How to collect and record continuous data, choosing appropriate equal class intervals over a sensible range to create frequency tables
- How to construct and interpret frequency diagrams

National Curriculum SATs questions

LEVEL 5

1 *1997 paper 2*

Some pupils wanted to find out if people liked a new biscuit.

They decided to do a survey and wrote a questionnaire.

a One question was:

How old are you (in years)?

☐ 20 or younger ☐ 20 to 30 ☐ 30 to 40 ☐ 40 to 50 ☐ 50 or over

Mary said:

> The labels for the middle three boxes need changing.

Explain why Mary was right.

b A different question was:

How much do you usually spend on biscuits each week?

☐ A lot ☐ A little ☐ Nothing ☐ Don't know

Mary said: 'Some of these labels need changing too.'
Write new labels for any boxes that need changing.
You may change as many labels as you want to.

The pupils decide to give their questionnaire to 50 people.

Jon said:

> Let's ask 50 pupils in our school.

c Give one disadvantage of Jon's suggestion.

d Give one advantage of Jon's suggestion.

2 *2001 Paper 1*

The diagrams show the number of hours of sunshine in two different months.

a How many days are there in month A?

28, 29, 30, 31 or not possible to tell

b How many days are there in month B?

28, 29, 30, 31 or not possible to tell

c Which month had more hours of sunshine?

Month A or Month B

Explain how you know.

Number of hours of sunshine in month A

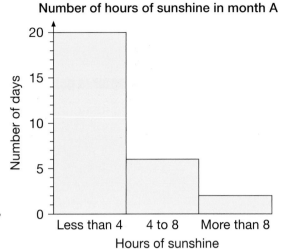

Number of hours of sunshine in month B

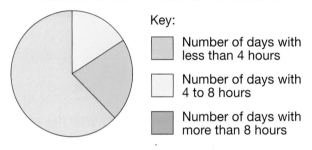

Key:

■ Number of days with less than 4 hours

□ Number of days with 4 to 8 hours

■ Number of days with more than 8 hours

LEVEL 6

3 *1994 Paper 1*

The two frequency diagrams below show the amount of rain that fell in two different months.

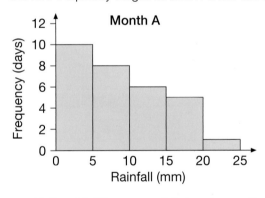
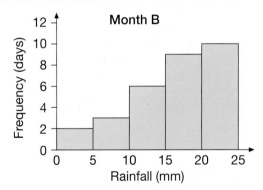

a Kath said: 'There were 30 days in month A.'

Explain how you know she was right.

b Carl asked five friends: 'How much rain fell during month A?'

They said: Jon — 5 mm   Dipta — 25 mm   Ian — 30 mm   Nerys — 75 mm   Sharon — 250 mm

Only one friend could have been right. You can tell who it is without trying to work out the total rainfall.

Which one of Carl's friends could have been right? Explain how you know.

c Sudi said: 'The diagram for month B shows that it rained more at the end of the month.'

Sudi is wrong. Explain why the diagram does not show this.

This chapter is going to show you

- how to round off positive whole numbers and decimals
- the order of operations
- how to multiply and divide a three-digit whole number by a two-digit whole number without a calculator
- how to use a calculator efficiently

What you should already know

- Tables up to 10 times 10
- Place value of the digits in a number such as 23.508

Rounding

What is wrong with this picture?

It shows that the woman's weight (60 kg) balances the man's weight (110 kg) when both weights are rounded to the nearest 100 kg!

This example highlights the need to round numbers *sensibly*, depending on the situation in which they occur.

But, we do not always need numbers to be precise, and it is easier to work with numbers that are rounded off.

Example 9.1 ▷ Round off each of these numbers to **i** the nearest 10 **ii** the nearest 100 **iii** the nearest 1000.

| **a** 937 | **b** 2363 | **c** 3799 | **d** 281 |

a 937 is 940 to nearest 10, 900 to the nearest 100 and 1000 to the nearest 1000.

b 2363 is 2360 to nearest 10, 2400 to the nearest 100, and 2000 to the nearest 1000.

c 3799 is 3800 to nearest 10, 3800 to the nearest 100, and 4000 to the nearest 1000.

d 281 is 280 to nearest 10, 300 to the nearest 100, and 0 to the nearest 1000.

Example 9.2

Round off each of these numbers to **i** the nearest whole number **ii** one decimal place **iii** two decimal places.

a 9.359   **b** 4.323   **c** 5.999

a 9.35 is 9 to the nearest whole number, 9.4 to 1 dp, and 9.36 to 2 dp.

b 4.323 is 4 to the nearest whole number, 4.3 to 1 dp, and 4.32 to 2 dp.

c 5.99 is 6 to the nearest whole number, 6.0 to 1 dp, and 6.00 to 2 dp.

Exercise 9A

1 Round off each of these numbers to **i** the nearest 10 **ii** the nearest 100 **iii** the nearest 1000.

a 3731	**b** 807	**c** 2111	**d** 4086	**e** 265	**f** 3457
g 4050	**h** 2999	**i** 1039	**j** 192	**k** 3192	**l** 964

2 Round off each of these numbers to **i** the nearest whole number **ii** one decimal place **iii** two decimal places.

a 4.721	**b** 3.073	**c** 2.634	**d** 1.932	**e** 0.785	**f** 0.927
g 3.925	**h** 2.648	**i** 3.182	**j** 3.475	**k** 1.459	**l** 1.863

3 **i** What is the mass being weighed by each scale to the nearest 100 g?

ii Estimate the mass being weighed to the nearest 10 g.

a  **b** 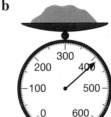 **c** 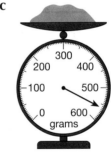 **d**

4 **i** What is the volume of the liquid in each measuring cylinder to the nearest 10 ml?

ii Estimate the volume of liquid to the nearest whole number.

a 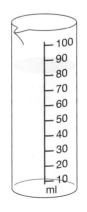 **b** 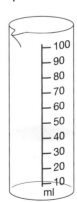 **c** 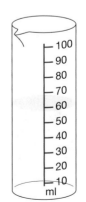 **d**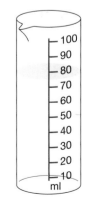

5 How long are each of these ropes to **i** the nearest 100 cm **ii** the nearest 10 cm **iii** the nearest cm **iv** the nearest mm?

a

| 176 | 177 | 178 | 179 cm |

b

| 62 | 63 | 64 | 65 | 66 cm |

c

| 278 | 279 | 280 | 281 | 282 cm |

d

| 3.4 | 3.5 | 3.6 | 3.7 | 3.8 m |

6 **a** The following are the diameters of the planets in kilometres. Round off each one to the nearest 1000 km. Then place the planets in order of size, starting with the smallest.

Planet	Earth	Jupiter	Mars	Mercury	Neptune	Pluto	Saturn	Uranus	Venus
Diameter (km)	12 800	142 800	6780	5120	49 500	2284	120 660	51 100	12 100

b What would happen if you rounded off the diameters to the nearest 10 000 km?

Extension Work

The headteacher says: 'All of our classes have about 30 pupils in them.'
Given this number is to the nearest 10, what is the smallest class there could be and what would be the largest?

The deputy head says: 'All of the cars driving past the school are doing about 30 mph.' Given this number is to the nearest 10, what is the lowest speed the cars could be doing and what would be the highest?

Why are these answers different?

Write down the smallest and largest values for each of the following.

a A crowd of people estimated at 80 to the nearest 10 people.

b The speed of a car estimated at 80 mph to the nearest 10 mph.

c The length of a leaf estimated at 8 cm to the nearest centimetre.

d The number of marbles in a bag estimated at 50 to the nearest 10 marbles.

e The number of marbles in a bag estimated at 50 to the nearest marble.

f The weight of some marbles in a bag estimated at 500 grams to the nearest 10 grams.

The four operations

Mr Jensen takes his family on a car ferry. The charge for the car is £40. On top of this he pays the standard adult fare for himself. Children are charged half the adult fare and pets are charged £5. The total cost for their crossing is £85. How much is the standard adult fare?

Example 9.3 ▸ **a** Find the product of 9 and 56. **b** Find the remainder when 345 is divided by 51.

a Product means 'multiply'. So, $9 \times 56 = 9 \times 50 + 9 \times 6 = 450 + 54 = 504$

b $345 \div 51 \approx 350 \div 50 = 7$. So, $7 \times 51 = 350 + 7 = 357$ which is too big.
$6 \times 51 = 306$, which gives $345 - 306 = 39$. The remainder is 39.

Example 9.4 ▸ A box of biscuits costs £1.99. How much will 28 boxes cost?

The easiest way to do this is: $28 \times £2$ minus $28p = £56 - 28p = £55.72$.

Example 9.5 ▸ Mr Smith travels from Edinburgh (E) to Liverpool (L) and then to Bristol (B). Mr Jones travels directly from Edinburgh to Bristol. Use the distance chart to find out how much further Mr Smith travelled than Mr Jones.

Mr Smith travels $226 + 237 = 463$ miles. Mr Jones travels 383 miles.
$463 - 383 = 80$
So, Mr Smith travels 80 miles further.

	E	L	B
E		226	383
L	226		237
B	383	237	

Exercise 9B

1 How long does a train journey take if the train leaves at ten thirty-two am and arrives at one twelve pm?

2 Which mark is better: seventeen out of twenty or forty out of fifty?

3 How much does it cost to fill a 51-litre petrol tank at 80p per litre?

4 a A company has 197 boxes to move by van. The van can carry 23 boxes at a time. How many trips must the van make to move all the boxes?

b The same van does 34 miles to the gallon of petrol. Each trip above is 31 miles. Can the van deliver all the boxes if it has 8 gallons of petrol in the tank?

5 Find the sum and product of **a** 5, 7 and 20 **b** 2, 38 and 50

6 Rajid has between 50 and 60 books. He arranged them in piles of four and found that he had one pile of three left over. He then arranged them in piles of five and found that he had one pile of four left over. How many books does Rajid have?

7 The local video shop is having a sale. Videos are £4.99 each or five for £20.

    a   What is the cost of three videos?

    b   What is the cost of ten videos?

    c   What is the greatest number of video you can buy with £37?

8 **a**   Three consecutive integers have a sum of 90. What are they?

    b   Two consecutive integers have a product of 132. What are they?

    c   Explain why there is more than one answer to this problem:

        Two consecutive integers have a difference of 1. What are they?

Extension Work

The magic number of this magic square is 50.

That means that the numbers in every row, in every column and in both diagonals add up to 50.

However, there are many more ways to make 50 by adding four numbers. For example, each of the following sets of 4 numbers from the magic square makes 50.

5	18	11	16
12	15	6	17
14	9	20	7
19	8	13	10

5	18
12	15

5		16
19		10

18	11
8	13

How many more arrangements of four numbers can you find that add up to 50?

BODMAS

The following are instructions for making a cup of tea.

Can you put them in the right order?

Drink tea	Empty teapot	Fill kettle	Put milk in cup	Put teabag in teapot
Switch on kettle	Wait for tea to brew	Rinse teapot with hot water	Pour boiling water in teapot	Pour out tea

It is important that things are done in the right order. In mathematical operations there are rules about this.

The order of operations is called **BODMAS**, which stands for **B** (Brackets), **O** (Order or pOwer), **D M** (Division and Multiplication) and **A S** (Addition and Subtraction).

Operations are always done in this order, which means that brackets are done first, followed by powers, then multiplication and division, and finally addition and subtraction.

Example 9.6 Circle the operation that you do first in each of these calculations. Then work out each one.

a $2 + 6 \div 2$ b $32 - 4 \times 5$ c $6 \div 3 - 1$ d $6 \div (3 - 1)$

a Division is done before addition, so you get $2 + 6 \div 2 = 2 + 3 = 5$

b Multiplication is done before subtraction, so you get $32 - 4 \otimes 5 = 32 - 20 = 12$

c Division is done before subtraction, so you get $6 \div 3 - 1 = 2 - 1 = 1$

d Brackets are done first, so you get $6 \div (3 - 1) = 6 \div 2 = 3$

Example 9.7 Work out each of the following, showing each step of the calculation.

a $1 + 3^2 \times 4 - 2$ b $(1 + 3)^2 \times (4 - 2)$

a The order will be power, multiplication, addition, subtraction (the last two can be interchanged). This gives
$$1 + 3^2 \times 4 - 2 = 1 + 9 \times 4 - 2 = 1 + 36 - 2 = 37 - 2 = 35$$

b The order will be brackets (both of them), power, multiplication. This gives
$$(1 + 3)^2 \times (4 - 2) = 4^2 \times 2 = 16 \times 2 = 32$$

Example 9.8 Add brackets to each of the following to make the calculation true.

a $5 + 1 \times 4 = 24$ b $1 + 3^2 - 4 = 12$ c $24 \div 6 - 2 = 6$

Decide which operation is done first.

a $(5 + 1) \times 4 = 24$

b $(1 + 3)^2 - 4 = 12$

c $24 \div (6 - 2) = 6$

Exercise 9C

1 Write down the operation that you do first in each of these calculations. Then work out each one.

a $2 + 3 \times 6$ b $12 - 6 \div 3$ c $5 \times 5 + 2$ d $12 \div 4 - 2$

e $(2 + 3) \times 6$ f $(12 - 3) \div 3$ g $5 \times (5 + 2)$ h $12 \div (4 - 2)$

2 Work out the following showing each step of the calculation.

a $2 \times 3 + 4$ b $2 \times (3 + 4)$ c $2 + 3 \times 4$ d $(2 + 3) \times 4$

e $4 \times 4 - 4$ f $5 + 3^2 + 6$ g $5 \times (3^2 + 6)$ h $3^2 - (5 - 2)$

i $(2 + 3) \times (4 + 5)$ j $(2^2 + 3) \times (4 + 5)$ k $4 \div 4 + 4 \div 4$

l $44 \div 4 + 4$ m $(6 + 2)^2$ n $6^2 + 2^2$ o $3^2 + 4 \times 6$

3 Add brackets to each of the following to make the calculation true.

a $2 \times 5 + 4 = 18$ b $2 + 6 \times 3 = 24$ c $2 + 3 \times 1 + 6 = 35$

d $5 + 2^2 \times 1 = 9$ e $3 + 2^2 = 25$ f $3 \times 4 + 3 + 7 = 28$

g $3 + 4 \times 7 + 1 = 35$ h $3 + 4 \times 7 + 1 = 50$ i $9 - 5 - 2 = 6$

j $9 - 5 \times 2 = 8$ k $4 + 4 + 4 \div 2 = 6$ l $1 + 4^2 - 9 - 2 = 18$

4 One of the calculations $2 \times 3^2 = 36$ and $2 \times 3^2 = 18$ is wrong. Which is it and how could you add brackets to make it true?

5 Work out the value of each of these.

a $(4 + 4) \div (4 + 4)$	**b** $(4 \times 4) \div (4 + 4)$	**c** $(4 + 4 + 4) \div 4$
d $4 \times (4 - 4) + 4$	**e** $(4 \times 4 + 4) \div 4$	**f** $(4 + 4 + 4) \div 2$
g $4 + 4 - 4 \div 4$	**h** $(4 + 4) \times (4 \div 4)$	**i** $(4 + 4) + 4 \div 4$

Extension Work

In Question 5, each calculation was made up of four 4s.

Work out the value of   **a** $44 \div 4 - 4$ **b** $4 \times 4 - 4 \div 4$ **c** $4 \times 4 + 4 - 4$

Can you make other calculations using four 4s to give answers that you have not yet obtained in Question 5 or in the three calculations above?

Do as many as you can and see whether you can make all the values up to 20.

Repeat with five 5s. For example:

$(5 + 5) \div 5 - 5 \div 5 = 1$ $(5 \times 5 - 5) \div (5 + 5) = 2$

Long multiplication and long division

Example 9.9

Work out 36×43.

Below are four examples of the ways this calculation can be done. The answer is 1548.

Box method (partitioning)

×	30	6	
40	1200	240	1440
3	90	18	108
			1548

Column method (expanded working)

$$\begin{array}{r} 36 \\ \times \quad 43 \\ \hline 18 \quad (3 \times 6) \\ 90 \quad (3 \times 30) \\ 240 \quad (40 \times 6) \\ 1200 \quad (40 \times 30) \\ \hline 1548 \end{array}$$

Column method (compacted working)

$$\begin{array}{r} 36 \\ \times \quad 43 \\ \hline 108 \quad (3 \times 36) \\ 1440 \quad (40 \times 36) \\ \hline 1548 \end{array}$$

Chinese method

Example 9.10

Work out $543 \div 31$.

Below are two examples of the ways this can be done. The answer is 17, remainder 16.

Subtracting multiples

$$\begin{array}{r} 543 \\ - 310 \quad (10 \times 31) \\ \hline 233 \\ - 155 \quad (5 \times 31) \\ \hline 78 \\ - 62 \quad (2 \times 31) \\ \hline 16 \end{array}$$

Traditional method

$$\begin{array}{r} 17 \\ 31 \overline{)543} \\ 31 \\ \hline 233 \\ 217 \\ \hline 16 \end{array}$$

1 Work out each of the following long multiplication problems. Use any method you are happy with.

a 17×23 b 32×42 c 19×45 d 56×46

e 12×346 f 32×541 g 27×147 h 39×213

2 Work out each of the following long division problems. Use any method you are happy with. Some of the problems will have a remainder.

a $684 \div 19$ b $966 \div 23$ c $972 \div 36$ d $625 \div 25$

e $930 \div 38$ f $642 \div 24$ g $950 \div 33$ h $800 \div 42$

Decide whether the following nine problems involve long multiplication or long division. Then do the appropriate calculation, showing your method clearly.

3 Each day 17 Jumbo jets fly from London to San Francisco. Each jet can carry up to 348 passengers. How many people can travel from London to San Francisco each day?

4 A company has 897 boxes to move by van. The van can carry 23 boxes at a time. How many trips must the van make to move all the boxes?

5 The same van does 34 miles to a gallon of petrol. How many miles can it do if the petrol tank holds 18 gallons?

6 The school photocopier can print 82 sheets a minute. If it runs without stopping for 45 minutes, how many sheets will it print?

7 The RE department has printed 525 sheets on Buddhism. These are put into folders in sets of 35. How many folders are there?

8 a To raise money, Wath Running Club are going to do a relay race from Wath to Edinburgh, which is 384 kilometres. Each runner will run 24 kilometres. How many runners will be needed to cover the distance?

b Sponsorship will bring in £32 per kilometre. How much money will the club raise?

9 Computer floppy disks are 45p each. How much will a box of 35 disks cost? Give your answer in pounds.

10 The daily newspaper sells advertising by the square inch. On Monday, it sells 232 square inches at £15 per square inch. How much money does it get from this advertising?

11 The local library has 13 000 books. Each shelf holds 52 books. How many shelves are there?

Another way of multiplying two two-digit numbers together is the 'Funny Face' method.

This shows how to do 26×57.

$$26 \times 57 = (20 + 6) \times (50 + 7)$$

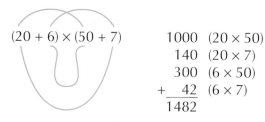

$(20 + 6) \times (50 + 7)$

1000	(20×50)
140	(20×7)
300	(6×50)
+ 42	(6×7)
1482	

Do a poster showing a calculation using the 'Funny Face' method.

Efficient calculations

You should have your own calculator, so that you can get used to it. Make sure that you understand how to use the basic functions ($\times$, $\div$, $+$, $-$) and the square, square root and brackets keys.

Example 9.11

Use a calculator to work out **a** $\dfrac{242 + 118}{88 - 72}$ **b** $\dfrac{63 \times 224}{32 \times 36}$

The line that separates the top numbers from the bottom numbers acts both as a divide sign ($\div$) and as brackets.

a Key the calculation as $(242 + 118) \div (88 - 72) = 22.5$

b Key the calculation as $(63 \times 224) \div (32 \times 36) = 12.25$

Example 9.12

Use a calculator to work out **a** $\sqrt{1764}$ **b** 23.4^2 **c** $52.3 - (30.4 - 17.3)$

a Some calculators need the square root after the number has been keyed, some need it before: $\sqrt{1764} = 42$

b Most calculators have a special key for squaring: $23.4^2 = 547.56$

c This can be keyed in exactly as it reads: $52.3 - (30.4 - 17.3) = 39.2$

Exercise 9E

1 Without using a calculator, work out the value of each of these.

a $\dfrac{17 + 8}{7 - 2}$

b $\dfrac{53 - 8}{3.5 - 2}$

c $\dfrac{19.2 - 1.7}{5.6 - 3.1}$

2 Use a calculator to do the calculations in Question 1. Do you get the same answers?

For each part, write down the sequence of keys that you pressed to get the answer.

3 Work out the value of each of these. Round off your answers to 1 dp.

a $\dfrac{194 + 866}{122 + 90}$ b $\dfrac{213 + 73}{63 - 19}$ c $\dfrac{132 + 88}{78 - 28}$ d $\dfrac{792 + 88}{54 - 21}$

e $\dfrac{790 \times 84}{24 \times 28}$ f $\dfrac{642 \times 24}{87 - 15}$ g $\dfrac{107 + 853}{24 \times 16}$ h $\dfrac{57 - 23}{18 - 7.8}$

4 Estimate the answer to $\dfrac{231 + 167}{78 - 32}$

Now use a calculator to work out the answer to 1 dp. Is it about the same?

5 Work out each of these.

a $\sqrt{42.25}$ b $\sqrt{68.89}$ c 2.6^2 d 3.9^2

e $\sqrt{(23.8 + 66.45)}$ f $\sqrt{(7 - 5.04)}$ g $(5.2 - 1.8)^2$ h $(2.5 + 6.1)^2$

6 Work out

a $8.3 - (4.2 - 1.9)$ b $12.3 + (3.2 - 1.7)^2$ c $(3.2 + 1.9)^2 - (5.2 - 2.1)^2$

7 Use a calculator to find the quotient and the remainder when

a 985 is divided by 23   b 802 is divided by 36

8 A calculator shows an answer of

2.33333333333

Write this as a mixed number or a top heavy fraction.

Extension Work

Time calculations are difficult to do on a calculator as there are not 100 minutes in an hour. So, you need to know either the decimal equivalents of all the divisions of an hour or the way to work them out. For example: 15 minutes is 0.25 of an hour.

Copy and complete this table for some of the decimal equivalents to fractions of an hour.

Time (min)	5	6	12	15	20	30	40	45	54	55
Fraction	$\frac{1}{12}$	$\frac{1}{10}$		$\frac{1}{4}$	$\frac{1}{3}$				$\frac{9}{10}$	
Decimal	0.083		0.2	0.25			0.667			0.917

When a time is given as a decimal and it is not one of those in the table above, you need a way to work it out in hours and minutes. For example:

3.4578 hours: subtract 3 to give 0.4578, then multiply by 60 to give 27.468

This is 27 minutes to the nearest minute. So, 3.4578 ≈ 3 hours 27 minutes.

1 Find each of the following decimal times as a time in hours and minutes.

a 2.5 h   b 3.25 h   c 4.75 h   d 3.1 h

e 4.6 h   f 3.3333 h   g 1.15 h   h 4.3 h

i 0.45 h   j 0.95 h   k 3.666 h

2 Find each of the following times in hours and minutes as a decimal time.

a 2 h 40 min   b 1 h 45 min   c 2 h 18 min   d 1 h 20 min

Calculating with measurements

The following table shows the relationship between the common metric units.

1000	100	10	1	0.1	0.01	0.001
km			m		cm	mm
kg			g			mg
			l		cl	ml

Example 9.13

Add together 1.23 m, 46 cm and 0.034 km.

First convert all the lengths to the same unit.

1000	100	10	1	0.1	0.01	0.001
km			m		cm	mm
			1	2	3	
				4	6	
0	0	3	4			

The answer is 0.035 69 km or 35.69 m or 3569 cm. 35.69 m is the sensible answer.

Example 9.14

A recipe needs 550 grams of flour to make a cake. How many 1 kg bags of flour will be needed to make six cakes?

Six cakes will need $6 \times 550 = 3300$ g, which will need four bags of flour.

Example 9.15

What unit would you use to measure each of these?

a   Width of a football field

b   Length of a pencil

c   Weight of a car

d   Spoonful of medicine

Choose a sensible unit. Sometimes there is more than one answer.

a   Metre   b   Centimetre   c   Kilogram   d   Millilitre

Example 9.16

Convert   a   6 cm to mm   b   1250 g to kg   c   5 l to cl

You need to know the conversion factors.

a   1 cm = 10 mm: $6 \times 10 = 60$ mm

b   1000 g = 1 kg: $1250 \div 1000 = 1.25$ kg

c   1 l = 100 cl: $5 l = 5 \times 100 = 500$ cl

1 Convert each of the following lengths to centimetres.

a 60 mm   **b** 2 m   **c** 743 mm   **d** 0.007 km   **e** 12.35 m

2 Convert each of the following lengths to kilometres.

a 456 m   **b** 7645 m   **c** 6532 cm   **d** 21 358 mm   **e** 54 m

3 Convert each of the following lengths to millimetres.

a 34 cm   **b** 3 m   **c** 3 km   **d** 35.6 cm   **e** 0.7 cm

4 Convert each of the following masses to kilograms.

a 3459 g   **b** 215 g   **c** 65 120 g   **d** 21 g   **e** 210 g

5 Convert each of the following masses to grams.

a 4 kg   **b** 4.32 kg   **c** 0.56 kg   **d** 0.007 kg   **e** 6.784 kg

6 Convert each of the following capacities to litres.

a 237 cl   **b** 3097 ml   **c** 1862 cl   **d** 48 cl   **e** 96 427 ml

7 Convert each of the following times to hours and minutes.

a 70 min   **b** 125 min   **c** 87 min   **d** 200 min   **e** 90 min

8 Add together each of the following groups of measurements and give the answer in an appropriate unit.

a 1.78 m, 39 cm, 0.006 km   **b** 0.234 kg, 60 g, 0.004 kg

c 2.3 l, 46 cl, 726 ml   **d** 0.000 6 km, 23 mm, 3.5 cm

9 Fill in each missing unit.

a A two-storey house is about 7...... high   **b** John weighs about 47......

c Mary lives about 2...... from school   **d** Ravid ran a marathon in 3......

10 Read the value from each of the following scales.

a    **b** 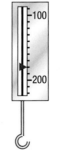   **c**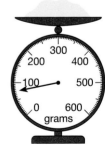

d 0   50   **e** 200   100   **f** 0   20

Area is measured in square millimetres (mm²), square centimetres (cm²), square metres (m²) and square kilometres (km²).

This square shows 1 square centimetre reproduced exactly.

You can fit 100 square millimetres inside this square because a 1 centimetre square is 10 mm by 10 mm.

10 mm

10 mm

How many square centimetres are there in 1 square metre?

How many square metres are there in 1 square kilometre?

1 What unit would you use to measure the area of each of these?

    a Football field   **b** Photograph   **c** Fingernail

    d National park   **e** Pacific Ocean   **f** Stamp

2 Convert **a** 24 cm² to mm²   **b** 6 km² to m²

                c 4000 mm² to cm²   **d** 3 456 000 m² to km²

3 Look up the areas of some countries on the Internet or in an encyclopaedia.

    a Which are the three biggest countries (in terms of area) in the world?

    b Which is the biggest country (in terms of area) in Europe?

Solving problems

MATHEMATICAL MICE

Mrs Farmer is frightened of mice. One day, she finds three mice in her kitchen. A large one, a medium-sized one and a small one.

She tries to scare them out but they are Mathematical Mice who will only leave when a dice is rolled.

When the dice shows 1 or 2, the small mouse goes through the door.

When the dice shows 3 or 4, the medium-sized mouse goes through the door.

When the dice shows 5 or 6, the big mouse goes through the door.

For example: Mrs Farmer rolls the dice. She gets 3, so the medium-sized mouse goes through the door. Next, she rolls 5, so the big mouse goes through the door. Next, she rolls 4, so the medium-sized mouse comes back through the door. Then she rolls 2, so the small mouse leaves. Finally, she rolls 4, so the medium-sized mouse leaves and all three are out of the kitchen.

Can you find a rule for the number of throws that it takes to get out all the mice?

What if there were two mice, or six mice?

Before you start, you should think about how you are going to record your results.

You should make sure that you explain in writing what you are going to do.

If you come up with an idea, you should write it down and explain it or test it.

What you need to know for level 5

- How to multiply and divide a three-digit whole number by a two-digit whole number
- The order in which the four operations must be used
- How to round numbers to one decimal place
- How to make estimates of calculations

What you need to know for level 6

- How to round numbers to two decimal places
- How to multiply integers and decimals, and understand where to position the decimal point

National Curriculum SATs questions

LEVEL 5

1 *1996 Paper 1*

Gwen makes kites to sell. She sells the kites for £4.75 each.

a Gwen sells 26 kites. How much does she get for the 26 kites?

b Gwen has a box of 250 staples. She uses 16 staples to make each kite.

How many complete kites can she make using the 250 staples?

2 *1997 Paper 1*

a A shop sells plants at 95p each. Find the cost of 35 plants.

b The shop also sells trees at £17 each. Mr Bailey has £250. He wants to buy as many trees as possible.

How many trees can Mr Bailey buy?

3 *1999 Paper 2*

This formula tells you how tall a boy is likely to be when he grows up.

> Add the mother's and father's heights.
> Divide by 2.
> Add 7 cm to the result.
> The boy is likely to be this height, plus or minus 10 cm.

Marc's mother is 168 cm tall. His father is 194 cm tall. What is the greatest height Marc is likely to be when he grows up?

4   *2000 Paper 2*

    a   A club wants to take 3000 people on a journey to London using coaches. Each coach can carry 52 people. How many coaches do they need?

    b   Each coach costs £420. What is the total cost of the coaches?

    c   How much is each person's share of the cost?

LEVEL 6

5   *2001 Paper 2*

The label on a pot of yoghurt shows this information.

How many grams of protein does 100g of yoghurt provide?

YOGHURT 125 g	
Each 125 g provides	
Energy	430 kJ
Protein	4.5 g
Carbohydrate	11.1 g
Fat	4.5 g

6   *1999 Paper 2*

A report on the police in 1995 said:

'There are 119 000 police officers. Almost 15% of them are women.'

    a   The percentage was rounded to the nearest whole number, 15. What is the smallest value the percentage could have been, to one decimal place?

    b   What is the smallest number of women police officers there might have been in 1995? Use your answer to part **a** to help you.

CHAPTER **10** Algebra **3**

This chapter is going to show you

- what square numbers and triangle numbers are
- how to use a calculator to find square roots
- how to draw graphs from functions
- how to use algebra to solve problems

What you should already know

- How to find the term-to-term rule in a sequence
- How to plot coordinates
- How to solve simple equations

Square numbers and square roots

When we multiply any number by itself, the answer is called the **square of the number** or the **number squared**. We call this operation **squaring**. We show it by putting a small 2 at the top right-hand corner of the number being squared. For example:

$$4 \times 4 = 4^2 = 16$$

The result of squaring a number is also called a **square number**. The first ten square numbers are shown below.

1×1	2×2	3×3	4×4	5×5	6×6	7×7	8×8	9×9	10×10
1^2	2^2	3^2	4^2	5^2	6^2	7^2	8^2	9^2	10^2
1	4	9	16	25	36	49	64	81	100

You need to learn all of these.

The **square root** of a number is that number which, when squared, gives the starting number. It is the opposite of finding the square of a number. There are always *two* square roots of a positive number: a positive value and its negative.

A square root is represented by the symbol $\sqrt{\ }$. For example:

$$\sqrt{1} = 1 \text{ and } -1 \quad \sqrt{4} = 2 \text{ and } -2 \quad \sqrt{9} = 3 \text{ and } -3 \quad \sqrt{16} = 4 \text{ and } -4 \quad \sqrt{25} = 5 \text{ and } -5$$

Only the square root of a square number will give an integer (whole number) as the answer.

Exercise 10A

1 Look at the pattern on the right.

   a Copy this pattern and draw the next two shapes in the pattern.

   b What is special about the total number of dots in each pattern number?

   c What is special about the number of blue dots in each pattern number?

   d What is special about the number of red dots in each pattern number?

   e Write down a connection between square numbers and odd numbers.

Pattern 1

1

Pattern 2

1 + 3
4

Pattern 3

4 + 5
9

2 $45 = 9 + 36 = 3^2 + 6^2$

Give each of the following numbers as the sum of two square numbers, as above.

a	29	**b**	34	**c**	65	**d**	100	**e**	82
f	25	**g**	85	**h**	73	**i**	106	**j**	58

3 You should have noticed from Question **2f** above that $3^2 + 4^2 = 5^2$.

This is a *special square sum* (made up of only square numbers). There are many to be found. See which of the following pairs of squares will give you a special square sum.

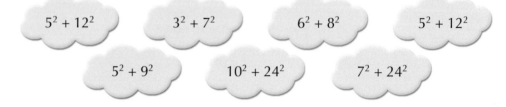

$5^2 + 12^2$ $3^2 + 7^2$ $6^2 + 8^2$ $5^2 + 12^2$

$5^2 + 9^2$ $10^2 + 24^2$ $7^2 + 24^2$

4 Write down the value represented by each of the following. Do not forget to write down the negative value, too. Do not use a calculator.

a	$\sqrt{16}$	**b**	$\sqrt{36}$	**c**	$\sqrt{4}$	**d**	$\sqrt{49}$	**e**	$\sqrt{1}$
f	$\sqrt{9}$	**g**	$\sqrt{100}$	**h**	$\sqrt{81}$	**i**	$\sqrt{25}$	**j**	$\sqrt{64}$

5 With the aid of a calculator, write down the value represented by each of the following.

a	$\sqrt{289}$	**b**	$\sqrt{961}$	**c**	$\sqrt{529}$	**d**	$\sqrt{2500}$	**e**	$\sqrt{1296}$
f	$\sqrt{729}$	**g**	$\sqrt{3249}$	**h**	$\sqrt{361}$	**i**	$\sqrt{3969}$	**j**	$\sqrt{1764}$

6 Make an estimate of each of the following square roots. Then use your calculator to see how many you got right.

a	$\sqrt{256}$	**b**	$\sqrt{1089}$	**c**	$\sqrt{625}$	**d**	$\sqrt{2704}$	**e**	$\sqrt{1444}$
f	$\sqrt{841}$	**g**	$\sqrt{3481}$	**h**	$\sqrt{441}$	**i**	$\sqrt{4096}$	**j**	$\sqrt{2025}$

7 The solutions to $x^2 = 9$ are $x = 3$ and $x = -3$. These can be written as $x = \pm 3$, which means $x = 3$ and $x = -3$.

Write down the full solution to each of these equations.

a	$x^2 = 16$	**b**	$x^2 = 36$	**c**	$x^2 = 100$	**d**	$x^2 = 1$
e	$x^2 + 1 = 10$	**f**	$x^2 - 3 = 46$	**g**	$x^2 + 7 = 11$		

8 Write down the full solution to each of these equations.

a	$2x^2 = 18$	**b**	$4x^2 = 100$	**c**	$3x^2 = 12$	**d**	$5x^2 = 45$
e	$3x^2 + 5 = 80$	**f**	$4x^2 - 7 = 29$	**g**	$2x^2 + 17 = 115$		

1 a Choose any two square numbers: for example, m and n.

  b Multiply them together: $m \times n = R$.

  c What is the square root of this result, $\sqrt{R}$?

  d Can you find a connection between this square root and the two starting numbers?

  e Try this again for more square numbers.

  f Is the connection the same no matter what two square numbers you choose?

2 See if you can find any more sets of the special square sums.

Triangle numbers

The number of dots used to make each triangle in this pattern form the sequence of **triangle numbers**.

The first few triangle numbers are   1   3   6

    1, 3, 6, 10, 15, 21, 28, 36, 45, ...

You need to remember how to generate the sequence of triangle numbers.

Exercise 10B

1 Look at the following sequence.

Pattern number	1	2	3	4	5	6	7
Number of blue dots	1	3	6				
Number of yellow dots	0	1	3				
Total number of dots	1	4	9				

  a Continue the sequence for the next three shapes.

  b Complete the table to show the number of dots in each shape.

  c What is special about the number of **blue** dots?

  d What is special about the number of **yellow** dots?

  e What is special about the **total number** of dots in each pattern number?

  f Write down a connection between triangle numbers and square numbers.

2 Look at the numbers in the box on the right.

Write down the numbers that are:

  a square numbers   **d** multiples of 5

  b triangle numbers   **e** factors of 100

  c even numbers   **f** prime numbers

1	2	3	5	6	9
10	13	15	18	21	
25	26	28	29	36	
38	64	75	93	100	

3 Each of the following numbers can be given as the sum of two triangle numbers. Write each sum in full.

a	7	**b**	24	**c**	16	**d**	31
e	21	**f**	25	**g**	36	**h**	42

4 **a** Write down the first 12 triangle numbers.

b How many of these numbers are **i** even **ii** odd.

c How many of these numbers are multiples of 3?

d Look at the numbers that are not multiples of 3. What is special about them all?

e Test parts **b** to **d** with the next 12 triangle numbers.

f What do you notice about your answers to part **e**?

Extension Work

36 is both a square number and a triangle number. Which are the next few numbers to be both square and triangular? You will find this easier if you use a spreadsheet to help you to search.

From mappings to graphs

Think about the function $x \to x + 1$. This represents the relationship 'Add on one'.

The equation $y = x + 1$ is another way of representing this function, and it is easier to use.

Putting these values together to form ordered pairs, we get:

$$(1,2), (2,3), (3,4), (4,5), (5,6)$$

We have chosen just five starting points, but we could have chosen many more.

x	$y = x + 1$
Input	**Output**
1	→ 2
2	→ 3
3	→ 4
4	→ 5
5	→ 6

We can use these ordered pairs as coordinates, and plot them on a pair of axes, as shown on the right.

We can join all the points with a straight line. Choose any point on the straight line. Use the first number of the pair of coordinates as the input to the function. You should find that the output is the second number of the coordinate pair.

Notice how we can extend the line into the negative axes. Check that the coordinates still satisfy the function.

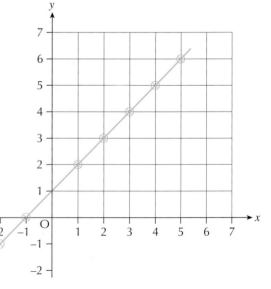

1 For each of the following functions:

  i Complete the arrow diagram.   **ii** Complete the coordinates alongside.

  iii Plot the coordinates and draw the graph, using the x-axis from -3 to 7.

a $y = x + 2$

x	$y = x + 2$	**Coordinates**
-1	⟶ 1	$(-1, 1)$
0	⟶ 2	$(0, 2)$
1	⟶	$(1,\ )$
2	⟶	$(2,\ )$
3	⟶	$(3,\ )$
4	⟶	$(4,\ )$

b $y = 2x$

x	$y = 2x$	**Coordinates**
-1	⟶ -2	$(-1, -2)$
0	⟶ 0	$(0, 0)$
1	⟶	$(1,\ )$
2	⟶	$(2,\ )$
3	⟶	$(3,\ )$
4	⟶	$(4,\ )$

c $y = 2x + 3$

x	$y = 2x + 3$	**Coordinates**
-1	⟶ 1	$(-1, 1)$
0	⟶ 3	$(0, 3)$
1	⟶	$(1,\ )$
2	⟶	$(2,\ )$
3	⟶	$(3,\ )$
4	⟶	$(4,\ )$

d $y = 3x - 2$

x	$y = 3x - 2$	**Coordinates**
-1	⟶ -5	$(-1, -5)$
0	⟶ -2	$(0, -2)$
1	⟶ 1	$(1, 1)$
2	⟶	$(2,\ )$
3	⟶	$(3,\ )$
4	⟶	$(4,\ )$

2 Choose some of your own starting points and create a graph from each of the following relationships.

  a $y = x + 3$ **b** $y = 3x + 2$ **c** $y = 2x - 3$ **d** $y = 4x - 3$

  e $y = 2x + 5$ **f** $y = 3x - 1$ **g** $y = 4x + 3$ **h** $y = 2x - 5$

Extension Work

a   Draw a mapping diagram for the function $x \to x^2$. Use the x-axis from -5 to 5.

b   Use the mapping to help you find some coordinates to draw the graph of $y = x^2$.

c   Use your graph to help ou to find $\sqrt{19}$, without using your calculator.

d   Check how accurate you were by working out $\sqrt{19}$ on your calculator.

More about graphs

What do you notice about the coordinates
$(-2, 3)$, $(-1, 3)$, $(0, 3)$, $(1, 3)$, $(2, 3)$, $(3, 3)$, $(4, 3)$?

The second number, the y-ordinate, is always 3.
In other words, $y = 3$.

Look what happens when we plot it.

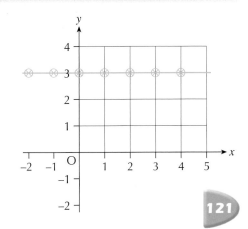

See also the graphs of $y = 2$ and $y = 5$, shown below.

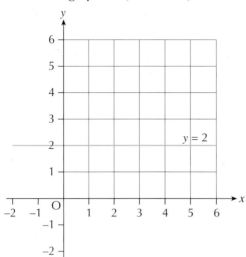 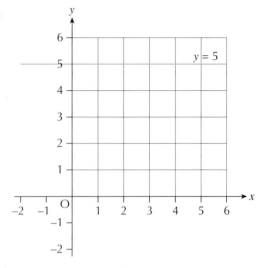

Note: the graphs are always horizontal lines for $y = A$, where A is any fixed number.

When we repeat this for an x-value, say $x = 2$, we get a vertical line, as shown.

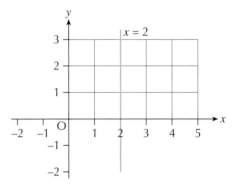

1 a Draw the following graphs on the same grid, and label them.

    i $y = 1$ **ii** $y = 4$ **iii** $y = -1$
    iv $x = 1$ **v** $x = 3$ **vi** $x = -2$

> **Axes**
> x-axis from –2 to 5
> y-axis from –2 to 5

b Write the coordinates of the point where each pair of lines cross.

    i $y = 1$ and $x = 3$ **ii** $y = 4$ and $x = 1$ **iii** $y = 6$ and $x = -4$

2 a For each of the equations in the box below, copy and complete the arrow diagram and the set of coordinates.

Start your arrow diagram as follows:

$x \longrightarrow$?	**Coordinates**
$-1 \longrightarrow$	$(-1, \ )$
$0 \longrightarrow$	$(0, \ )$
$1 \longrightarrow$	$(1, \ )$
$2 \longrightarrow$	$(2, \ )$
$3 \longrightarrow$	$(3, \ )$
$4 \longrightarrow$	$(4, \ )$

> $y = x$
> $y = 2x$
> $y = 3x$
> $y = 4x$
> $y = 5x$

b For each set of coordinates, draw a graph on the same pair of axes as those for the other equations. Not all your points will fit on the grid, so plot the points that will fit on, and join them.

> **Axes**
> x-axis from –2 to 5
> y-axis from –2 to 12

c Explain what you notice.

d Try putting the graph of $y = 7x$ on your diagram without calculating the coordinates.

3 a For each of the equations in the box below, copy and complete the arrow diagram and the set of coordinates.

Start your arrow diagram as follows:

$x \longrightarrow$?	**Coordinates**
$-1 \longrightarrow$	$(-1, \ )$
$0 \longrightarrow$	$(0, \ )$
$1 \longrightarrow$	$(1, \ )$
$2 \longrightarrow$	$(2, \ )$
$3 \longrightarrow$	$(3, \ )$
$4 \longrightarrow$	$(4, \ )$

> $y = x$
>
> $y = x + 1$
>
> $y = x + 2$
>
> $y = x + 3$
>
> $y = x + 4$

b For each set of coordinates, draw a graph on the same pair of axes as those for the other equations. Not all your points will fit on the grid, so plot the points that will fit on, and join them.

> **Axes**
> x-axis from -2 to 5
> y-axis from -2 to 10

c Explain what you notice.

d Try putting the graph of $y = x + 5$ on your diagram.

Extension Work

1 Use a spreadsheet to draw the graph of $y = 2x + 3$.

2 Use a graphics calculator to draw all the graphs in Exercise 10D.

Questions about graphs

Example 10.1

Which of the points $(2, 5)$ and $(3, 9)$ are on the graph of $y = 2x + 3$?

Look at $(2, 5)$. When $x = 2$:

$y = 2x + 3 = 2 \times 2 + 3 = 7$ (which is not 5)

So, the point $(2, 5)$ is not on the line $y = 2x + 3$.

Look at $(3, 9)$. When $x = 3$:

$y = 2x + 3 = 2 \times 3 + 3 = 9$

So, the point $(3, 9)$ is on the line $y = 2x + 3$.

You can check this by looking on the graph of $y = 2x + 3$.

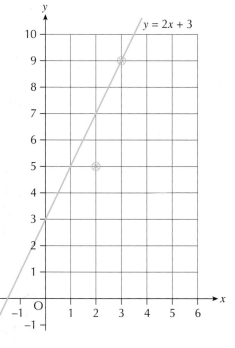

Answer the first five questions without drawing graphs.

1 **a**   Is the point (3, 5) on the graph of $y = x + 2$?
   b   Is the point (4, 2) on the graph of $y = x - 2$?
   c   Is the point (−3, 3) on the graph of $y = x + 3$?
   d   Is the point (2, 10) on the graph of $y = 5x$?
   e   Is the point (3, 8) on the graph of $y = 3x$?
   f   Is the point (−2, −8) on the graph of $y = 4x$?

2 Which of the following lines does the point (2, 3) lie on?

$y = x - 1$ $y = x + 1$ $y = 2x$ $y = 3x$

3 Which of the following lines does the point (3, 6) lie on?

$y = x + 2$ $y = x + 3$ $y = 2x$ $y = 3x$

4 Write down two functions whose graphs will pass through the point (1, 3).

5 Write down two functions whose graphs will pass through the point (2, 8).

6 Find, by drawing the two graphs, the coordinates of the point where the graphs of $y = x + 1$ and $y = 2x$ intersect (cross).

> **Axes**
> x-axis from 0 to 3
> y-axis from 0 to 7

Extension Work

1 Two numbers, x and y, add up to 8. We are told that x is 3 more than y.
   a   Use the statement 'x and y add up to 8' to create an equation of the form $y = \ldots\ldots$
   b   Use the statement 'x is 3 more than y' to create an equation of the form $y = \ldots\ldots$

> **Axes**
> x-axis from 0 to 9
> y-axis from 0 to 9

   c   Draw graphs of the above two equations on the same grid.
   d   What are the coordinates of the point where the two graphs cross?
   e   Use your answer to part **c** to enable you to state the values of x and y.

2 I think of two non-integer numbers, x and y, where x is smaller than y. The two numbers add together to make 6.
   a   Write down an equation involving y, x and 6 of the form $y = \ldots\ldots$

> **Axes**
> x-axis from 0 to 7
> y-axis from 0 to 7

   The larger number is three times the smaller number.
   b   Write down an equation involving y, x and 3 of the form $y = \ldots\ldots$
   c   Draw graphs of these two equations on the same pair of axes.
   d   What are the coordinates of the point where the two graphs cross?
   e   Use the answer to part **d** to say what the two numbers are.

What you need to know for level 5

- How to generate coordinates from a simple linear rule
- How to plot the graphs of simple linear functions, where y is given in terms of x

What you need to know for level 6

- How to plot negative coordinates
- How to use coordinates to interpret the general features of the graphs of simple linear functions

National Curriculum SATs questions

LEVEL 5

1 *2002 Paper 1*

The graph shows a straight line. The equation of the line is $y = 3x$.

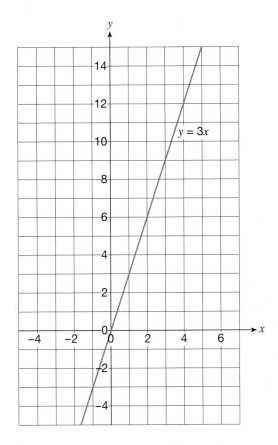

Does the point (25, 75) lie on the straight line $y = 3x$? Answer Yes or No.

Explain how you know.

2 *2000 Paper 1*

These straight line graphs all pass through the point (10, 10).

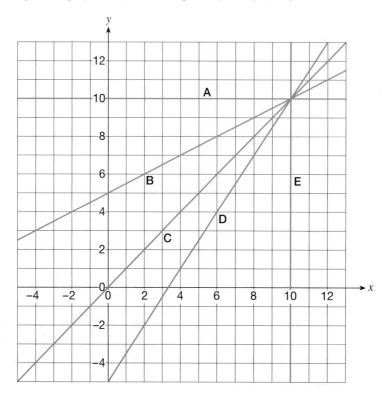

a Which line has the equation $x = 10$?

b Which line has the equation $y = 10$?

c Which line has the equation $y = x$?

d Which line has the equation $y = 1.5x - 5$?

e Which line has the equation $y = 0.5x + 5$?

3 *2002 Paper 2*

Each point on the straight line $x + y = 12$ has an x-coordinate and a y-coordinate that add together to make 12.

Draw the straight line $x + y = 12$ on a copy of this grid.

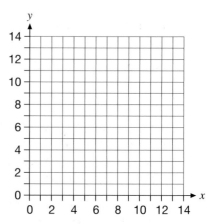

CHAPTER 11

Shape, Space and Measures **3**

This chapter is going to show you	What you should already know
○ how to measure and draw angles ○ how to construct triangles and other shapes ○ how to construct the perpendicular bisector of a straight line ○ how to construct the bisector of an angle ○ the geometrical properties of triangles and quadrilaterals	○ How to use a protractor to measure and draw angles ○ How to calculate angles on a straight line and around a point ○ How to calculate angles in a triangle

Measuring and drawing angles

Notice that on a semicircular protractor there are two scales. The outer scale goes from 0° to 180°, and the inner one goes from 180° to 0°. It is important that you use the correct scale.

When measuring or drawing an angle, always decide first whether it is an acute angle or an obtuse angle.

Example 11.1 ▷   First, decide whether the angle to be measured is acute or obtuse. This is an acute angle (less than 90°).

Place the centre of the protractor at the corner of the angle, as in the diagram.

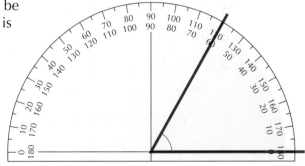

The two angles shown on the protractor scales are 60° and 120°. Since you are measuring an acute angle, the angle is 60° (to the nearest degree).

Example 11.2 ▷   Measure the size of this reflex angle.

First, measure the inside or interior angle. This is an obtuse angle.

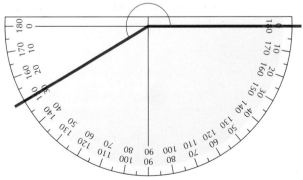

The two angles shown on the protractor scales are 30° and 150°. Since you are measuring an obtuse angle, the angle is 150°.

The size of the reflex angle is found by subtracting this angle from 360°. The reflex angle is therefore 360° − 150°, which is 210° (to the nearest degree).

1 Measure the size of each of the following angles, giving your answer to the nearest degree.

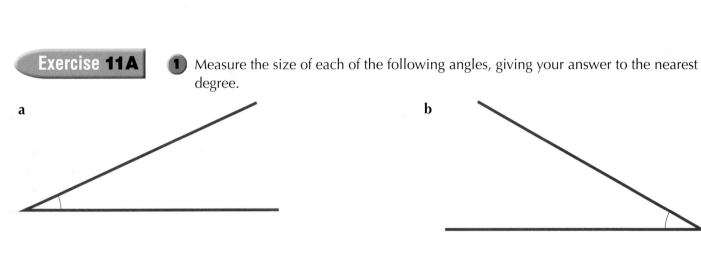

a

b

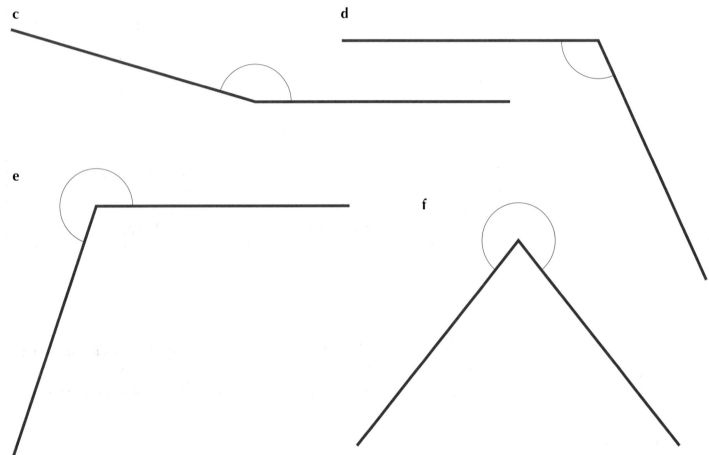

c

d

e

f

2 Draw and label each of the following angles.

a	20°	**b**	35°	**c**	72°	**d**	100°	**e**	145°
f	168°	**g**	220°	**h**	258°	**i**	300°	**j**	347°

3 a Measure the five angles in the pentagon ABCDE.

b Add the five angles together.

c Comment on your answer.

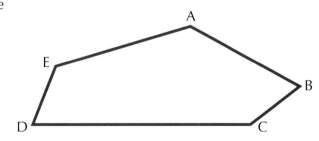

Estimating angles

- Copy the table below.

Angle	Estimate	Actual	Difference
1			
2			
3			
4			

- Estimate the size of each of the four angles below and complete the Estimate column in the table.

1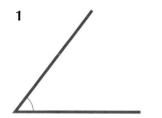

2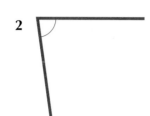

3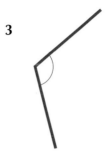

4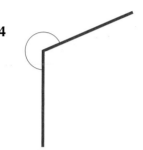

- Now measure the size of each angle to the nearest degree and complete the Actual column.
- Work out the difference between your estimate and the actual measurement for each angle and complete the Difference column.

Constructions

You need to be able to draw a shape exactly from information given on a diagram, using a ruler, a protractor and compasses. This is known as **constructing a shape**.

When constructing a shape you need to draw lines to the nearest millimetre and the angles to the nearest degree.

Example 11.3

Construct the triangle ABC.
- Draw line BC 7.5 cm long.
- Draw an angle of 50° at B.
- Draw line AB 4.1 cm long.
- Join AC to complete the triangle.

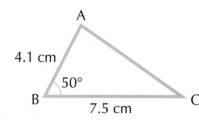

The completed, full-sized triangle is given below.

This is an example of constructing a triangle given two sides and the included angle – SAS.

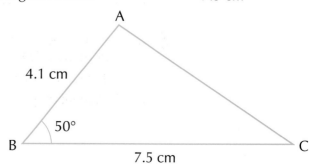

Example 11.4 ▷   Construct the triangle XYZ.
- Draw line YZ 8.3 cm long.
- Draw an angle of 42° at Y.
- Draw an angle of 51° at Z.
- Extend both angle lines to intersect at X to complete the triangle.

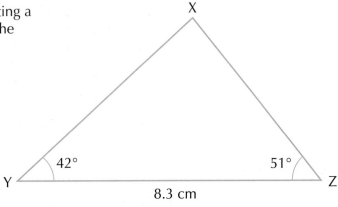

The completed, full-sized triangle is given below.

This is an example of constructing a triangle given two angles and the included side – ASA.

Example 11.5 ▷   Construct the triangle PQR.
- Draw line QR 6 cm long.
- Set the compasses to a radius of 4 cm and, with centre at Q, draw a long arc above QR.
- Set the compasses to a radius of 5 cm and, with centre at R, draw a long arc to intersect the first arc.
- The intersection of the arcs is P.
- Join QP and RP to complete the triangle.

This is an example of constructing a triangle given three sides – SSS.

The construction lines should be left on the diagram.

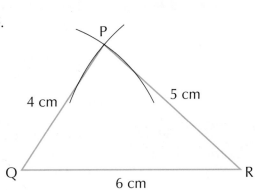

Example 11.6 To construct the mid-point and the perpendicular bisector of a line segment.
- Draw a line segment AB of any length.
- Set the compasses to any radius which is greater than half the length of AB.
- Draw two arcs with their centre at A, above and below AB.
- With the compasses set at the same radius, draw two arcs with their centre at B, to intersect the first two arcs at C and D.
- Join C and D to intersect AB at X.
- X is the mid-point of the line AB.
- The line CD is the perpendicular bisector of the line AB.

All construction lines should be left on the diagram.

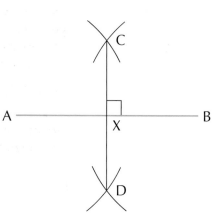

Example 11.7 To construct the bisector of ∠ABC.
- Draw an angle ABC of any size.
- Set the compasses to any radius and, with centre at B, draw an arc to intersect BC at X and AB at Y.
- With the compasses set to any radius, draw two arcs with centres at X and Y, to intersect at Z.
- Join BZ.
- BZ is the bisector of ∠ABC.
- ∠ABZ = ∠CBZ.

All construction lines should be left on the diagram.

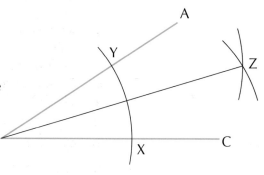

Exercise 11B

1 Construct each of the following triangles. Remember to label all lines and angles.

a
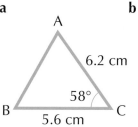

b
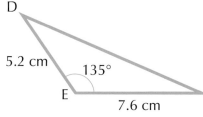

c
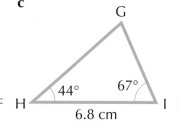

d
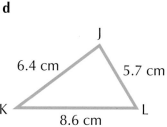

2 a Construct the triangle PQR.
b Measure the size of ∠P and ∠R to the nearest degree.
c Measure the length of the line PR to the nearest millimetre.

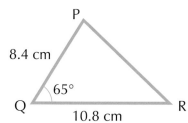

3 **a** Construct the triangle ABC with ∠A = 100°, ∠B = 36° and AB = 8.4 cm.

b Construct the triangle XYZ with XY = 6.5 cm, XZ = 4.3 cm and YZ = 5.8 cm.

4 **a** Construct the trapezium ABCD.

b Measure the size of ∠B to the nearest degree.

c Measure the length of the lines AB and BC to the nearest millimetre.

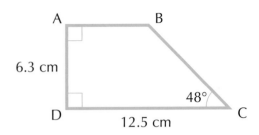

5 **a** Draw a line AB 6 cm long. Construct the perpendicular bisector of AB.

b Draw a line CD 8.5 cm long. Construct the perpendicular bisector of CD.

6 **a** Draw an angle of 48°. Construct the bisector of the angle.

b Draw an angle of 90°. Construct the bisector of the angle.

c Draw an angle of 120°. Construct the bisector of the angle.

Extension Work

1 Construct the parallelogram ABCD with AB = 7.4 cm, AD = 6.4 cm, ∠A = 50° and ∠B = 130°.

2 **a** Construct the quadrilateral PQRS.

b Measure ∠P and ∠Q to the nearest degree.

c Measure the length of the line PQ to the nearest millimetre.

3 If you have access to ICT facilities, find out how to draw triangles using computer software packages such as LOGO.

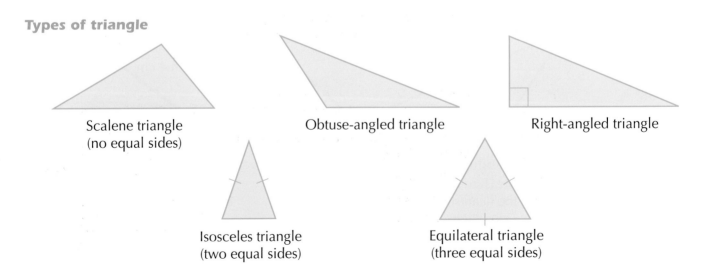

Solving geometrical problems

Types of triangle

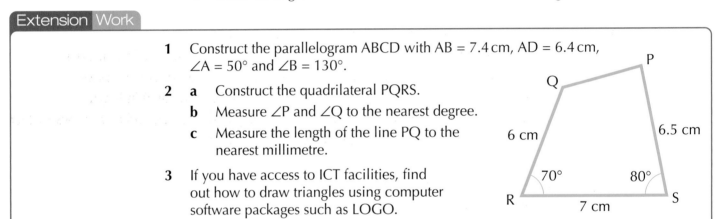

Scalene triangle
(no equal sides)

Obtuse-angled triangle

Right-angled triangle

Isosceles triangle
(two equal sides)

Equilateral triangle
(three equal sides)

Types of quadrilateral

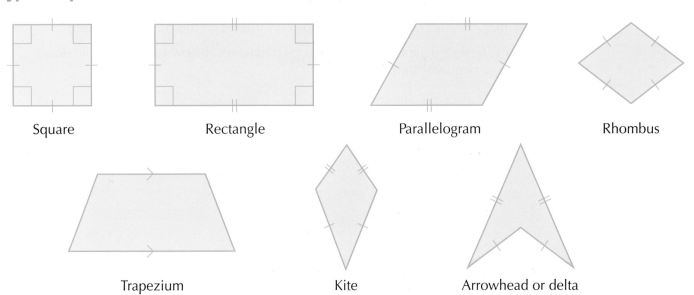

Square

Rectangle

Parallelogram

Rhombus

Trapezium

Kite

Arrowhead or delta

1 Which quadrilaterals have the following properties?

  a Four equal sides   **b** Two different pairs of equal sides

  c Two pairs of parallel sides   **d** Only one pair of parallel sides

  e Adjacent sides equal   **f** Diagonals are equal in length

  g Diagonals bisect each other **h** Diagonals are perpendicular to each other

  i Diagonals intersect at right angles outside the shape

2 Explain the difference between:

  a a square and a rectangle

  b a rhombus and a parallelogram

  c a kite and an arrowhead

3 How many different triangles can be constructed on this 3 by 3 pin-board?

  Use square dotted paper to record your triangles. Below each one, write down what type of triangle it is.

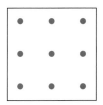

4 Copy this square on a piece of card. Then draw in the two diagonals and cut out the four triangles.

  How many different triangles or quadrilaterals can you make with the following?

  a Four of the triangles

  b Three of the triangles

  c Two of the triangles

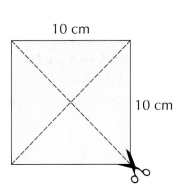

10 cm

10 cm

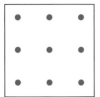

How many distinct quadrilaterals can be constructed on this 3 by 3 pin-board?

Use square dotted paper to record your quadrilaterals. Below each one, write down what type of quadrilateral it is.

What you need to know for level 5

- How to draw and measure angles
- How to construct triangles from given information
- Understand the geometrical properties of 2-D shapes

What you need to know for level 6

- How to construct the mid-point and the perpendicular bisector of a straight line
- How to construct the bisector of an angle
- How to solve problems using the geometrical properties of triangles and quadrilaterals

National Curriculum SATs questions

LEVEL 5

1 *1997 Paper 2*

Here is a rough sketch of a sector of a circle.

Make an accurate, full size drawing of this sector.

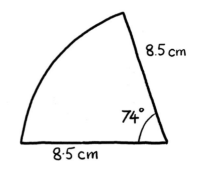

8.5 cm

8·5 cm

74°

Not to scale

2 *1995 Paper 2*

Julie wants to make a card with a picture of a boat.

The boat will stand up as the card
is opened.

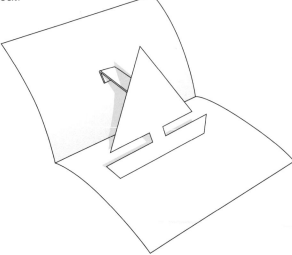

Julie makes a rough sketch of the boat.
It is made out of a triangle and a trapezium.

a Make an accurate full-sized drawing of
the triangle.

b Make an accurate full-sized drawing of
the trapezium for the boat.

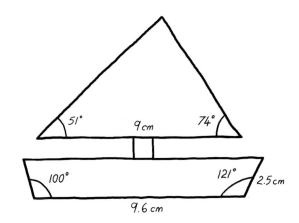

LEVEL 6

3 *1995 Paper 2*

Shape A is an equilateral triangle.

The instructions to draw shape A are:

    FORWARD 5
    TURN RIGHT 120°
    FORWARD 5
    TURN RIGHT 120°
    FORWARD 5

a Write instructions to draw a triangle that
has sides double those of shape A.

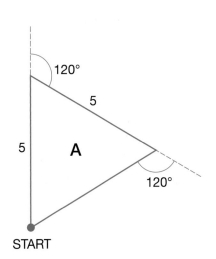

Shape B is a parallelogram.

b Copy and complete the instructions to draw shape B.

FORWARD 8

......

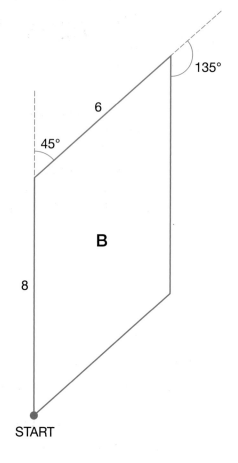

This chapter is going to show you

- how to find percentages and use them to compare proportions
- how to work out ratio, leading into simple direct proportion
- how to solve problems using ratio

What you should already know

- How to find equivalent fractions, percentages and decimals
- How to find multiples of 10% of a quantity
- Division facts from tables up to 10×10

Percentages

One of these labels is from a packet of porridge oats. The other is from a toffee cake.

Compare the percentages of protein, carbohydrates, fat and fibre.

PORRIDGE OATS	
Typical values	**per 100 g**
Energy	1555 kJ/ 372 kcal
Protein	7.5 g
Carbohydrates	71 g
Fat	6.0 g
Fibre	6.0 g
Sodium	0.3 g

TOFFEE CAKE	
Typical values	**per 100 g**
Energy	1421 kJ/ 340 kcal
Protein	2.9 g
Carbohydrates	39.1 g
Fat	19.1 g
Fibre	0.3 g
Sodium	0.2 g

Example 12.1 Without using a calculator find **a** 12% of £260 **b** 39% of 32

a 12% = 10% + 1% + 1%, so 12% of £260 = 26 + 2.6 + 2.6 = £31.20

b 39% = 10% + 10% + 10% + 10% − 1%,
so 39% of 32 = 4 × 3.2 − 0.32 = 12.8 − 0.32 = 12.48

Example 12.2 Work out **a** 6% of £190 **b** 63% of 75 eggs

a (6 ÷ 100) × 190 = £11.40

b (63 ÷ 100) × 75 = 47.25 = 47 eggs

Example 12.3 Which is greater, 42% of 560 or 62% of 390?

(42 ÷ 100) × 560 = 235.2 (62 ÷ 100) × 390 = 241.8

62% of 390 is greater.

1. Write down or work out the equivalent percentage and decimal to each of these fractions.

   a $\frac{2}{5}$ **b** $\frac{1}{4}$ **c** $\frac{3}{8}$ **d** $\frac{11}{20}$ **e** $\frac{21}{25}$

2. Write down or work out the equivalent percentage and fraction to each of these decimals.

   a 0.1   **b** 0.75   **c** 0.34   **d** 0.85   **e** 0.31

3. Write down or work out the equivalent fraction and decimal to each of these percentages.

   a 15%   **b** 62.5%   **c** 8%   **d** 66.6%   **e** 80%

4. Without using a calculator, work out each of these.

   a 12% of 320   **b** 49% of 45   **c** 31% of 260   **d** 18% of 68
   e 11% of 12   **f** 28% of 280   **g** 52% of 36   **h** 99% of 206

5. Work out each of these.

   a 13% of £560   **b** 46% of 64 books   **c** 73% of 190 chairs
   d 34% of £212   **e** 64% of 996 pupils   **f** 57% of 120 buses
   g 37% of 109 plants   **h** 78% of 345 bottles   **i** 62% of 365 days
   j 93% of 2564 people   **k** 54% of 456 fish   **l** 45% of £45
   m 65% of 366 eggs   **n** 7% of £684   **o** 9% of 568 chickens

6. Which is bigger:

   a 45% of 68 or 34% of 92?   **b** 22% of £86 or 82% of £26?
   c 28% of 79 or 69% of 31?   **d** 32% of 435 or 43% of 325?

7. Javid scores 17 out of 25 on a maths test, 14 out of 20 on a science test and 33 out of 50 on an English test. Work out each score as a percentage.

8. Arrange these numbers in order of increasing size.

   a 21%, $\frac{6}{25}$, 0.2   **b** 0.39, 38%, $\frac{3}{8}$ **c** $\frac{11}{20}$, 54%, 0.53

Extension Work

The pie chart shows the percentage of each constituent of the toffee cake given in the label on page 137.

Draw a pie chart to show the percentage of each constituent of the porridge oats given on the same page.

Obtain labels from a variety of cereals and other food items. Draw a pie chart for each of them.

What types of food have the most fat? What types of food have the most energy?

Is there a connection between the energy of food and the fat and carbohydrate content?

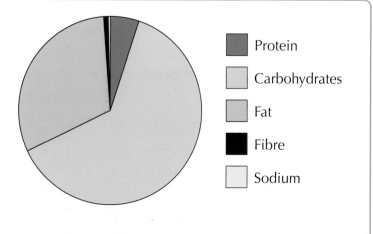

Protein
Carbohydrates
Fat
Fibre
Sodium

Ratio and proportion

Look at the fish tank. There are three types of fish – plain, striped and spotted.

What proportion of the fish are plain? What proportion are striped? What proportion are spotted?

What is the ratio of plain fish to striped fish?

What is the ratio of striped fish to spotted fish?

What is the ratio of plain fish to striped fish?

Proportion is a way of comparing the parts of a quantity to the whole quantity.

Example 12.4 ▷ What proportion of this metre rule is shaded? What is the ratio of the shaded part to the unshaded part?

40 cm out of 100 cm are shaded. This is 40% (or 0.4 or $\frac{2}{5}$). The ratio of shaded to unshaded is $40:60 = 2:3$.

Example 12.5 ▷ A fruit drink is made by mixing 20 cl of orange juice with 60 cl of pineapple juice. What is the proportion of orange juice in the drink?

Total volume of drink is $20 + 60 = 80$ cl

The proportion of orange is 20 out of $80 = \frac{20}{80} = \frac{1}{4}$

Example 12.6 ▷ Another fruit drink is made by mixing orange juice and grapefruit juice. The proportion of orange is 40%. 60 cl of orange juice is used. What proportion of grapefruit is used? How much grapefruit juice is used?

The proportion of grapefruit is $100\% - 40\% = 60\%$. Now 40% = 60 cl, so 10% = 15 cl. So, 60% = 90 cl of grapefruit juice.

Example 12.7 ▷ Five pens cost £3.25. How much do 8 pens cost?

First, work out cost of 1 pen: £3.25 ÷ 5 = £0.65
So, 8 pens cost 8 × £0.65 = £5.20

Exercise 12B

① For each of these metre rules:
  i What proportion of the rule is shaded?
  ii What is the ratio of the shaded part to the unshaded part?

2 For each bag of black and white balls:

    i   What proportion of the balls are black?

    ii   What is the ratio of black to white balls?

    a   **b**   **c**   **d**

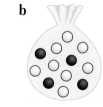 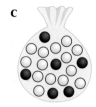 

3 Tom and Jerry have some coins. This table shows the coins they have.

	1p	2p	5p	10p	20p	50p
Tom	15	45	50	80	20	40
Jerry	18	36	72	24	20	30

    a   How much do they each have altogether?

    b   How many coins do they each have?

    c   Copy and complete the table below, which shows the proportion of each coin that they have.

	1p	2p	5p	10p	20p	50p
Tom	6%	18%				
Jerry						

    d   Add up the proportions for Tom and for Jerry. Explain your answer.

4 Three bars of soap cost £1.80. How much would **a** 12 bars cost? **b** 30 bars cost?

5 One litre of fruit squash contains 24 cl of fruit concentrate and the rest is water.

    a   What proportion of the drink is fruit concentrate?

    b   What proportion of the drink is water?

6 One euro is worth £0.62. How many pounds will I get for each of the following numbers of euros?

    a   5 euros   **b**   8 euros   **c**   600 euros

7 These are the ingredients to make four pancakes.

    a   How much of each ingredient will be needed to make 12 pancakes?

    b   How much of each ingredient will be needed to make six pancakes?

> 1 egg
> 3 ounces of plain flour
> 5 fluid ounces of milk

8 The ratio of British cars to foreign cars in the staff car park is 1 : 4. Explain why the proportion of British cars is 20% and not 25%.

9 Steve wears only red or black socks. The ratio of red to black pairs that he owns is 1 : 3. If he doesn't favour any particular colour, what proportion of days will he wear red socks?

Extension Work

Direct proportion can be used to solve problems such as: In 6 hours, a woman earns £42. How much would she earn in 5 hours?

First, you have to work out how much she earns in 1 hour: 42 ÷ 6 = £7. Then multiply this by 5 to get how much she earns in 5 hours: 5 × £7 = £35.

Answer the following questions but be careful! Two of them are trick questions.

1 3 kg of sugar cost £1.80. How much do 4 kg of sugar cost?

2 A man can run 10 km in 40 minutes. How long does he take to run 12 km?

3 In two days my watch loses 20 seconds. How much time does it lose in a week?

4 It takes me 5 seconds to dial the 10 digit number of a friend who lives 100 km away. How long does it take me to dial the 10 digit number of a friend who lives 200 miles away?

5 A jet aircraft with 240 people on board takes 2 h 30 min to fly 1000 km. How long would the same aircraft take to fly 1500 km when it had only 120 people on board?

Calculating ratios and proportions

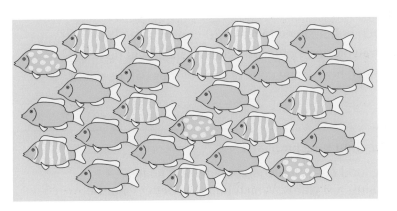

The fish have been breeding!

What is the ratio of striped fish to spotted fish?

What is the ratio of plain fish to spotted fish?

What is the ratio of plain fish to striped fish?

If five more plain fish are added to the tank, how many more striped fish would have to be added to keep the ratio of plain to striped the same?

Example 12.8 Reduce the following ratios to their simplest form : **a** 4 : 6 **b** 5 : 25

a The highest common factor of 4 and 6 is 2. So, divide 2 into both values, giving 4 : 6 = 2 : 3.

b The highest common factor of 5 and 25 is 5. So, divide 5 into both values, giving 5 : 25 = 1 : 5.

Example 12.9 A fruit drink is made by mixing 20 cl of orange juice with 60 cl of pineapple juice. What is the ratio of orange juice to pineapple juice?

Orange : pineapple = 20 : 60 = 1 : 3 (cancel by 20).

Example 12.10 ▶ Another fruit drink is made by mixing orange juice and grapefruit juice in the ratio 2 : 5. 60 cl of orange juice are used. How much grapefruit juice is needed?

The problem is 60 : ? = 2 : 5. You will see that, instead of cancelling, your need to multiply by 30. So, 2 : 5 = 60 : 150.

So, 150 cl of grapefruit juice will be needed.

Exercise **12C**

1 Reduce each of the following ratios to its simplest form.

a 4 : 8	**b** 3 : 9	**c** 2 : 10	**d** 9 : 12	**e** 5 : 20	**f** 8 : 10
g 4 : 6	**h** 10 : 15	**i** 2 : 14	**j** 4 : 14	**k** 6 : 10	**l** 25 : 30

2 Write down the ratio of shaded : unshaded from each of these metre rules.

a

b

c

3 There are 300 lights on a Christmas tree. 120 are white, 60 are blue, 45 are green and the rest are yellow.

a Write down the percentage of each colour.
b Write down each of the following ratios in its simplest form.
   i   white : blue   ii   blue : green
   iii green : yellow   iv   white : blue : green : yellow

4 To make jam, Josh uses strawberries to preserving sugar in the ratio 3 cups : 1 cup.

a How many cups of each will he need to make 20 cups of jam altogether?
b If he has 12 cups of strawberries, how many cups of sugar will he need?
c If he has $2\frac{1}{2}$ cups of sugar, how many cups of strawberries will he need?

Extension Work

Proportion can be used to solve 'best buy' problems.

For example: A large tin of dog food costs 96p and contains 500 grams.
A small tin costs 64p and contains 300 grams. Which tin is the better value?
For each tin, work out how much 1 gram costs.

Large tin: 500 ÷ 96 = 5.2 grams per penny.
Small tin: 300 ÷ 64 = 4.7 grams per penny. So, the large tin is the better buy.

1 A bottle of shampoo costs £2.62 and contains 30 cl. A different bottle of the same shampoo costs £1.50 and contains 20 cl. Which is the better buy?

2 A large roll of Sellotape has 25 metres of tape and costs 75p. A small roll of Sellotape has 15 metres of tape and costs 55p. Which roll is better value?

3 A pad of A4 paper costs £1.10 and has 120 sheets. A thicker pad of A4 paper costs £1.50 and has 150 sheets. Which pad is the better buy?

4 A small tin of peas contains 250 grams and costs 34p. A large tin costs 70p and contains 454 grams. Which tin is the better buy?

Solving problems

A painter has a 5-litre can of blue paint and 3 litres of yellow paint in a 5-litre can (Picture 1).

Picture 1

Picture 2

Picture 3

He pours 2 litres of blue paint into the other can (Picture 2) and mixes it thoroughly.

He then pours 1 litre from the second can back into the first can (Picture 3) and mixes it thoroughly.

How much blue paint is in the first can now?

Example 12.11 Divide £150 in the ratio 1:5.

There are 1 + 5 = 6 portions. This gives £150 ÷ 6 = £25 per portion. So one share of the £150 is 1 × 25 = £25, and the other share is 5 × £25 = £125.

Example 12.12 Two-fifths of a packet of bulbs are daffodils. The rest are tulips. What is the ratio of daffodils to tulips?

Ratio is $\frac{2}{5} : \frac{3}{5}$ = 2:3

Exercise 12D

1. Divide £100 in the ratio

   a   2:3   b   1:9   c   3:7   d   1:3   e   9:11

2. There are 350 pupils in a primary school. The ratio of girls to boys is 3:2. How many boys and girls are there in the school?

3. Freda has 120 CDs. The ratio of pop CDs to dance CDs is 5:7. How many of each type of CD are there?

4. James is saving 50p coins and £1 coins. He has 75 coins. The ratio of 50p coins to £1 coins is 7:8. How much money does he have altogether?

5. Mr Smith has 24 calculators in a box. The ratio of ordinary calculators to scientific calculators is 5:1. How many of each type of calculator does he have?

6. An exam consists of three parts. A mental test, a non-calculator paper and a calculator paper. The ratio of marks for each is 1:3:4. The whole exam is worth 120 marks. How many marks does each part of the exam get?

7. a   There are 15 bottles on the wall. The ratio of green bottles to brown bottles is 1:4. How many green bottles are there on the wall?

   b   One green bottle accidentally falls. What is the ratio of green to brown bottles now?

8 a Forty-nine trains pass through Barnsley station each day. They go to Huddersfield or Leeds in the ratio 3 : 4. How many trains go to Huddersfield?

b One day, due to driver shortages, six of the Huddersfield trains are cancelled and three of the Leeds trains are cancelled. What is the ratio of Huddersfield trains to Leeds trains that day?

Extension Work

Uncle Fred has decided to give his nephew and niece, Jack and Jill, £100 between them. He decides to split the £100 in the ratio of their ages. Jack is 4 and Jill is 6.

a How much do each get?

b The following year he does the same thing with another £100. How much do each get now?

c He continues to give them £100 shared in the ratio of their ages for another 8 years. How much will each get each year?

d After the 10 years, how much of the £1000 given in total will Jack have? How much will Jill have?

What you need to know for level 5

○ How to solve simple problems using ratio and direct proportion

○ The link between a proportion and the equivalent decimal, fraction and percentage

What you need to know for level 6

○ How to use percentage in problems involving increase and decrease

○ How to calculate with ratios

National Curriculum SATs questions

LEVEL 5

1 *1999 Paper 2*

a Nigel pours 1 carton of apple juice and 3 cartons of orange juice into a big jug. What is the ratio of apple juice to orange juice in Nigel's jug?

b Lesley pours 1 carton of apple juice and $1\frac{1}{2}$ cartons of orange juice into another big jug. What is the ratio of apple juice to orange juice in Lesley's jug?

c Tandi pours 1 carton of apple juice and 1 carton of orange juice into another big jug. She wants only half as much apple juice as orange juice in her jug. What should Tandi pour into her jug now?

2   *2000 Paper 1*

The table shows some percentages of amounts of money.

Use the table to work out

	£10	£30	£45
5%	50p	£1.50	£2.25
10%	£1	£3	£4.50

a   15% of £30 = ...

b   £6.75 = 15% of ......

c   £3.50 = ... % of £10

d   25p = 5% of ......

3   *2000 Paper 2*

Calculate   **a**   8% of £26.50   **b** $12\frac{1}{2}$% of £98

LEVEL 6

4   *1996 Paper 2*

Emlyn is doing a project on world population. He has found some data about the population of the world in 1950 and 1990.

Region	Population (millions) 1950	Population (millions) 1990
Africa	222	642
Asia	1558	3402
Europe	393	498
Latin America	166	448
North America	166	276
Oceania	13	26
World	2518	5292

a   In 1950, what percentage of the world's population lived in Asia?

b   In 1990, for every person who lived in North America how many people lived in Asia?

c   For every person who lived in Africa in 1950, how many people lived in Africa in 1990?

d   Emlyn thinks that from 1950 to 1990 the population of Oceania went up by 100%. Is Emlyn right?

5   *1998 Paper 2*

The table shows the land area of each of the world's continents.

Continent	Land area in 1000 km²
Africa	30 264
Antarctica	13 209
Asia	44 250
Europe	9 907
North America	24 398
Oceania	8 534
South America	17 793
World	148 355

a   Which continent is approximately 12% of the world's land area?

b   What percentage of the world's land area is Antarctica?

c   About 30% of the world's area is land. The rest is water. The amount of land in the world is about 150 million km². Work out the approximate total area (land and water) of the world.

This chapter is going to show you

- how to solve different types of problem using algebra

What you should already know

- Understand the conventions of algebra
- How to use letters in place of numbers
- How to solve equations

Solving 'brick wall' problems

Example 13.1 ▷ The numbers in two 'bricks' which are side by side (adjacent) are added together. The answer is written in the 'brick' above. Find the number missing from the 'brick' in the bottom layer.

	21	
8		3

Let the missing number be x. This gives:

	21	
$x + 8$		$x + 3$
8	x	3

Adding the terms in adjacent 'bricks' gives:

$$(x + 8) + (x + 3) = 21$$
$$x + 8 + x + 3 = 21$$
$$2x + 11 = 21$$
$$2x + 11 - 11 = 21 - 11 \text{ (Take 11 from both sides)}$$
$$2x = 10$$
$$\frac{2x}{2} = \frac{10}{2} \text{ (Divide both sides by 2)}$$
$$x = 5$$

So, the missing number is 5.

Exercise 13A Find the unknown number x in each of these 'brick wall' problems.

1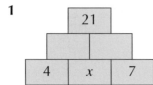

2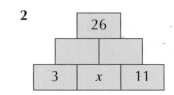

3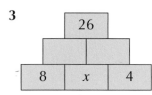

4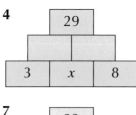
29
| 3 | x | 8 |

5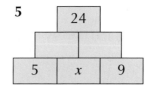
24
| 5 | x | 9 |

6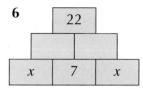
22
| x | 7 | x |

7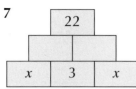
22
| x | 3 | x |

8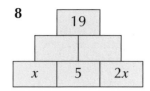
19
| x | 5 | $2x$ |

9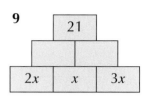
21
| $2x$ | x | $3x$ |

10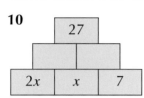
27
| $2x$ | x | 7 |

11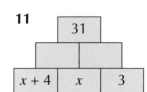
31
| $x + 4$ | x | 3 |

12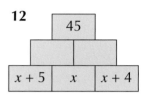
45
| $x + 5$ | x | $x + 4$ |

1 Find the value of x.

2 Make up some of your own 'brick wall' problems.

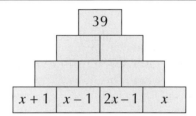
39
| $x + 1$ | $x - 1$ | $2x - 1$ | x |

Square-and-circle problems

The number in each square is the sum of the numbers in the two circles on either side of the square.

Example 13.2

The values of A, B, C and D are to be positive integers. Can you work out all possible values of A, B, C and D?

First, write down four equations from this diagram:

$A + B = 10$
$B + C = 12$
$C + D = 13$
$D + A = 11$

There may be more than one solution to this problem. So, continue by asking yourself: 'What if I let $A = 1$?'

$A = 1$ gives $B = 10 - 1 = 9$
$B = 9$ gives $C = 12 - 9 = 3$
$C = 3$ gives $D = 13 - 3 = 10$
$D = 10$ gives $A = 11 - 10 = 1$, which is the starting value, $A = 1$

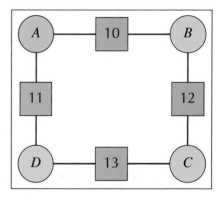

Example 13.2

continued

This gives one of a series of possible solutions to this problem. So, set up a table to calculate and display these solutions, which are called the **solution set**.

A	B	C	D	A (check)
1	9	3	10	1
2	8	4	9	2
3	7	5	8	3
4	6	6	7	4
5	5	7	6	5
6	4	8	5	6
7	3	9	4	7
8	2	10	3	8
9	1	11	2	9

Note The last column is used as a check.

Such a table allows you to look at all possible solutions.

Example 13.3

Again, the values of *A*, *B*, *C* and *D* are to be positive integers.

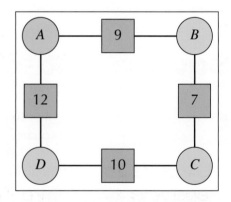

Starting with *A* = 1, gives *B* = 8, which makes *C* negative. Since you are looking only for positive solutions, you cannot have *A* = 1. So try *A* = 2. This will give *C* = 0, so you cannot use *A* = 2.

This will lead to the following solution set.

A	B	C	D	A (check)
3	6	1	9	3
4	5	2	8	4
5	4	3	7	5
6	3	4	6	6
7	2	5	5	7
8	1	6	4	8

1 Find the solution set to each of the following square-and-circle puzzles. All solutions must use positive numbers.

a

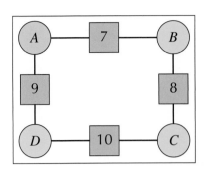

b

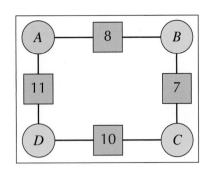

c

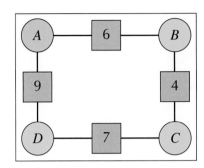

2 Find the solution set to each of the following square-and-circle puzzles. All solutions must use positive numbers.

a

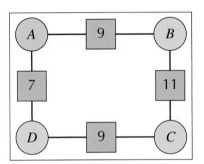

b

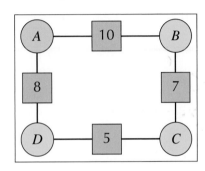

c

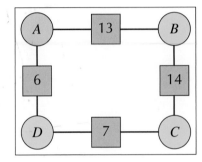

Extension Work

Make up your own square-and-circle problem that has only one solution.

Other types of problem

Follow through Example 13.4.

Example 13.4

The total cost of five pens and eight pencils is £2.38. The pens cost 19p more than the pencils. Find the price of each.

Let the price of a pencil be x pence. So, the price of a pen will be $(x + 19)$ pence.

The total cost of the pencils and pens is £2.38, which gives:

$$8x + 5(x + 19) = 238$$

(Remember: the units in an equation must all be the same, which is why we change £2.38 to pence.)

Expanding and simplifying the equation gives:

$$8x + 5x + 95 = 238$$
$$13x + 95 - 95 = 238 - 95$$
$$13x = 143$$
$$x = 143 \div 13 = 11$$

So, the price of a pencil is 11p, which means the price of a pen is 30p.

Now check the answer:

$$5 \times 30p + 8 \times 11p = 150p + 88p = 238p = £2.38$$

1) Brian bought 2 saucers and 4 cups. Each cup cost 40p more than each saucer. He paid £8.50 altogether. Find the cost of a cup.

2) The total cost of 3 fish and 4 chips is £7.55. Each fish costs 65p more than a portion of chips. How much does each fish cost?

3) Sophia goes to the cinema with 4 other children and 3 adults. An adult ticket is 45p more than a child ticket. The total cost of all 8 tickets is £24.95. What is the price of a child's ticket?

4) Mr Brennan bought 20 new basic and 30 new scientific calculators for the department, paying £170 for the lot. A scientific calculator cost £2.50 more than a basic one. What was the price of a scientific calculator?

5) Joy bought 3 rabbits and 5 guinea pigs. Each rabbit cost £4 more than each guinea pig. She paid a total of £72. What was the cost of a rabbit?

6) Nick sent his Christmas presents by post at a total cost of £56.90. He sent 5 small parcels (all the same size) and 7 large parcels (all the same size) and a large parcel cost £3.50 more to send than a small parcel. What was the cost of sending a large parcel?

7) The total cost of 6 packets of crisps and 5 drinks was £4.56. Each drink cost 12p more than a packet of crisps. How much did a drink cost?

8) The sum of two consecutive numbers is 123. What is the larger number?

9) The sum of two consecutive numbers is 235. What is the larger number?

Extension Work

There were 50 more pupils who took the mathematics exam than took the geology exam. A fifth of those who took the mathematics exam were girls and a quarter of those who took the geology exam were girls. If the number of girls who took the mathematics exam was six more than the number of girls who took the geology exam, find the number of pupils who took the mathematics exam.

What you need to know for level 5

- How to construct simple formulae from problems
- How to express simple problems algebraically
- How to use algebra to help to solve problems

What you need to know for level 6

- How to use algebra to solve more complicated problems

National Curriculum SATs questions

LEVEL 5

1 *1996 Paper 1*

Four people play a game with counters.

Each person starts with one or more bags of counters.

Each bag has m counters in it.

The table shows what happened during the game.

Write an expression to show what Cal and Fiona had at the end of the game.

Write each expression as simply as possible.

Lisa   Ben   Cal   Fiona

	Start	During game	End of game
Lisa	3 bags	lost 5 counters	$3m - 5$
Ben	2 bags	won 3 counters	$2m + 3$
Cal	1 bags	lost 2 counters	
Fiona	4 bags	won 6 counters, and lost 2 counters	

LEVEL 6

2 *1997 Paper 2*

In these walls each brick is made by adding the two bricks underneath it.

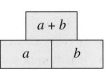

a Write an expression for the top brick in this wall. Write your expression as simply as possible.

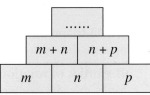

b Write down the missing expressions for these walls. Write your expressions as simply as possible.

   i

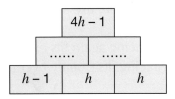

   ii

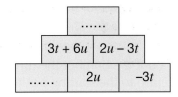

<table>
<tr><td>

This chapter is going to show you

- how to use line and rotation symmetry
- how to reflect shapes in a mirror line
- how to rotate shapes about a point
- how to translate shapes
- how to enlarge shapes by a scale factor

</td><td>

What you should already know

- Be able to recognise shapes that have reflective symmetry
- Be able to recognise shapes that have been translated

</td></tr>
</table>

Line symmetry and rotational symmetry

A 2-D shape has a **line of symmetry** when one half of the shape fits exactly over the other half when the shape is folded along that line.

A mirror or tracing paper can be used to check whether a shape has a line of symmetry. Some shapes have no lines of symmetry while others have more than one.

A line of symmetry is also called a **mirror line** or an **axis of reflection**.

Example 14.1

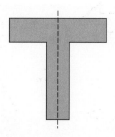 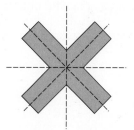 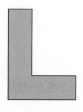

a This T-shape has one line of symmetry, as shown.

b This cross has four lines of symmetry, as shown.

c This L-shape has no lines of symmetry.

A 2-D shape has **rotational symmetry** when it can be rotated about a point to look exactly the same in a new position.

The **order of rotational symmetry** is the number of different positions in which the shape looks the same when it is rotated about the point through one complete turn (360°).

A shape has no rotational symmetry when it has to be rotated through one complete turn to look exactly the same. So it is said to have rotational symmetry of order 1.

To find the order of rotational symmetry of a shape, use tracing paper.
- First, trace the shape.
- Then rotate the tracing paper until the tracing again fits exactly over the shape.
- Count the number the times that the tracing fits exactly over the shape until you return to the starting position.
- The number of times that the tracing fits is the order of rotational symmetry.

Example 14.2

a This shape has rotational symmetry of order 3.

b This shape has rotational symmetry of order 4.

c This shape has no rotational symmetry. Therefore, it has rotational symmetry of order 1.

Exercise 14A

1 Copy each of these shapes and draw its lines of symmetry. Write below each shape the number of lines of symmetry it has.

a Isosceles triangle   **b** Equilateral triangle   **c** Square   **d** Rectangle   **e** Parallelogram   **f** Kite

2 Write down the number of lines of symmetry for each of the following shapes.

a

b
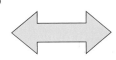
c

d

e

f

g

h

3 Copy each of these capital letters and write below its order of rotational symmetry.

a H   **b** M   **c** N   **d** S   **e** W   **f** X

4 Write down the order of rotational symmetry for each of the shapes below.

a

b

c

d

e

f

5 Copy and complete the table for each of the following regular polygons.

a  b c 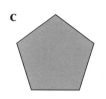 d 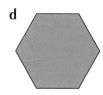 e

Shape		Number of lines of symmetry	Order of rotational symmetry
a	Equilateral triangle		
b	Square		
c	Regular pentagon		
d	Regular hexagon		
e	Regular octagon		

What do you notice?

1 **Symmetry squares**

Two squares can be put together along their sides to make a shape that has line symmetry.

One symmetrical arrangement for two squares

Three squares can be put together along their sides to make 2 different shapes that have line symmetry.

Investigate how many different symmetrical arrangements there are for four squares. What about five squares?

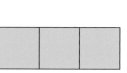

Two symmetrical arrangements for three squares

2 a Make eight copies of this shape on square dotty paper.

b Cut them out and arrange them to make a pattern with rotational symmetry of order 8.

c Design your own pattern which has rotational symmetry of order 8.

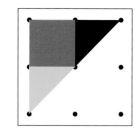

Reflections

The picture shows an L-shape reflected in a mirror.

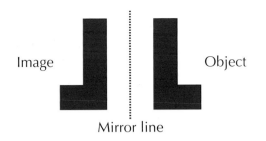

Image   Object

Mirror line

You can also draw the picture without the mirror, as here.

The **object** is reflected in the mirror line to give the **image**. The mirror line becomes a line of symmetry. So, if the paper is folded along the mirror line, the object will fit exactly over the image. The image is the same distance from the mirror line as the object.

A reflection is an example of a **transformation**. A transformation is a way of changing the position or the size of a shape.

Example 14.3

Reflect this shape in the given mirror line.

Notice that the image is the same size as the object, and that the mirror line becomes a line of symmetry.

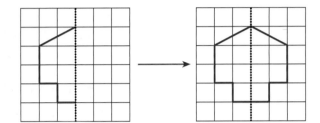

Example 14.4

Triangle A′B′C′ is the reflection of triangle ABC in the given mirror line.

When we change the position of a shape, we sometimes use the term **map**. Here we could write:

△ABC is mapped onto △A′B′C′ by a reflection in the mirror line.

Notice that the line joining A to A′ is perpendicular to the mirror line. This is true for all corresponding points on the object and the image. Also, all corresponding points on the object and image are at the same perpendicular distance from the mirror line.

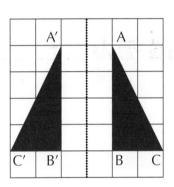

Example 14.5

Reflect this rectangle in the mirror line shown.

Use tracing paper to check the reflection.

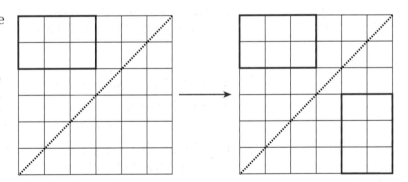

Exercise 14B

1 Copy each of these diagrams onto squared paper and draw its reflection in the given mirror line.

a   b   c   d

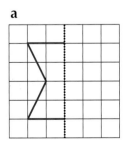
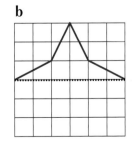
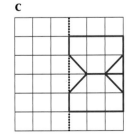
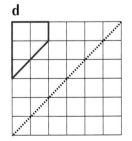

2 Copy each of these shapes onto squared paper and draw its reflection in the given mirror line.

a   b   c   d

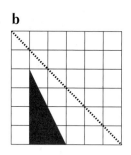

3 The points A(1, 2), B(2, 5), C(4, 4) and D(6, 1) are shown on the grid.

  a Copy the grid onto squared paper and plot the points A, B, C and D. Draw the mirror line.

  b Reflect the points in the mirror line and label them A′, B′, C′ and D′.

  c Write down the coordinates of the image points.

  d The point E(12, 6) is mapped onto E′ by a reflection in the mirror line. What are the coordinates of E′?

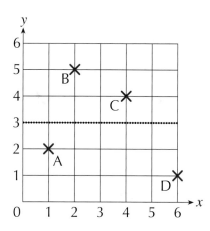

Extension Work

1   a Copy the diagram onto squared paper and reflect the triangle in the series of parallel mirrors.

    b Make up your own patterns using a series of parallel mirrors.

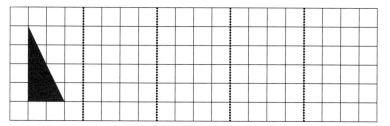

2   a Copy the grid onto squared paper and draw the triangle ABC. Write down the coordinates of A, B and C.

    b Reflect the triangle in the *x*-axis. Label the vertices of the image A′, B′ and C′. What are the coordinates of A′, B′ and C′?

    c Reflect triangle A′B′C′ in the *y*-axis. Label the vertices of this image A″, B″ and C″. What are the coordinates of A″, B″ and C″?

    d Reflect triangle A″B″C″ in the *x*-axis. Label the vertices A‴, B‴ and C‴. What are the coordinates of A‴B‴C‴?

    e Describe the reflection that maps triangle A‴B‴C‴ onto triangle ABC.

3 Use ICT software, such as LOGO, to reflect shapes in mirror lines.

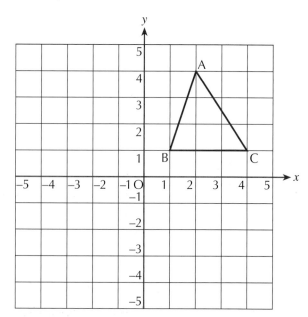

Rotations

Another type of transformation in geometry is **rotation**.

To describe the rotation of a 2-D shape, three facts must be known:
- **Centre of rotation** – the point about which the shape rotates.
- **Angle of rotation** – this is usually 90° ($\frac{1}{4}$ turn), 180° ($\frac{1}{2}$ turn) or 270° ($\frac{3}{4}$ turn).
- **Direction of rotation** – clockwise or anticlockwise.

When you rotate a shape, it is a good idea to use tracing paper.

As with reflections, the original shape is called the object, and the rotated shape is called the image.

Example 14.6

The flag is rotated through 90° clockwise about the point X.

Notice that this is the same as rotating the flag through 270° anticlockwise about the point X.

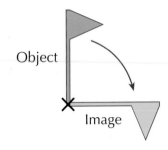

Example 14.7

This right-angled triangle is rotated through 180° clockwise about the point X.

Notice that this triangle can be rotated either clockwise or anticlockwise when turning through 180°.

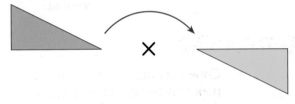

Example 14.8

△ABC has been mapped onto △A′B′C′ by a rotation of 90° anticlockwise about the point X.

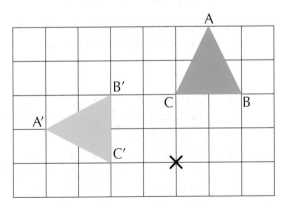

Exercise 14C

1. Copy each of the flags below and draw the image after each one has been rotated about the point marked X through the angle indicated. Use tracing paper to help.

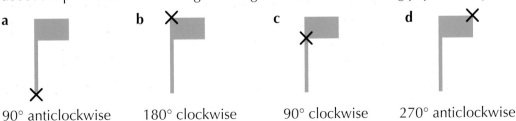

a   90° anticlockwise   b   180° clockwise   c   90° clockwise   d   270° anticlockwise

2 Copy each of the shapes below onto a square grid. Draw the image after each one has been rotated about the point marked X through the angle indicated. Use tracing paper to help.

a

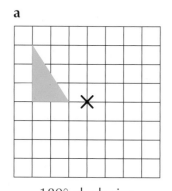

180° clockwise

b

90° anticlockwise

c

180° anticlockwise

d

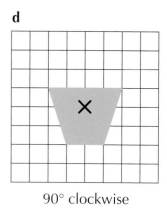

90° clockwise

3 **a** Rotate the rectangle ABCD through 90° clockwise about the point (1,2) to give the image A'B'C'D'.

b Write down the coordinates of A', B', C' and D'.

c Which coordinate point remains fixed throughout the rotation?

d What rotation will map the rectangle A'B'C'D' onto the rectangle ABCD?

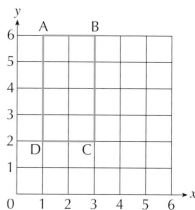

Extension Work

1 **Inverse rotations**

The **inverse** of a rotation is that rotation required to map the image back onto the object, using the same centre of rotation. Investigate inverse rotations by drawing your own shapes and using different rotations.

Write down any properties you discover about inverse rotations.

2 Use ICT software, such as LOGO, to rotate shapes about different centres of rotation.

Translations

A translation is the movement of a 2-D shape from one position to another without reflecting it or rotating it.

The distance and direction of the translation are given by the number of unit squares moved to the right or left, followed by the number of unit squares moved up or down.

As with reflections and rotations, the original shape is called the object, and the translated shape is called the image.

Example 14.9 Triangle A has been mapped onto triangle B by a translation 3 units right, followed by 2 units up.

Points on triangle A are mapped by the same translation onto triangle B, as shown by the arrows.

When an object is translated onto its image, every point on the object moves the same distance.

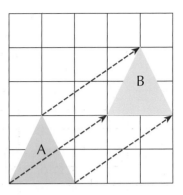

Example 14.10 The rectangle ABCD has been mapped onto rectangle A'B'C'D' by a translation 3 units left, followed by 3 units down.

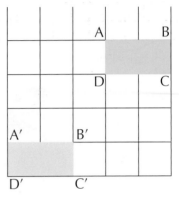

Exercise 14D

1 Describe each of the following translations:

   a   from A to B

   b   from A to C

   c   from A to D

   d   from A to E

   e   from B to D

   f   from C to E

   g   from D to E

   h   from E to A

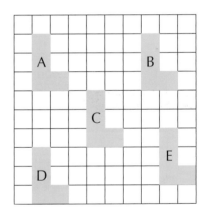

2 Copy the triangle ABC onto squared paper. Label it P.

   a   Write down the coordinates of the vertices of triangle P.

   b   Translate triangle P 6 units left and 2 units down. Label the new triangle Q.

   c   Write down the coordinates of the vertices of triangle Q.

   d   Translate triangle Q 5 units right and 4 units down. Label the new triangle R.

   e   Write down the coordinates of the vertices of triangle R.

   f   Describe the translation which maps triangle R onto triangle P.

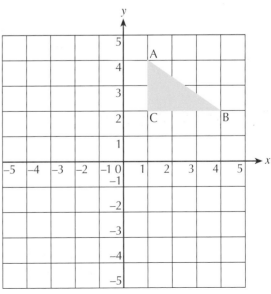

1 Use squared dotty paper or a pin-board for this investigation.

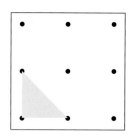

   a How many different translations of the triangle are possible on this 3 by 3 grid?

   b How many different translations of this triangle are possible on a 4 by 4 grid?

   c Investigate the number of translations that are possible on any size grid.

2 **Combining transformations**

Copy the following triangles A, B, C, D, E, and F onto a square grid.

   a Find a single transformation that will map:

      i A onto B   **ii** E onto F

      iii B onto E   **iv** C onto B

   b Find a combination of two transformations that will map:

      i A onto C   **ii** B onto F

      iii F onto D   **iv** B onto E

   c Find other examples of combined transformations for different pairs of triangles.

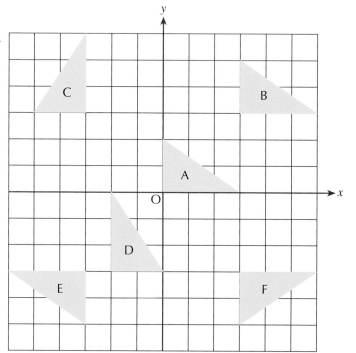

3 Use ICT software, such as LOGO, to transform shapes by using various combinations of reflections.

Enlargements

The three transformations you have met so far: reflections, rotations and translations, have not changed the size of the object. You are now going to look at a transformation that does change the size of an object: **an enlargement**.

The diagram below shows triangle ABC enlarged to give triangle A'B'C'.

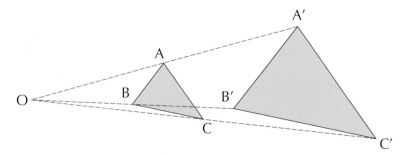

All the sides of triangle A'B'C' are twice as long as the sides of triangle ABC. Notice also that OA' = 2 × OA, OB' = 2 × OB and OC' = 2 × OC.

We say that triangle ABC has been enlarged by a scale factor of 2 about the centre of enlargement O to give the image triangle A'B'C'. The dotted lines are called the guidelines, or rays, for the enlargement. To enlarge a shape we need: a centre of enlargement and a scale factor.

Example 14.11

Enlarge the triangle XYZ by a scale factor of 2 about the centre of enlargement O.

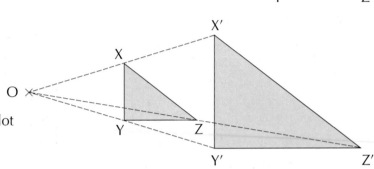

Draw rays OX, OY and OZ.

Measure the length of the three rays and multiply each of these lengths by 2. Extend each of the rays to these new lengths measured from O and plot the points X', Y' and Z'.

Join X', Y' and Z'.

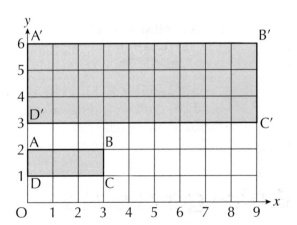

Triangle X'Y'Z' is the enlargement of triangle XYZ by a scale factor of 2 about the centre of enlargement O.

Example 14.12

The rectangle ABCD on the coordinate grid on the right has been enlarged by a scale factor of 3 about the origin O to give the image rectangle A'B'C'D'.

The coordinates of the object are: A(0, 2), B(3, 2), C(3, 1) and D(0, 1).

The coordinates of the image are: A'(0, 6), B'(9, 6), C'(9, 3) and D'(0, 3).

Notice that if a shape is enlarged by a scale factor about the origin on a coordinate grid, the coordinates of the enlarged shape are multiplied by the scale factor.

Exercise 14E

1 Draw copies of the following shapes below and enlarge each one by the given scale factor about the centre of enlargement O.

a Scale factor 2

O ×

b Scale factor 3

O ×

c Scale factor 2

d Scale factor 3

(NB × is the centre of square)

O ×

2 Copy the diagrams below onto centimetre squared paper and enlarge each one by the given scale factor about the origin O.

a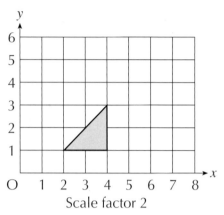

Scale factor 2

b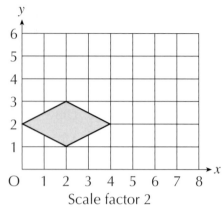

Scale factor 2

c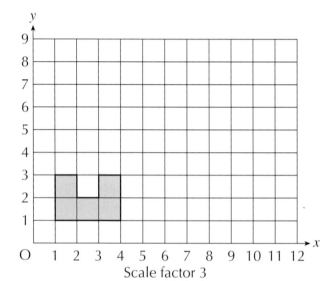

Scale factor 3

3 Draw axes for *x* and *y* from 0 to 10 on centimetre squared paper. Plot the points A(4, 6), B(5, 4), C(4, 1) and D(3, 4) and join them together to form the kite ABCD. Enlarge the kite by a scale factor of 2 about the point (1, 2).

Extension Work

1 a Draw axes for *x* and *y* from 0 to 12 on centimetre squared paper. Plot the points A(1, 3), B(3, 3), C(3, 1) and D(1, 1) and join them together to form the square ABCD.

b Write down the area of the square.

c Enlarge the square ABCD by a scale factor of 2 about the origin. What is the area of the enlarged square?

d Enlarge the square ABCD by a scale factor of 3 about the origin. What is the area of the enlarged square?

e Enlarge the square ABCD by a scale factor of 4 about the origin. What is the area of the enlarged square?

f Write down anything you notice about the increase in area of the enlarged squares. Can you write down a rule to explain what is happening?

g Repeat the above using your own shapes. Does your rule still work?

2 Use ICT software, such as LOGO, to enlarge shapes by different scale factors and using different centres of enlargement.

What you need to know for level 5

- Be able to recognise and visualise transformations of 2-D shapes:
  - reflections
  - rotations
  - translations

What you need to know for level 6

- Be able to identify all the symmetries of 2-D shapes
- How to transform 2-D shapes by a combination of reflections, rotations or translations
- How to enlarge 2-D shapes by a scale factor

National Curriculum SATs questions

LEVEL 5

1   *1999 Paper 2*

   a   Copy the diagram onto squared paper. You can rotate triangle A onto triangle B.

        Put a cross on the centre of rotation. You may use tracing paper to help you.

   b   You can rotate triangle A onto triangle B. The rotation is anticlockwise. What is the angle of rotation?

   c   Copy the diagram onto squared paper. Reflect triangle A in the mirror line. You may use a mirror or tracing paper to help you.

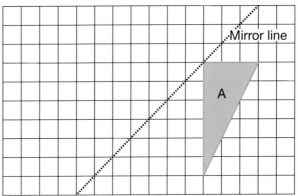

2   *1999 Paper 1*

Write the letter of each shape in the correct space in a copy of the table below. You may use a mirror or tracing paper to help you. The letters for the first two shapes have been written for you.

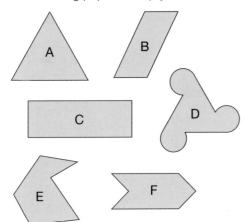

<table>
<tr><td rowspan="2" colspan="2"></td><td colspan="4">Number of lines of symmetry</td></tr>
<tr><td>0</td><td>1</td><td>2</td><td>3</td></tr>
<tr><td rowspan="4">Order of rotational symmetry</td><td>1</td><td></td><td></td><td></td><td></td></tr>
<tr><td>2</td><td>B</td><td></td><td></td><td></td></tr>
<tr><td>3</td><td></td><td></td><td></td><td>A</td></tr>
<tr><td></td><td></td><td></td><td></td><td></td></tr>
</table>

3   *1996 Paper 1*

Julie has written a computer program to transform pictures of tiles.

There are only two instructions in her program,

> Reflect vertical
> or
> Rotate 90° clockwise

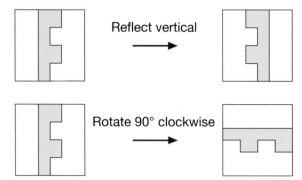

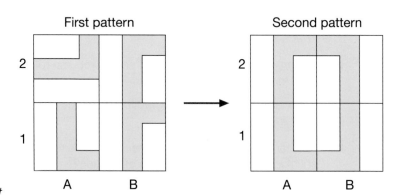

a   Julie wants to transform the first pattern to the second pattern.

Copy and complete the instructions to transform the tiles B1 and B2. You must use only Reflect vertical or Rotate 90° clockwise.

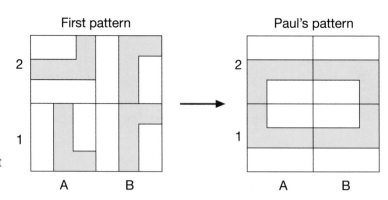

A1   *Tile is in the correct position*

A2   *Reflect vertical, and then Rotate 90° clockwise.*

B1   *Rotate 90° clockwise, and then ......*

B2   *......*

b   Paul starts with the first pattern that was on the screen.

Copy and complete the instructions for the transformations of A2, B1 and B2 to make Paul's pattern.

You must use only Reflect vertical or Rotate 90° clockwise.

A1   *Reflect vertical, and then Rotate 90° clockwise.*

A2   *Rotate 90° clockwise, and then ......*

B1   *......*

B2   *......*

CHAPTER 15

Handling Data **3**

<table>
<thead>
<tr><th>This chapter is going to show you</th><th>What you should already know</th></tr>
</thead>
<tbody>
<tr>
<td>

- how to draw pie charts from frequency tables
- when to use mean, median, mode and range
- how to compare distributions using range and mean

</td>
<td>

- How to draw pie charts
- How to calculate the mean of a set of data
- How to find the range of a set of data

</td>
</tr>
</tbody>
</table>

Pie charts

Sometimes you will have to interpret pie charts that are already drawn and sometimes you will be asked to draw a pie chart.

Example 15.1 ▷ Draw a pie chart to represent the following set of data showing how a group of people travel to work.

Type of travel	Walk	Car	Bus	Train	Cycle
Frequency	24	84	52	48	32

It is easier to set out your workings in a table.

Type of travel	Frequency	Calculation	Angle
Walk	24	$\frac{24}{240} \times 360 = 36°$	36°
Car	84	$\frac{84}{240} \times 360 = 126°$	126°
Bus	52	$\frac{52}{240} \times 360 = 78°$	78°
Train	48	$\frac{48}{240} \times 360 = 72°$	72°
Cycle	32	$\frac{32}{240} \times 360 = 48°$	48°
TOTAL	240		360°

We work out the angle for each sector using

$$\frac{\text{Frequency}}{\text{Total frequency}} \times 360°$$

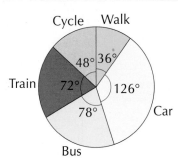

Example 15.2

The pie chart shows the types of housing on a new estate. Altogether there were 540 new houses built.

How many are

a   detached?   b   semi-detached?
c   bungalows?   d   terraced?

You need to work out the fraction of 540 that each sector represents.

a $\frac{90}{360} \times 540 = 135$ detached

b $\frac{120}{360} \times 540 = 180$ semi-detached

c $\frac{40}{360} \times 540 = 60$ bungalows

d $\frac{110}{360} \times 540 = 165$ terraced

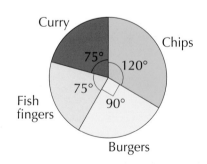

Exercise 15A

1   Draw pie charts to represent the following data.

a   The favourite subject of 36 pupils.

Subject	Maths	English	Science	Languages	Other
Frequency	12	7	8	4	5

b   The type of food that 40 people usually eat for breakfast.

Food	Cereal	Toast	Fruit	Cooked	Other	None
Frequency	11	8	6	9	2	4

c   The number of goals scored by an ice hockey team in 24 matches.

Goals	0	1	2	3	4	5 or more
Frequency	3	4	7	5	4	1

d   The favourite colour of 60 year 7 pupils.

Colour	Red	Green	Blue	Yellow	Other
Frequency	17	8	21	3	11

2   The pie chart shows the results of a survey of 216 children about their favourite foods.

How many chose

a   chips?   b   burgers?
c   fish fingers?   d   curry?

Extension Work

Design a poster showing information about the pupils in your class. Either include pie charts that you have drawn yourself or use a spreadsheet to produce the pie charts. Make sure that any pie chart you produce has labels and is easy to understand.

Comparing data

Look at the queue of people. Why is it impossible to find the most common height?

	Advantages	Disadvantages	Example
Mean	Uses every piece of data. Probably the most used average.	May not be representative if the data contains extreme values.	2, 2, 2, 2, 4, 12 Mean $= \dfrac{2 + 2 + 2 + 2 + 4 + 12}{6} = 6$ which is a higher value than most of the data.
Median	Only looks at the middle value, so it is a better average to use if the data contains extreme values.	Not all values are considered. The median might not be a central value and so could be misleading.	1, 1, 3, 5, 10, 15, 20 Median = 4th value = 5. Note that above the median the numbers are a long way from the median but below the median they are very close.
Mode	It is the most popular value.	If the mode is an extreme value it may be misleading to use it as an average.	Weekly wages of a boss and his 4 staff: £150, £150, £150, £150, £1000. Mode is £150 but mean is £320.
Modal class for continuous data	This is the largest class in a frequency table. For continuous data the actual values could all be different so the informtaion is clearer when grouped together.	The actual values may not be centrally placed in the class.	<table><tr><td>Time (T) minutes</td><td>Frequency</td></tr><tr><td>0<T≤5</td><td>2</td></tr><tr><td>5<T≤10</td><td>3</td></tr><tr><td>10<T≤15</td><td>6</td></tr><tr><td>15<T≤20</td><td>1</td></tr></table> The modal class is 10<T≤15, but all 6 values may be close to 15.
Range	It looks at how the data is spread out.	It only looks at the two extreme values.	1, 2, 5, 7, 9, 40. The range is 40 − 1 = 39 without the last value (40) the range would be only 8.

Example 15.3 ▷ You are organising a ten-pin bowling match. You have one team place to fill.

These are the last five scores for Carol and Doris.

Carol	122	131	114	162	146
Doris	210	91	135	99	151

Who would you pick to be in the team and why?

The mean for Carol is 135 and the range is 48.
The mean for Doris is 137.2 and the range is 119.

You could pick Doris as she has the greater mean, or you could pick Carol as she is more consistent.

Example 15.4 ▷ Your teacher thinks that the girls in the class are absent more often than the boys.

There are 10 boys in your class. Their days absent over last term were:

    5   0   3   4   6   3   0   8   6   5

There are 12 girls in the class. Their days absent over last term were:

    2   1   0   0   5   3   1   2   3   50   2   3

Is your teacher correct? Explain your answer.

The mean for the boys is 4 and the range is 8.
The mean for the girls is 6 and the range is 50.

It looks as though your teacher is correct. But if you take out the girl who was absent 50 times because she was in hospital, the mean for the girls becomes 2 and the range 5. In that case, your teacher would be wrong.

Exercise 15B

1 Each day at break I buy a bag of biscuits from the school canteen. I can buy them from canteen A or canteen B. I made a note of how many biscuits were in each bag I got from each canteen.

Canteen A	12	11	14	10	13	12	9	12	15	12
Canteen B	5	18	13	15	10	15	17	8	11	13

  a Work out the mean for Canteen A.   **b** Work out the range for Canteen A.
  c Work out the mean for Canteen B.   **d** Work out the range for Canteen B.
  e Which canteen should I buy my biscuits from and why?

2 You have to choose someone for a quiz team. The last ten quiz scores (out of 20) for Bryan and Ryan are:

Bryan	1	19	2	12	20	13	2	6	5	10
Ryan	8	7	9	12	13	8	7	11	7	8

  a Work out the mean for Bryan.   **b** Work out the range for Bryan.
  c Work out the mean for Ryan.   **d** Work out the range for Ryan.
  e Who would you choose for the quiz team and why?

3 Look at each set of data and give a reason why the chosen average is suitable or not.

a 2, 3, 5, 7, 8, 10   Mean
b 0, 1, 2, 2, 2, 4, 6   Mode
c 1, 4, 7, 8, 10, 11, 12   Median
d 2, 3, 6, 7, 10, 10, 10   Mode
e 2, 2, 2, 2, 4, 6, 8   Median
f 1, 2, 4, 6, 9, 30   Mean

4 Look at each set of data and decide whether the range is suitable or not for measuring how spread out it is. Explain your answer.

a 1, 2, 4, 7, 9, 10
b 1, 10, 10, 10, 10
c 1, 1, 1, 2, 10
d 1, 3, 5, 6, 7, 10
e 1, 1, 1, 7, 10, 10, 10
f 2, 5, 8, 10, 14

Extension Work

Get two different makes of scientific calculator.

Use each of them to generate 100 random digits. (Some calculators give a number such as 0.786 when the random button is pressed. In this case take the three digits after the decimal point as three separate, random numbers. For example: for 0.786, record 7, 8 and 6; for 0.78 (= 0.780), record 7, 8 and 0.)

Work out the mean and the range for each set of numbers. The range should be 9 (smallest digit should be zero and largest 9). The mean should be 4.5.

Which calculator is better at generating random numbers?

Statistical surveys

You are about to carry out your own statistical survey and write a report on your findings.

Once you have chosen a problem to investigate, you will first need to plan how you intend to carry out the survey and decide how you are going to collect your data.

When you have done this, you may want to write down any statements which you want to test and the responses you might expect to receive from your survey. These will be your hypotheses.

Your data may be obtained in one of the following ways.

- A survey of a sample of people. Your sample size should be more than 30. To collect data from your chosen sample, you will need to use a data collection sheet or a questionnaire.
- Carrying out experiments. You will need to keep a record of your observations on a data collection sheet.
- Searching secondary sources. Examples are reference books, newspapers, ICT databases and the Internet.

If you plan to use a data collection sheet, remember the following points:

- Decide what types of data you need to collect.
- Design the layout of your sheet before you start the survey.
- Keep a tally of your results in a table.

If you plan to use a questionnaire, remember the following points:

- Make the questions short and simple.
- Choose questions that require simple responses. For example: Yes, No, Don't know. Or use tick boxes with a set of multichoice answers.
- Avoid personal and embarrassing questions.
- Never ask a leading question designed to get a particular response.

When you have collected all your data, you are ready to write a report on your findings.

Your report should be short and based only on the evidence you have collected. Use statistics, such as the mean, the median, the mode and the range, to help give an overall picture of the facts. Also, use statistical diagrams to illustrate your results and to make them easier to understand. For example, you might draw bar charts, line graphs or pie charts. Try to give a reason why you have chosen to use a particular type of diagram.

To give your report a more professional look, use ICT software to illustrate the data.

Finally, you will need to write a short conclusion based on your evidence. This may require you to refer to your original hypotheses. You should include a reference to any averages you have calculated or to any diagrams you have drawn.

Exercise 15C

Write your own statistical report on one or more of the following problems.

Remember:

- Write down any hypotheses for the problem.
- Decide on your sample size.
- Decide whether you need to use a data collection sheet or a questionnaire.
- Find any relevant averages.
- Illustrate your report with suitable diagrams or graphs, and explain why you have used them.
- Write a short conclusion based on all the evidence.

The data can be collected from people in your class or year group, but it may be possible to collect the data from other sources, friends and family outside school.

1 The amount of TV young people watch.

2 The types of sport young people take part in outside school.

3 The musical likes and dislikes of Year 7 students.

4 Investigate the young woman's statement.

Taller people have a larger head circumference.

5 'More people are taking holidays abroad this year.' Investigate this statement.

Write your own statistical report on one or more of the following problems.
For these problems, you will need to use secondary sources to collect the data.

1   Do football teams in the First Division score more goals than teams in
    the Second Division?

2   Compare the frequency of letters in the English language to the frequency
    of letters in the French language.

3   Compare the prices of second-hand cars using different motoring
    magazines.

Comparing experimental and theoretical probabilities

This section will remind you how to calculate the probabilities of events where the
outcomes are equally likely. You will also see how to compare your calculations with
what happens in practice by carrying out experiments to find the experimental
probabilities of these events.

The **theoretical probability** of an event predicts what is likely to happen when you know
all the possible outcomes of the event. You can use theoretical probability only when all
the outcomes are equally likely.

For theoretical probability:

$$P(\text{event}) = \frac{\text{Number of ways the event can happen}}{\text{Total number of all possible outcomes}}$$

Finding the **experimental probability** of an event lets you check the theoretical
probability and see whether an experiment is fair or unfair. To calculate the experimental
probability, you carry out a sequence of repeated experiments or **trials**.

For experimental probability:

$$P(\text{event}) = \frac{\text{Number of events in the trials}}{\text{Total number of trials}}$$

Remember: the more trials you carry out, the closer the experimental probability gets to
the theoretical probability.

Example 15.5

Josie wants to compare the experimental probability for the event Heads happening
when she tosses a coin with the theoretical probability to see whether the coin she is
using is a fair one.

Josie decides to carry out 50 trials and completes the frequency table given below.

	Tally	Frequency
Heads	┼┼┼┼ ┼┼┼┼ ┼┼┼┼ ┼┼┼┼ ┼┼┼┼ I I	27
Tails	┼┼┼┼ ┼┼┼┼ ┼┼┼┼ ┼┼┼┼ I I I	23

Example 15.5

continued

The experimental probability for the event Heads is

$$P(\text{Heads}) = \frac{27}{50}$$

Josie knows that there are two equally likely outcomes, Heads or Tails, when she tosses a coin. So, the theoretical trial probability is given by:

$$P(\text{Heads}) = \frac{1}{2}$$

She can now compare the two probabilities. To do this, she needs to change each probability fraction into a decimal to make the comparison easier.

$$\frac{27}{50} = 0.54 \text{ and } \frac{1}{2} = 0.5$$

The two decimals are close. So she concludes that the coin is a fair one.

Exercise 15D

1 **a** Working in pairs, throw a four-sided dice 40 times and record your results on a copy of the following frequency table.

Score	Tally	Frequency
1		
2		
3		
4		

Use your results to find the experimental probability of getting
  i 4   **ii** an even number

b Write down the theoretical probability of getting
  i 4   **ii** an even number

c By writing your answers to parts **a** and **b** as decimals, state whether you think the dice is a fair one or not.

2 Put ten cards numbered 1 to 10 in a box. Working in pairs, pick a card from the box and note its number. Replace it, shake the box and pick another card. Repeat the experiment 20 times and record your results in a frequency table.

a Use your results to find the experimental probability of getting
  i 10   **ii** an odd number

b Write down the theoretical probability of getting
  i 10   **ii** an odd number

c Compare your answers to parts **a** and **b**, and state any conclusions you make about the experiment.

3 You will need a box or a bag containing two red counters, three green counters and five blue counters.

a Working in pairs, pick a counter from the box and note its colour. Replace it, shake the box and pick another counter. Repeat the experiment 50 times and record your results on a copy of the following frequency table.

Colour	Tally	Frequency
Red		
Green		
Blue		

Use your results to find the experimental probability of getting

   i   a red counter   **ii**   a green counter   **iii**   a blue counter

b   Write down the theoretical probability of getting

   i   a red counter   **ii**   a green counter   **iii**   a blue counter

c   By writing your answers to parts **a** and **b** as decimals, state whether you think the experiment is fair or not.

4 Two fair dice are thrown.

   a   Copy and complete the sample space diagram for the total scores.

   b   What is the theoretical probability of a double?

   c   Design and carry out an experiment to test whether you think the two dice are fair.

   d   If you repeated the experiment using more trials, what would you expect to happen to the estimate of probability?

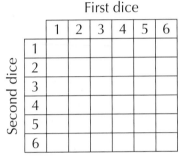

Second dice / First dice

	1	2	3	4	5	6
1						
2						
3						
4						
5						
6						

Extension Work

For this activity, you will need to work in pairs or groups.

On a large sheet of paper or card, draw a square measuring 40 cm by 40 cm. Divide into 100 squares, each measuring 4 cm by 4 cm.

- Each person rolls a 2p coin onto the sheet 50 times.
- If the coin lands completely inside a small square, score 1 point.
- If the coin touches or covers any line when it lands, score 0 point.
- The winner is the person who gets the most points.
- Work out the experimental probability of coin landing completely inside a small square.
- You often see games like this one at fun fairs and village fêtes. Do you think these games are fair?

What you need to know for level 5

- How to compare two distributions using the mean and the range, and to draw conclusions
- How to construct and interpret pie charts
- How to calculate probabilities based on experimental evidence

What you need to know for level 6

- To construct pie charts
- To construct and interpret frequency diagrams
- When dealing with a combination of two experiments, identify all the outcomes, using diagrams or tables

National Curriculum SATs questions

LEVEL 5

1 *1993 Paper 2*

Rita and Yoko counted the numbers of chips they got from two school dinner servers. This is what they found out:

	Number of chips									
Server 1	32	33	34	35	33	31	34	33	35	30
Server 2	39	26	25	26	39	27	40	39	39	40

They worked out the mean for each server.

They decided server 2 was better because the mean was bigger.

	Mean
Server 1	33
Server 2	34

Then they worked out the range for each server.

Say why the low range for server 1 was good.

	Range
Server 1	5
Server 2	15

2 *1998 Paper 2*

These pie charts show some information about the ages of people in Greece and in Ireland.

There are about 10 million people in Greece, and there are about 3.5 million people in Ireland.

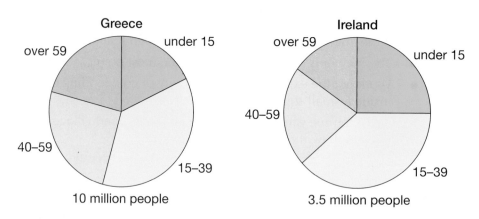

a Roughly what percentage of people in Greece are aged 40–59?

b There are about 10 million people in Greece. Use your percentage from part **a** to work out roughly how many people in Greece are aged 40–59.

c Dewi says:

The charts show that there are more people under 15 in Ireland than in Greece.

Dewi is wrong. Explain why the charts do not show this.

174

d There are about 60 million people in the UK. The table shows roughly what percentage of people in the UK are of different ages.

Under 15	15–39	40–59	Over 59
20%	35%	25%	20%

Draw on a copy of the pie chart the information in the table. Label each section of your pie chart clearly with the ages.

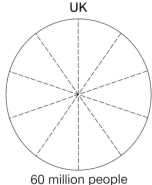

UK

60 million people

3 *2000 Paper 2*

A school has a new canteen. A special person will be chosen to perform the opening ceremony.

The names of all the pupils, all the teachers and all the canteen staff are put into a box. One name is taken out at random.

A pupil says:

'There are only three choices. It could be a pupil, a teacher or one of the canteen staff. The probabiliy of it being a pupil is $\frac{1}{3}$.'

The pupil is wrong. Explain why.

LEVEL 6

4 *2001 Paper 2*

A teacher asked two different classes:

'What type of book is your favourite?'

a Results from class A (total 20 pupils):

Type of book	Frequency
Crime	3
Non-fiction	13
Fantasy	4

Copy and complete the pie chart to show this information. Show your working and draw your angles accurately.

Class A

Crime

b The pie chart below shows the results from all of class B.

Each pupil had only one vote.

The sector for Non-fiction represents 11 pupils.

How many pupils are in class B?

Show your working.

Class B

Crime

Romance

Fantasy

165°

Non-fiction

This chapter is going to show you	What you should already know
o how to multiply and divide decimals o how to use the memory keys on a calculator o how to use the square root and sign change keys on a calculator o how to calculate fractions and percentages of quantities	o How to do long and short multiplication and division o Equivalence of fractions, decimals and percentages o How to use a calculator efficiently, including the use of brackets

Multiplying decimals

This section will show you how to easily work out the correct number of decimal places in your answer when multiplying with decimals.

Example 16.1 ▷ Work out **a** 0.8×0.7 **b** 0.02×0.7

a $8 \times 7 = 56$, so $0.\underline{8} \times 0.\underline{7} = 0.\underline{56}$ because the number of decimal places in the answer is always the same as in the original calculation.

b $2 \times 7 = 14$, and there are three decimal places in the original calculation, so $0.02 \times 0.7 = 0.014$.

Notice that a zero has been put in to make-up the correct number of decimal places.

Example 16.2 ▷ Work out **a** 2000×0.07 **b** $0.06 \times 50\,000$

a $2000 \times 0.07 = 200 \times 0.7 = 20 \times 7 = 140$

If we divide one number by 10 and multiply the other by 10, then their product will remain the same.

b $0.06 \times 50\,000 = 0.6 \times 5000 = 6 \times 500$

These are all equivalent calculations, so the answer is $6 \times 500 = 3000$.

Exercise 16A

1 Without using a calculator, write down the answer to each of these.

a	0.2×0.3	**b**	0.4×0.2	**c**	0.6×0.6	**d**	0.7×0.2
e	0.02×0.4	**f**	0.8×0.04	**g**	0.06×0.1	**h**	0.3×0.03
i	0.7×0.8	**j**	0.07×0.08	**k**	0.9×0.3	**l**	0.006×0.9
m	0.5×0.09	**n**	0.5×0.5	**o**	0.8×0.005	**p**	0.06×0.03

2 Without using a calculator, work out each of these.

a 300×0.8	**b** 0.06×200	**c** 0.6×500	**d** 0.02×600
e 0.03×400	**f** 0.004×500	**g** 0.007×200	**h** 0.002×9000
i 0.005×8000	**j** 200×0.006	**k** 300×0.01	**l** 800×0.06
m 500×0.5	**n** 400×0.05	**o** 300×0.005	**p** 200×0.0005

3 Without using a calculator, work out each of these.

a $0.006 \times 400 \times 200$	**b** $0.04 \times 0.06 \times 50\,000$	**c** $0.2 \times 0.04 \times 300$
d $300 \times 200 \times 0.08$	**e** $20 \times 0.008 \times 40$	**f** $0.1 \times 0.07 \times 2000$

4 Bolts cost 0.06. An engineering company orders 20 000 bolts. How much will this cost?

5 A grain of sand weighs 0.006 grams. How much would 500 000 grains weigh?

6 A kilogram of uranium ore contains 0.000002 kg of plutonium.

a How much plutonium is in a tonne of ore?

b In a year, 2 million tonnes of ore are mined. How much plutonium will this give?

Extension Work

1 Work out each of these:

a 0.1×0.1 **b** $0.1 \times 0.1 \times 0.1$ **c** $0.1 \times 0.1 \times 0.1 \times 0.1$

2 Using your answers to **1**, write each of these as a decimal.

a 0.1^5 **b** 0.1^6 **c** 0.1^7 **d** 0.1^{10}

3 Write down the answer to each of these.

a 0.2^2	**b** 0.3^2	**c** 0.4^2	**d** 0.5^2	**e** 0.8^2
f 0.2^3	**g** 0.3^3	**h** 0.4^3	**o** 0.5^3	**j** 0.8^3

Dividing decimals

Example 16.3   Work out   **a** $0.08 \div 0.2$ **b** $20 \div 0.05$

a Rewrite as equivalent divisions.

$$0.08 \div 0.2 = 0.8 \div 2 = 0.4$$

We have shifted the decimal point in both of the numbers by the same amount, in the same direction.

b Rewrite as equivalent divisions.

$$20 \div 0.05 = 200 \div 0.5 = 2000 \div 5 = 400$$

Example 16.4 ▷ Work out **a** $4.8 \div 80$ **b** $24 \div 3000$

a Because we are dividing 4.8 by a multiple of 10, we first reduce it by a factor of 10 by moving the decimal point to the left. This produces an easier division calculation.

$$4.8 \div 80 = 0.48 \div 8 = 0.06$$

You can set the last step out as a short division problem if you want, being sure to keep the decimal points lined up.

$$\frac{0.06}{8\sqrt{0.48}}$$

b $24 \div 3000 = 2.4 \div 300 = 0.24 \div 30 = 0.024 \div 3$

$$\frac{0.008}{3\sqrt{0.024}}$$

So $24 \div 3000 = 0.008$

Exercise 16B

1 Without using a calculator, work out each of these.

a $0.04 \div 0.02$	**b** $0.8 \div 0.5$	**c** $0.06 \div 0.1$	**d** $0.9 \div 0.03$
e $0.2 \div 0.01$	**f** $0.06 \div 0.02$	**g** $0.09 \div 0.3$	**h** $0.12 \div 0.3$
i $0.16 \div 0.2$	**j** $0.8 \div 0.02$	**k** $0.8 \div 0.1$	**l** $0.24 \div 0.08$
m $0.2 \div 0.2$	**n** $0.08 \div 0.8$	**o** $0.9 \div 0.09$	**p** $0.4 \div 0.001$

2 Without using a calculator, work out each of these.

a $200 \div 0.4$	**b** $300 \div 0.2$	**c** $40 \div 0.08$	**d** $200 \div 0.02$
e $90 \div 0.3$	**f** $40 \div 0.04$	**g** $50 \div 0.1$	**h** $400 \div 0.2$
i $300 \div 0.5$	**j** $400 \div 0.05$	**k** $400 \div 0.1$	**l** $200 \div 0.01$
m $30 \div 0.5$	**n** $50 \div 0.5$	**o** $60 \div 0.5$	**p** $400 \div 0.5$

3 Without using a calculator, work out each of these.

a $3.2 \div 20$	**b** $2.4 \div 400$	**c** $12 \div 400$	**d** $3.6 \div 90$
e $24 \div 800$	**f** $2.4 \div 2000$	**g** $1.4 \div 70$	**h** $1.6 \div 40$
i $32 \div 2000$	**j** $0.18 \div 300$	**k** $0.24 \div 0.2$	**l** $0.032 \div 4000$

4 Screws cost £0.03. How many can I buy with £6000?

5 Grains of salt weigh 0.002 g. How many grains are in a kilogram of salt?

6 How many gallons of sea water will produce 3 kg of gold if each gallon contains 0.000 002 kg of gold?

Extension Work

1 Given that $46 \times 34 = 1564$, write down the answer to
    a 4.6×34 **b** 4.6×3.4 **c** $1564 \div 3.4$ **d** $15.64 \div 0.034$

2 Given that $57 \times 32 = 1824$, write down the answer to
    a 5.7×0.032 **b** 0.57×32000 **c** 5700×0.32 **d** 0.0057×32

3 Given that $2.8 \times 0.55 = 1.54$, write down the answer to
    a 28×55 **b** $154 \div 55$ **c** $15.4 \div 0.028$ **d** 0.028×5500

Using a calculator

Your calculator is broken. Only the keys shown are working. Using just these keys, can you make all the numbers up to 25? For example:

$$1 = 4 - 3 \qquad 12 = 3 \times 4 \qquad 15 = 4 + 4 + 7$$

You have already met brackets on a calculator in Chapter 9 (page 110). With the most recent calculators, using brackets is probably the best way to do lengthy calculations. The problem with keying in a calculation using brackets is that there is no intermediate working to check where you made mistakes. One way round this is to use the memory keys, or to write down the intermediate values. (This is what examiners call 'working'.)

The memory is a location inside the calculator where a number can be stored.

The memory keys are not exactly the same on different makes of calculators, but they all do the same things. Let's look at the four main keys:

Min This key puts the value in the display into the memory and the contents of the memory are lost. This is STO on some calculators.

M+ This key adds the contents of the display to the contents of the memory.

M– This key subtracts the contents of the display from the contents of the memory. This is SHIFT M+ on some calculators.

MR This key recalls the contents of the memory and puts it in the display. The contents of the display will disappear but may still be involved in the calculation.

Example 16.5 Calculate **a** $\dfrac{16.8 + 28.8}{23.8 - 16.2}$ **b** $60.3 \div (16.3 - 9.6)$

a Type in 23.8 – 16.2 =, which gives an answer of 7.6. Store this in the memory with Min.

Type in 16.8 + 28.8 =, which gives 45.6 in the display. Type ÷ MR =. This should give an answer of 6.

b Type in 16.3 – 9.6 =, which gives an answer of 6.7. Store this with Min.

Type in 60.3 ÷ MR =, which should give an answer of 9.

Two other very useful keys are the square root key √ and the sign change key +/– .

Note that not all calculators have a sign change key. Some have (–) . Also, the square root key has to be pressed before the number on some calculators and after the number on others.

The best thing to do is to get your own calculator and learn how to use it.

Example 16.6 Calculate **a** $\sqrt{432}$ **b** $180 - (32 + 65)$

a Typing either √ 432 = or 432 √ should give 20.78460969. Round this off to 20.78.

b Type in 32 + 65 =, which should give 97. Press the sign change key and the display should change to –97. Type in + 180 =, which should give 83.

The sign change key is also used to input a negative number. For example, on some calculators, typing 2 +/– will give a display of –2.

1 Use the memory keys to work out each of the following. Write down any values that you store in the memory.

a $\dfrac{17.8 + 25.6}{14.5 - 8.3}$ b $\dfrac{35.7 - 19.2}{34.9 - 19.9}$ c $\dfrac{16.9 + 23.6}{16.8 - 14.1}$ d $\dfrac{47.2 - 19.6}{11.1 - 8.8}$

e $45.6 - (23.4 - 6.9)$ f $44.8 \div (12.8 - 7.2)$ g $(4 \times 28.8) \div (9.5 - 3.1)$

2 Use the sign change key to enter the first negative number. Then use the calculator to work out the value of each of these.

a $-2 + 3 - 7$ b $-4 - 6 + 8$ c $-6 + 7 - 8 + 2$ d $-5 + 3 - 8 + 9$

3 Use the square root key to work out

a $\sqrt{400}$ b $\sqrt{300}$ c $\sqrt{150}$ d $\sqrt{10}$

4 What happens if you press the sign key twice in succession?

5 If you start with 16 and press the square root key twice in succession, the display shows 2. If you start with 81 and press the square root key twice in succession, the display shows 3.

Explain what numbers are shown in the display.

6 Calculate each of the following **i** using the brackets keys, and **ii** using the memory keys.

Write out the key presses for each. Which method uses fewer key presses?

a $\dfrac{12.9 + 42.9}{23.7 - 14.4}$ b $\dfrac{72.4 - 30.8}{16.85 - 13.6}$ c $25.6 \div (6.7 - 3.5)$

Extension Work

It helps to understand how a calculator works if you can think like a calculator. So, do the following without using a calculator.

You are told what the number in the memory and the number in the display are.

After each series of operations shown below, what number will be in the display and what number will be in the memory? The first one has been done as an example.

	Starting number in display	Starting number in memory	Operations	Final number in display	Final number in memory
	6	10	M+, M+, M+	6	28
a	6	10	Min, M+, M+		
b	6	10	M–, MR		
c	12	5	M+, MR, M+		
d	10	6	M+, M+, M+, MR		
e	10	6	MR, M+, M+		
f	8	8	M–, M+, MR, M+		
g	15	20	M–, M–, MR, M+		
h	10	6	MR, M–		
i	15	0	M+, M+, MR, M+		
j	0	15	M+, M+, MR, M+		

Fractions of quantities

This section is going to help you to revise the rules for working with fractions.

Example 16.7 Find **a** $\frac{2}{7}$ of £28   **b** $\frac{3}{5}$ of 45 sweets   **c** $1\frac{2}{3}$ of 15 m

a First, find $\frac{1}{7}$ of £28: $28 \div 7 = 4$. So, $\frac{2}{7}$ of £28 $= 2 \times 4 = £8$.

b First, find $\frac{1}{5}$ of 45 sweets: $45 \div 5 = 9$. So, $\frac{3}{5}$ of 45 sweets $= 3 \times 9 = 27$ sweets.

c Either calculate $\frac{2}{3}$ of 15 and add it to 15, or make $1\frac{2}{3}$ into a top-heavy fraction and work out $\frac{5}{3}$ of 15.

$15 \div 3 = 5$, so $\frac{2}{3}$ of 15 $= 10$. So, $1\frac{2}{3}$ of 15 m $= 15 + 10 = 25$ m.
$15 \div 3 = 5$, so $\frac{5}{3}$ of 15 $= 25$ m.

Example 16.8 Find **a** $7 \times \frac{3}{4}$ **b** $8 \times \frac{2}{3}$ **c** $5 \times 1\frac{3}{5}$

a $7 \times \frac{3}{4} = \frac{21}{4} = 5\frac{1}{4}$.

b $8 \times \frac{2}{3} = \frac{16}{3} = 5\frac{1}{3}$.

c $5 \times 1\frac{3}{5} = 5 \times \frac{8}{5} = \frac{40}{5} = 8$.

Example 16.9 A magazine has 96 pages. $\frac{5}{12}$ of the pages have adverts on them. How many pages have adverts on them?

$\frac{1}{12}$ of 96 $= 8$. So, $\frac{5}{12}$ of 96 $= 5 \times 8 = 40$ pages.

Exercise 16D

1 Find each of these.

  a $\frac{2}{3}$ of £27   **b** $\frac{3}{5}$ of 75 kg   **c** $1\frac{2}{3}$ of 18 metres **d** $\frac{4}{9}$ of £18

  e $\frac{3}{10}$ of £46   **f** $\frac{5}{8}$ of 840 houses   **g** $\frac{3}{7}$ of 21 litres   **h** $1\frac{2}{5}$ of 45 minutes

  i $\frac{5}{6}$ of £63   **j** $\frac{3}{8}$ of 1600 loaves   **k** $1\frac{4}{7}$ of 35 km   **l** $\frac{7}{10}$ of 600 crows

  m $\frac{2}{9}$ of £1.26   **n** $\frac{4}{9}$ of 540 children   **o** $\frac{7}{12}$ of 144 miles **p** $3\frac{3}{11}$ of £22.

2 Find each of these as a mixed number.

  a $5 \times \frac{3}{4}$ **b** $8 \times \frac{2}{7}$ **c** $6 \times 1\frac{2}{3}$ **d** $4 \times \frac{3}{8}$

  e $9 \times \frac{1}{4}$ **f** $5 \times 1\frac{5}{6}$ **g** $9 \times \frac{4}{5}$ **h** $7 \times 2\frac{3}{4}$

  i $3 \times 3\frac{3}{7}$ **j** $8 \times \frac{2}{11}$ **k** $4 \times 1\frac{2}{7}$ **l** $6 \times \frac{7}{9}$

  m $2 \times 3\frac{3}{4}$ **n** $3 \times \frac{7}{10}$ **o** $5 \times 1\frac{3}{10}$ **p** $2 \times 10\frac{5}{8}$

3 A bag of rice weighed 1300 g. $\frac{2}{5}$ of it was used to make a meal. How much was left?

4 Mrs Smith weighed 96 kg. She lost $\frac{3}{8}$ of her weight due to a diet. How much did she weigh after the diet?

5 A petrol tank holds 52 litres. $\frac{3}{4}$ is used on a journey. How many litres are left?

6 A GCSE textbook has 448 pages. $\frac{3}{28}$ of the pages are the answers. How many pages of answers are there?

7 A bar of chocolate weighs $\frac{5}{8}$ of a kilogram. How much do seven bars weigh?

8 A Smartie machine produces 1400 Smarties a minute. $\frac{2}{7}$ of them are red. How many red Smarties will the machine produce in an hour?

9 A farmer has nine cows. Each cow eats $1\frac{2}{3}$ bales of silage a week. How much do they eat altogether?

10 A cake recipe requires $\frac{2}{3}$ of a cup of walnuts. How many cups of walnuts will be needed for five cakes?

Extension Work

This is about dividing fractions by a whole number.

Dividing a fraction by 2 has the same effect as halving the fraction. For example:

$$\frac{2}{7} \div 2 = \frac{2}{7} \times \frac{1}{2} = \frac{1}{7}$$

Work out each of the following as a fraction.

a	$\frac{2}{3} \div 2$	**b**	$\frac{3}{4} \div 2$	**c**	$\frac{4}{5} \div 2$	**d**	$\frac{7}{8} \div 2$
e	$\frac{4}{7} \div 3$	**f**	$\frac{2}{5} \div 5$	**g**	$\frac{3}{8} \div 4$	**h**	$\frac{3}{10} \div 5$
i	$\frac{3}{4} \div 6$	**j**	$\frac{2}{3} \div 3$	**k**	$\frac{2}{11} \div 10$	**l**	$\frac{3}{8} \div 8$
m	$\frac{3}{7} \div 4$	**n**	$\frac{3}{4} \div 5$	**o**	$\frac{7}{8} \div 3$	**p**	$\frac{4}{5} \div 9$

Percentages of quantities

This section will help you to revise the equivalence between fractions, percentages and decimals. It will also show you how to calculate simple percentages of quantities.

Example 16.10 ▷ Write down the equivalent percentage and fraction for each of these decimals.

a 0.6 **b** 0.28

To change a decimal to a percentage, multiply by 100. This gives: **a** 60% **b** 28%

To change a decimal to a fraction, multiply and divide by 10, 100, 1000 as appropriate and cancel if possible. This gives:

a $0.6 = \frac{6}{10} = \frac{3}{5}$ **b** $0.28 = \frac{28}{100} = \frac{7}{25}$

Example 16.11 ▶ Write down the equivalent percentage and decimal for each of these fractions.

a $\frac{7}{20}$ b $\frac{9}{25}$

To change a fraction into a percentage, make the denominator 100. This gives:

a $\frac{7}{20} = \frac{35}{100} = 35\%$ b $\frac{9}{25} = \frac{36}{100} = 36\%$

To change a fraction into a decimal, divide the top by the bottom, or make into a percentage, then divide by 100. This gives:

a 0.35 b 0.36

Example 16.12 ▶ Write down the equivalent decimal and fraction for each of these percentages.

a 95% b 26%

To convert a percentage to a decimal, divide by 100. This gives: **a** 0.95 **b** 0.26

To convert a percentage to a fraction, make a fraction over 100 then cancel if possible. This gives:

a $95\% = \frac{95}{100} = \frac{19}{20}$ b $26\% = \frac{26}{100} = \frac{13}{50}$

Example 16.13 ▶ Calculate **a** 15% of £670 **b** 40% of £34

Calculate 10%, then use multiples of this.

a 10% of £670 = £67, 5% = 33.50. So, 15% of £670 = 67 + 33.5 = £100.50.

b 10% of £34 = £3.40. So, 40% of £34 = 4 × 3.40 = £13.60.

Exercise 16E

1 Copy and complete this table.

	a	b	c	d	e	f	g	h	i	j
Decimal	0.45			0.76			0.36			0.85
Fraction	$\frac{9}{20}$	$\frac{3}{5}$			$\frac{4}{25}$			$\frac{3}{50}$		
Percentage	45%		32%			37.5%			65%	

2 Calculate

a 35% of £340 b 15% of £250 c 60% of £18 d 20% of £14.40
e 45% of £440 f 5% of £45 g 40% of £5.60 h 25% of £24.40

3 A bus garage holds 50 buses. 34% are single-deckers, the rest are double-deckers.

a How many single-deckers are there?
b How many double-deckers are there?
c What percentage are double-deckers?

4 A Jumbo Jet carries 400 passengers. On one trip, 52% of the passengers were British, 17% were American, 12% were French and the rest were German.

a How many people of each nationality were on the plane?
b What percentage were German?

5 Copy the cross-number puzzle. Use the clues to fill it in. Then use the puzzle to fill in the missing numbers in the clues.

Across		Down	
1	71% of 300	**1**	96% of ......
3	73% of 200	**2**	81% of ......
5	107% of 200	**3**	50% of 24
8	58% of	**4**	25% of 596
9	88% of 400	**6**	61% of 200
		7	100% of 63

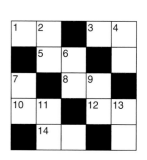

Extension Work

Copy the cross-number puzzle. Work out each percentage.
Then use the puzzle to fill in the missing numbers in the clues.

Across		Down	
1	54 out of 200	**2**	...... out of 400
3	33 out of 50	**4**	134 out of 200
5	13 out of 25	**6**	...... out of 300
8	99 out of 100	**7**	100 out of 400
10	...... out of 200	**9**	...... out of 20
12	27 out of 50	**11**	110 out of 1000
14	38 out of 200	**13**	23 out of 50

Solving problems

Below are two investigations. Before you start either of these, read the question carefully and think about how you are going to record your results. Show all your working clearly.

Who wants to be a millionaire?

You have won a prize in a lottery. You have a choice of how to take the prize.

You can either:

Take £10 000 in the first year, 10% less (£9000) in the second year, 10% less than the second year's amount (£8100) in the third year, and so on for 10 years.

Or

Take £1000 in the first year, 50% more (£1500) in the second year, 50% more than the second year's amount (£1500) in the third year, and so on for 10 years.

Which would you choose? You will probably need to use a calculator and round off the amounts to the nearest penny.

Would your choice change if the second method gave 40% more each year? Would your choice change if the second method started with £10 000?

Chocolate bars

Eight children, Alf, Betty, Charles, Des, Ethel, Fred, George and Helen, are lined up outside a room in alphabetical order.

Inside the room are three tables. Each table has eight chairs around it.

On the first table is one chocolate bar, on the second table are two chocolate bars, and on the third table are three chocolate bars.

The children go into the room one at a time and sit at one of the tables. After they are all seated they share out the chocolate bars on the table at which they are seated.

Where should Alf sit to make sure he gets the most chocolate?

What you need to know for level 5

- How to identify and obtain the necessary information to solve mathematical problems
- How to check results and describe situations using mathematical symbols, words and diagrams
- How to calculate fractions and percentages of quantities and of measurements

What you need to know for level 6

- How to use equivalent fractions, decimals and percentages to solve problems
- How to divide and multiply integers and decimals
- How to use the memory and bracket functions on a calculator

National Curriculum SATs questions

LEVEL 5

1 *1998 Paper 2*

You can make different colours of paint by mixing red, blue and yellow in different proportions. For example, you can make green by mixing one part blue to one part yellow.

a To make purple, you mix 3 parts red to 7 parts blue.

How much of each colour do you need to make 20 litres of purple paint?

b To make orange, you mix 13 parts yellow to 7 parts red.

How much of each colour do you need to make 10 litres of orange paint?

2 *1998 Paper 1*

a A teacher needs 220 booklets. The booklets are in packs of 16.

How many packs must the teacher order?

b Each booklet weighs 48 g. How much do the 220 booklets weigh altogether? Give your answer in kg.

3 *1997 Paper 2*

The cost of an old toy vehicle depends on its condition and on whether it is in the original box. The table shows how to work out the value of a vehicle as a percentage of its original price.

Condition	Value
Excellent and in its box	100%
Good and in its box	85%
Poor and in its box	50%
Excellent but not in its box	65%
Good but not in its box	32%
Poor but not in its box	15%

A mail van in excellent condition, and in its box, costs £125.

a How much is a mail van in good condition, and in its box?

b How much is a mail van in good condition but not in its box?

c A petrol tanker in excellent condition, and in its box, costs £152.

Another petrol tanker should be sold for £98.80.

Using the table, what is its condition and does it have its box?

CHAPTER 17 Algebra 5

This chapter is going to show you

- how to use the algebraic ideas given in previous chapters
- how to extend these ideas into more difficult problems

What you should already know

- How to solve simple equations
- How to use simple formulae and derive a formula
- How to find the term-to-term rule in a sequence
- How to plot coordinates and draw graphs
- How to use algebra to solve simple problems

Solving equations

In Chapter 6 (page 73) you were shown how to solve some simple equations. Examples 17.1 and 17.2 introduce two further types of equation.

Example 17.1

Solve $5(2x + 3) = 47$.

Multiply out the bracket:

$$10x + 15 = 47$$

Subtract 15 from both sides:

$$10x + 15 - 15 = 47 - 15$$
$$10x = 32$$

Divide both sides by 10:

$$10x \div 10 = 32 \div 10$$
$$x = 3.2$$

Example 17.2

Solve $5x + 4 = 6 - 3x$.

Add $3x$ to both sides:

$$5x + 4 + 3x = 6 - 3x + 3x$$
$$8x + 4 = 6$$

Subtract 4 from both sides:

$$8x + 4 - 4 = 6 - 4$$
$$8x = 2$$

Divide both sides by 8:

$$8x \div 8 = 2 \div 8$$
$$x = 0.25$$

1 Solve the following equations.

a	$12x + 3 = 51$	**b**	$21x + 5 = 257$	**c**	$13x + 4 = 108$
d	$32x + 7 = 359$	**e**	$14m + 1 = 253$	**f**	$15k + 6 = 81$
g	$4n + 9 = 65$	**h**	$12x + 7 = 199$	**i**	$6h + 5 = 119$
j	$7t + 5 = 68$	**k**	$8x + 3 = 107$	**l**	$5y + 3 = 33$
m	$17x + 3 = 292$	**n**	$42t + 7 = 427$	**p**	$23x + 8 = 353$
q	$8m + 3 = 51$				

2 Solve the following equations.

a	$12x + 3 = 87$	**b**	$13x + 4 = 56$	**c**	$15x - 1 = 194$
d	$14x - 3 = 137$	**e**	$13m - 2 = 24$	**f**	$15m + 4 = 184$
g	$17m + 3 = 105$	**h**	$14m - 5 = 219$	**i**	$16k + 1 = 129$
j	$15k - 3 = 162$	**k**	$13k - 1 = 38$	**l**	$12k + 5 = 173$
m	$17x - 4 = 285$	**n**	$14x + 3 = 73$	**p**	$15x + 6 = 231$
q	$19x - 4 = 167$				

3 Solve the following equations.

a	$2(3x + 5) = 34$	**b**	$4(2x - 3) = 52$	**c**	$5(3x + 1) = 41$
d	$3(4x - 5) = 15$	**e**	$2(3x + 4) = 17$	**f**	$4(5x - 2) = 57$
g	$5(2x - 1) = 21$	**h**	$3(5x + 2) = 111$	**i**	$2(3x - 2) = 17$
j	$4(7x + 3) = 54$	**k**	$5(4x + 3) = 79$	**l**	$3(4x - 1) = 201$

4 Solve the following equations.

a	$6x + 5 = 2x + 17$	**b**	$5x + 3 = 3x + 8$	**c**	$4x - 3 = x + 18$
d	$3x - 7 = x + 2$	**e**	$5x + 4 = 16 - x$	**f**	$2x - 3 = 9 - 2x$
g	$6x - 5 = 2x + 1$	**h**	$7x + 1 = 2x + 7$	**i**	$4x - 1 = 2x + 10$
j	$x - 3 = 7 - 3x$				

Extension Work

1 The sum of ten consecutive numbers is the same as the number of days in a non-leap year. What is the smallest of the numbers?

2 I multiply a number by 8 then subtract 14 to obtain the number of weeks in a year. What is my starting number?

3 Make up some similar problems to these using numbers in times or dates.

Formulae

Formulae occur in many situations, some of which you have already met. You need to be able to use formulae to calculate a variety of quantities.

Example 17.3

One rule to find the area of a triangle is to take half of the length of its base and multiply it by the vertical height of the triangle. This rule, written as a formula is

$$A = \tfrac{1}{2}bh$$

where A = area, b = base length, and h = vertical height.

Using this formula to calculate the area of a triangle with a base length of 7 cm and a vertical height of 16 cm gives

$$A = \tfrac{1}{2} \times 7 \times 16 = 56 \text{ cm}^2$$

Exercise 17B

1. The average of three numbers is given by the formula

    $$A = \frac{m + n + p}{3}$$

    where A is the average and m, n and p are the numbers.

    a   Use the formula to find the average of 4, 8 and 15.
    b   What is the average of 32, 43 and 54?

2. The average speed of a car is given by the formula

    $$A = \frac{d}{t}$$

    where A is the average speed in miles per hour, d is the number of miles travelled, and t is the number of hours taken for the journey.

    a   Find the average speed of a car which travels 220 miles in 4 hours.
    b   In 8 hours a car covered 360 miles. What was the average speed?

3. The speed, v m/s, of a train t seconds after passing through a station with a speed of u m/s, is given by the formula

    $$v = u + 5t$$

    a   What is the speed 4 seconds after leaving a station with a speed of 12 m/s?
    b   What is the speed 10 seconds after leaving a station with a speed of 8 m/s?

4. The speed, v, of a land speed car can be calculated using the following formula

    $$v = u + at$$

    where v is the speed after t seconds, u is the initial speed, and a is the acceleration.

    a   Calculate the speed of the car with 10 m/s² acceleration 8 seconds after it had a speed of 12 m/s.
    b   Calculate the speed of a car with 5 m/s² acceleration 12 seconds after it had a speed of 15 m/s.

5 To change a temperature in degrees Celsius to degrees Fahrenheit, we use the formula

$$F = 32 + 1.8C$$

where F is the temperature in degrees Fahrenheit and C is the temperature in degrees Celsius.

Change each of the following temperatures to degrees Fahrenheit.

a   45 °C   **b**   40 °C   **c**   65 °C   **d**   100 °C

6 When a stone is dropped from the top of a cliff, the distance, d metres, that it falls in t seconds is given by the formula

$$d = 4.9t^2$$

Calculate the distance a stone has fallen 8 seconds after being dropped from the top of a cliff.

7 The distance, D km, which you can see out to sea from the shore line, at a height of h metres above sea level, is given by the formula

$$D = \sqrt{(12.5h)}$$

How far out to sea can you see from the top of a cliff, 112 metres above sea level?

Extension Work

Here are some cards with expressions written on them.

| n^2 | $4 \div n$ | $n + 4$ | $n + n + n + n$ | n |

| $4n$ | $n - 4$ | $n \div 4$ | n^3 | $3n + n$ |

1   Which cards always give the same answer as $4 \times n$ when you substitute a number into them?

2   Two of the expressions add together to give double the value of another expression. Which are these three cards?

3   When $n = 4$, which cards have the same value as each other?

Dotty investigations

1 Look at the following two shapes drawn on a dotted square grid.

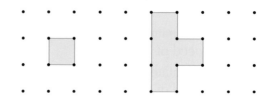

By drawing some of your own shapes (with no dots inside each shape), complete the table below, giving the number of dots on each perimeter and the area of each shape.

Number of dots on perimeter	Area of shape
4	1 cm²
6	
8	
10	4 cm²
12	
14	
16	

2 What is special about the number of dots on the perimeter of all the shapes in the table in Question 1?

3 For a shape with no dots inside, one way to calculate the area of the shape from the number of dots on the perimeter is to

Divide the number of dots by two, then subtract 1

a Check that this rule works for all the shapes drawn in Question 1.

b Write this rule as a formula, where A is the area of a shape and D is the number of dots on its perimeter.

4 Look at the following two shapes drawn on a dotted square grid. They both have one dot inside.

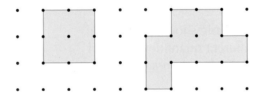

By drawing some of your own shapes (with only one dot inside each shape), complete the table below.

Number of dots on perimeter	Dots inside	Area of shape
4	1	
6	1	
8	1	4 cm²
10	1	
12	1	
14	1	
16	1	

5 For the shapes in Question 4, find a formula to connect A, the area of each shape with D, the number of dots on its perimeter.

6 a Draw some shapes with an even number of dots on each perimeter and two dots inside each shape.

  b Find the formula connecting A, the area of each shape, with D, the number of dots on its perimeter.

7 a Draw some shapes with an even number of dots on each perimeter and three dots inside each shape.

  b Find the formula connecting A, the area of each shape, with D, the number of dots on its perimeter.

8 Find the formula connecting area to number of perimeter dots for shapes that have an even number of perimeter dots, and eight dots inside each shape.

Extension Work

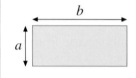

The perimeter of the rectangle is $2a + 2b$.

Draw shapes that have the following perimeter.

1	$4a$	**2**	$3b$	**3**	$a + 2b$	**4**	$2a + 2b$
5	$5b$	**6**	$6a$	**7**	$3a + 3b$	**8**	$b + 3a$

Graphs from the real world

When you fill your car with petrol, both the amount of petrol you've taken and its cost are displayed on the pump. One litre of petrol costs about 80p, but this rate does change from time to time.

The table shows the costs of different quantities of petrol as displayed on a petrol pump.

Petrol (litres)	5	10	15	20	25	30
Cost (£)	4	8	12	16	20	24

This information can also be represented by the following ordered pairs:

(5, 4)   (10, 8)   (15, 12)   (20, 16)   (25, 20)   (30, 24)

On the right, these pairs have been plotted to give a graph which relates the cost of petrol to the quantity bought.

This is an example of a **conversion graph**. You can use it to find the cost of any quantity of petrol, or to find how much petrol can be bought for a given amount of money.

Conversion graphs are usually straight-line graphs.

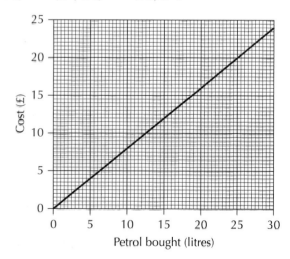

1

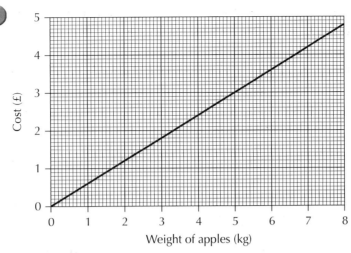

Use the graph to answer these questions
a Find the cost of each quantity of apples.
  i 3 kg   ii 7 kg
b What weight of apples can be bought for:
  i £3   ii £2.40?

2 The graph below shows the distance travelled by a car during an interval of 5 minutes.

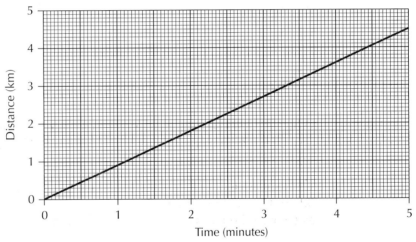

a Find the distance travelled during the second minute of the journey.
b Find the time taken to travel 3 km.

3 Here is a kilometre–mile conversion graph.

a Express each of the following distances in km:
  i 3 miles
  ii 4.5 miles
b Express each of the following distances in miles:
  i 2 km
  ii 4 km
  iii 6 km

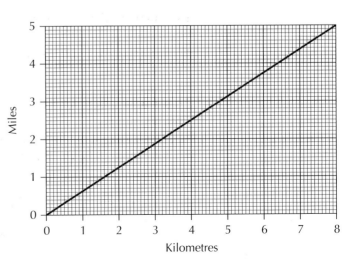

4 **a** Copy and complete the following table for the exchange rate of the euro.

Euros (€)	1	5	10	15	20
Pounds (£)	0.60	3.00			

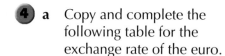

b Use the data from this table to draw a conversion graph from pounds to euros.

c Use your graph to convert each of the following to pounds.

   i €7   **ii** €16   **iii** €17.50

d Use your graph to convert each of the following to euros.

   i £9   **ii** £12   **iii** £10.80

5 A box weighs 2 kg. Packets of juice, each weighing 425 g, are packed into it.

a Draw a graph to show the weight of the box plus the packets of juice and the number of packets of fruit juice put into the box.

b Find, from the graph, the number of packets of juice that make the weight of the box and packets as close to 5 kg as possible.

Extension Work

A particular car could travel 6 km for every litre of petrol used by its engine. Draw a graph to show the relationship between the distance travelled (*d*) and the number of litres of petrol used (*p*). Use your graph to find each of the following.

a The distance travelled after using 12 litres of petrol.

b The amount of petrol used by the car after travelling 90 km.

c The equation relating the distance travelled to the amount of petrol used.

Triangle-and-circle problems

Look at the diagram on the right. The number in each box is the sum of the two numbers in the circles on either side of the box.

The values of *A*, *B* and *C* are positive integers and no two are the same. What are they?

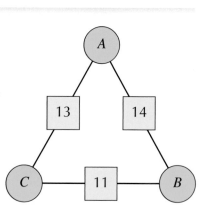

The values of *A*, *B* and *C* can be found by using algebraic equations, as shown below.

Three equations can be written down from the diagram. They are:

$A + B = 14$ (1) $B + C = 11$ (2) $A + C = 13$ (3)

First, add together equation (1) and equation (2). This gives

$$A + B + B + C = 14 + 11$$
$$A + 2B + C = 25 \quad (4)$$

Next, subtract equation (3) from both sides of equation (4):

$$A + 2B + C - (A + C) = 25 - 13$$
$$2B = 12$$
$$B = 6$$

Finally, substitute $B = 6$ in equations (1) and (2), to obtain $A = 8$ and $C = 5$.

1 Use algebra to solve each of these triangle-and-circle problems. All the solutions are positive integers.

a
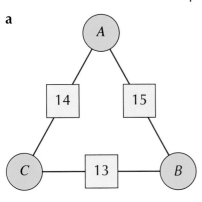

b
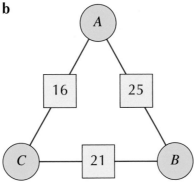

c
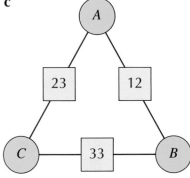

2 Use algebra to solve each of these triangle-and-circle problems. The solutions are positive and negative integers.

a
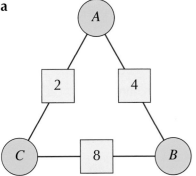

b
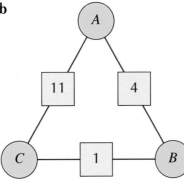

c
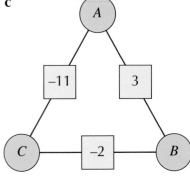

Extension Work

1 Use algebra to solve this triangle-and-circle problem. The solutions are positive and negative numbers.

2 Make up your own triangle-and-circle problem which uses negative numbers, and challenge a classmate to solve it.

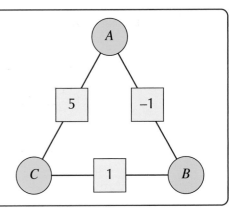

What you need to know for level 5

○ How to construct and use simple formulae
○ How to use and interpret coordinates derived from real-life situations
○ How to solve equations involving two stages
○ How to solve simple problems using algebra

What you need to know for level 6

○ How to solve equations with the variable on both sides
○ How to substitute into formulae involving squares and square roots

National Curriculum SATs questions

LEVEL 5

1 *1996 Paper 2*

Steve is making a series of patterns with black and grey square tiles.

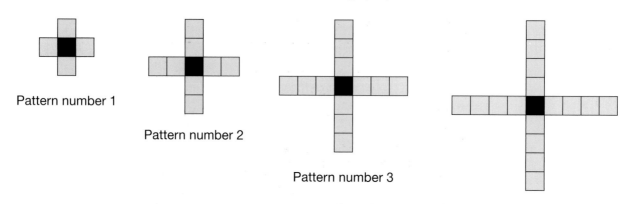

Pattern number 1

Pattern number 2

Pattern number 3

Pattern number 4

a Each pattern has one black tile at the centre.

Each new pattern has more grey tiles than the one before.

How many more grey tiles does Steve add each time he makes a new pattern?

b Steve says:

The rule for finding the number of tiles in pattern number *N* is:
Number of tiles = 4 × *N* + 1

The 1 in Steve's rule represents the black tile. What does the 4 × *N* represent?

c Steve wants to make pattern number 15. How many black tiles and how many grey tiles does he need?

d Steve uses 41 tiles altogether to make a pattern. What is the number of the pattern he makes?

e Steve has 12 black tiles and 80 grey tiles. What is the number of the biggest pattern Steve can make?

LEVEL 6

2 *Paper 1 2002*

a When $x = 5$, work out the values of the expressions below.

$2x + 13 = $ ......

$5x - 5 = $ ......

$3 + 6x = $ ......

b When $2y + 11 = 17$, work out the value of y. Show your working.

c Solve the equation $9y + 3 = 5y + 13$. Show your working.

3 *Paper 1 2002*

You can often use algebra to show why a number puzzle works. Copy this puzzle and fill in the missing expressions.

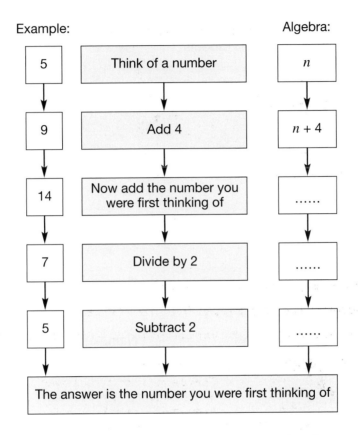

Example:

Algebra:

| 5 | Think of a number | n |

| 9 | Add 4 | $n + 4$ |

| 14 | Now add the number you were first thinking of | ...... |

| 7 | Divide by 2 | ...... |

| 5 | Subtract 2 | ...... |

The answer is the number you were first thinking of

This chapter is going to show you

- the names and properties of polygons
- how to tessellate 2-D shapes
- how to make 3-D models

What you should already know

- How to reflect, rotate, translate and enlarge shapes
- How to draw and measure angles
- How to calculate the angles on a straight line, in a triangle and around a point
- How to draw nets for 3-D shapes

Polygons

A **polygon** is any closed 2-D shape that has straight sides.

The names of the most common polygons are given in the table below.

Number of sides	Name of polygon
3	Triangle
4	Quadrilateral
5	Pentagon
6	Hexagon
7	Heptagon
8	Octagon
9	Nonagon
10	Decagon

A **convex polygon** has all its diagonals inside the polygon.

A **concave polygon** has at least one diagonal outside the polygon.

Example 18.1

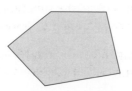

A convex pentagon
(all diagonals inside)

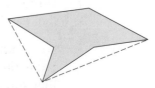

A concave hexagon
(two diagonals outside)

A polygon is **regular** when all its interior angles are equal and all its sides have the same length.

Example 18.2 ▷ A regular octagon has eight lines of symmetry and rotational symmetry of order 8.

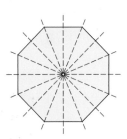

Exercise 18A

1 Which shapes below are polygons? If they are, write down their names.

a 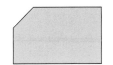 b  c  d   e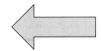

2 Which shapes below are regular polygons?

a   b   c   d   e

3 State whether each of the shapes below is a convex polygon or a concave polygon.

a   b   c   d   e

4 Draw, if possible, a pentagon which has

    a no reflex angles   **b** one reflex angle

    c two reflex angles   **d** three reflex angles

5 Draw hexagons which have exactly

    a no lines of symmetry   **b** one line of symmetry

    c two lines of symmetry   **d** three lines of symmetry

6 a Write down the names of all the different shapes that can be made by overlapping two squares.

    For example: a pentagon can be made, as shown. Draw diagrams to show all the different shapes that you have made.

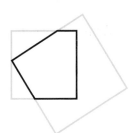

    b What shapes can be made by overlapping three squares?

7 The interior angle of a regular pentagon is 108°.
Calculate the size of the angles *a*, *b* and *c* in the diagram.

8 ABCDEF is a regular hexagon. ∠DEF is 120°.

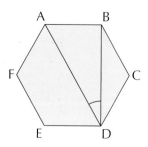

Calculate the size of ∠ADB.

Extension Work

1 How to construct a regular hexagon.

a Draw a circle of radius 5 cm.

b With your compasses still set to a radius of 5 cm, go round the circumference of the circle making marks 5 cm apart.

c Use a ruler to join the points where the marks cross the circle.

2 A triangle has no diagonals. A quadrilateral has two diagonals.

Investigate the total number of diagonals that can be drawn inside convex polygons.

3 Use ICT to draw regular polygons.

a These instructions draw a square using LOGO:

```
fd 50 rt 90
fd 50 rt 90
fd 50 rt 90
fd 50 rt 90
```

b These instructions draw a regular pentagon using LOGO:

```
repeat 5 [fd 50 rt 72]
```

Investigate how to draw other regular polygons using LOGO.

Tessellations

A **tessellation** is a pattern made by fitting together identical shapes without leaving any gaps.

When drawing a tessellation, use a square or a triangular grid, as in the examples below.

To show a tessellation, it is usual to draw up to about ten repeating shapes.

Example 18.3 ▷

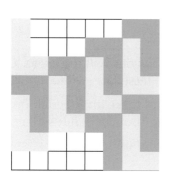 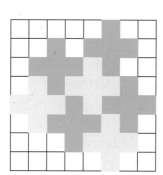

Two different shapes which each make a tessellation on a square grid.

Example 18.4 ▷

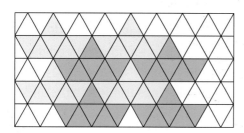

This shape tessellates on a triangular grid.

Example 18.5 ▷

Circles *do not* tessellate.

However you try to fit circles together, there will always be gaps.

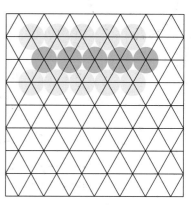

Exercise 18B

1. Make a tessellation for each of the following shapes. Use a square grid.

   a   b   c   d

2. Make a tessellation for each of the following shapes. Use a triangular grid.

   a   b   c    d

1 Design a tessellation of your own. Working in pairs or groups, make an attractive poster to show all your different tessellations.

2 Here is a tessellation which uses curves. Can you design a different curved tessellation?

3 Investigate which of the regular polygons will tessellate. Can you find a rule to predict if a regular polygon will tessellate, without having to try it out?

4 Any quadrilateral will tessellate. So, make an irregular quadrilateral tile cut from card. Then use your tile to show how it tessellates.

Can you explain why it is that *any* quadrilateral will tessellate?

Constructing 3-D shapes

A net is a 2-D shape which can be cut out and folded up to make a 3-D shape.

To make the nets overleaf into 3-D shapes you will need the following equipment: a sharp pencil, a ruler, a protractor, a pair of scissors and a glue-stick or sticky tape.

Always score the card along the fold-lines using scissors and a ruler. This makes the card much easier to fold properly.

You can glue the edges together using the tabs or you can just use sticky tape. If you decide to use glue, then always keep one face of the shape free of tabs and glue down this face last.

Example 18.6 **Constructing a square-based pyramid**

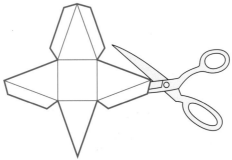

1 Carefully cut out the net using scissors.

2 Score along each fold-line using a ruler and scissors.

3 Fold along each fold-line and stick the shape together by gluing each tab.

4 The last face to stick down is the one without any tabs.

Draw each of the following nets accurately on card. Cut out the net and construct the 3-D shape.

1 **Regular tetrahedron**

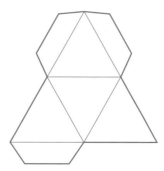

Each equilateral triangle has these measurements:

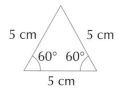

5 cm 5 cm

60° 60°

5 cm

2 **Square-based pyramid**

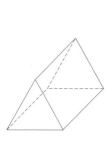

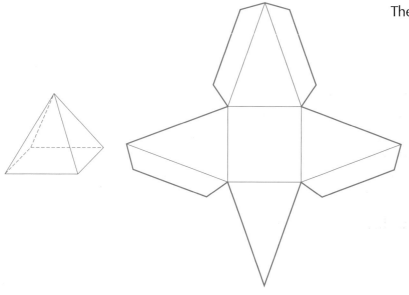

The square has these measurements:

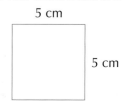

5 cm

5 cm

The isosceles triangle has these measurements:

70° 70°

5 cm

3 **Triangular prism**

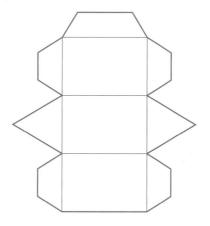

Each rectangle has these measurements:

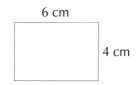

6 cm

4 cm

Each equilateral triangle has these measurements:

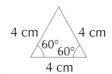

4 cm 4 cm

60° 60°

4 cm

The following nets are for more complex 3-D shapes. Choose suitable measurements and make each shape from card.

1 Octahedron

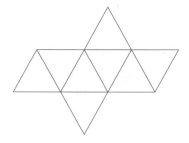

2 Regular hexagonal prism

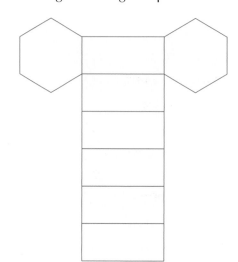

3 Truncated square-based pyramid

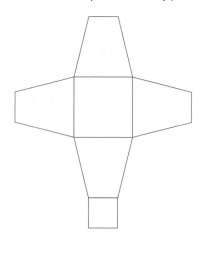

4 Regular dodecahedron

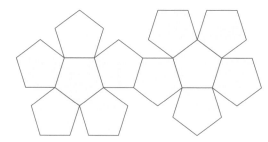

What you need to know for level 5

- Be able to identify the symmetry of 2-D shapes
- How to use the geometrical properties of 2-D shapes
- How to construct more complex 3-D shapes

What you need to know for level 6

- How to use the properties of quadrilaterals
- Be able to solve problems using angle and symmetry properties of polygons
- How to write instructions for a computer to generate and transform shapes

National Curriculum SATs questions

LEVEL 5

1 *2000 Paper 1*

The sketch shows the net of a triangular prism.

The net is folded up and glued to make the prism.

a Which edge is tab 1 glued to? On a copy of the diagram, label this edge A.

b Which edge is tab 2 glued to? Label this edge B.

c The corner marked ● meets two other corners. Label these two other corners ●.

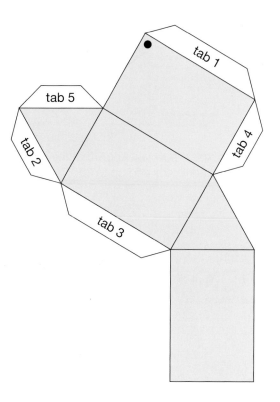

2 *2001 Paper 1*

The diagram shows a box. Draw the net for the box on a square grid.

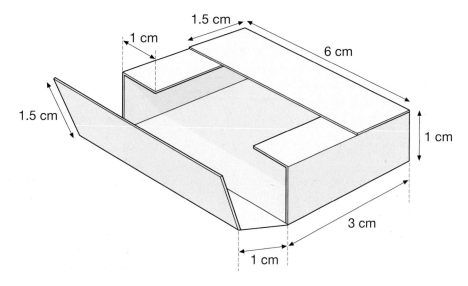

3   *2000 Paper 2*

    a   Any quadrilateral can be split into 2 triangles.

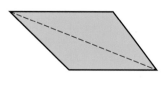

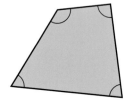

        Explain how you know that the angles inside a
quadrilateral add up to 360°

    b   What do the angles inside a pentagon add up to?

    c   What do the angles inside a heptagon (7-sided
shape) add up to?

        Show your working.

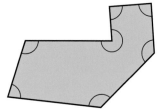

Published by HarperCollins*Publishers* Limited
77–85 Fulham Palace Road
Hammersmith
London
W6 8JB

www.**Collins**Education.com
Online support for schools and colleges

10 9 8 7 6 5 4

ISBN 0 00 713857 1

Keith Gordon, Kevin Evans, Trevor Senior and Brian Speed assert
their moral rights to be identified as the authors of this work.

British Library Cataloguing in Publication Data
A Catalogue record for this publication is available from the
British Library

Commissioned by Mark Jordan
Edited by John Day
Design and typesetting by Jordan Publishing Design
Project Management by Helen Parr
Covers by Tim Byrne
Illustrations by Nigel Jordan and Tony Wilkins
Additional proofreading by Sam Holmes and Genevieve Sabin
Production by Jack Murphy
Printed and bound by Printing Express Ltd.

The publishers would like to thank the many teachers and
advisers whose feedback helped to shape *Maths
Frameworking*.

The publishers thank the Qualifications and Curriculum
Authority for granting permission to reproduce questions from
past SAT papers for Key Stage 3.

Every effort has been made to trace copyright holders and to
obtain their permission for the use of copyright material. The
author and publishers will gladly receive any information
enabling them to rectify any error or omission in subsequent
editions.

You might also like to visit:
www.**fire**and**water**.com
The book lover's website